# Launching the Imagination

## A Guide to Two-Dimensional Design

third edition
# Mary Stewart

McGraw Hill

Boston   Burr Ridge, IL   Dubuque, IA   Madison, WI   New York   San Francisco   St. Louis
Bangkok   Bogotá   Caracas   Kuala Lumpur   Lisbon   London   Madrid   Mexico City
Milan   Montreal   New Delhi   Santiago   Seoul   Singapore   Sydney   Taipei   Toronto

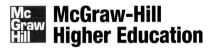
Published by McGraw-Hill, an imprint of The McGraw-Hill Companies, Inc., 1221 Avenue of the Americas, New York, NY 10020. Copyright © 2008, 2006, 2002. All rights reserved. No part of this publication may be reproduced or distributed in any form or by any means, or stored in a database or retrieval system, without the prior written consent of The McGraw-Hill Companies, Inc., including, but not limited to, in any network or other electronic storage or transmission, or broadcast for distance learning.

3 4 5 6 7 8 9 0 DOW /DOW 0 9

ISBN: 978-0-07-332730-3
MHID: 0-07-332730-1

Editor-in-chief: *Michael Ryan*
Publisher: *Lisa Moore*
Executive editor: *Lisa Pinto*
Development editors: *Nadia Bidwell* and *Nicole Caddigan Bridge*
Marketing manager: *Pamela Cooper*
Media producer: *Jocelyn Spielberger*
Media project manager: *Thomas Brierly*
Production editor: *Anne Fuzellier*
Art director: *Jeanne M. Schreiber*
Design manager: *Kim Menning*
Cover designer: *William Stanton*
Interior designer: *Glenda King*
Art manager: *Emma Ghiselli*
Production supervisor: *Randy Hurst*
Photo research coordinator: *Alexandra Ambrose*
Photo research: *Photo Search, Inc., New York*
Production service: *Jean Dal Porto*
Composition: *10.5/14 Palatino by Prographics*
Printing: *70# Sterling Ultra Web Dull, R.R. Donnelley & Sons*

Cover images: Top: © Jacey, Début Art Ltd & The Coningsby Gallery, London.
Right: Courtesy of Joel Peter Johnson.
Center: Courtesy of Georgiana Nehl.
Bottom: Courtesy of Roger Shimomura.

Credits: *The credits section for this book begins on page 191 and is considered an extension of the copyright page.*

**Library of Congress Cataloging-in-Publication Data**

Stewart, Mary, 1952-
    Launching the imagination : A comprehensive guide to basic design / Mary Stewart.—3rd ed.
        p. cm.
    Also issued in parts titled: Launching the imagination: A guide to two-dimensional design, and Launching the imagination: A guide to three-dimensional design.
    Includes bibliographical references and index.
    ISBN-13: 978-0-07-352648-5 (set: alk. paper)
    ISBN-10: 0-07-352648-7 (set: alk. paper)
    ISBN-13: 978-0-07-332730-3 (v.1: alk. paper)
    ISBN-10: 0-07-332730-1 (v.1: alk. paper)
    ISBN-13: 978-0-07-332731-0 (v.2: alk. paper)
    ISBN-10: 0-07-332731-X (v.2: alk. paper)
    1. Design. I. Title.
NK1510.S74 2008
745.4—dc22

                                                                  2007032452

The Internet addresses listed in the text were accurate at the time of publication. The inclusion of a Web site does not indicate an endorsement by the authors or McGraw-Hill, and McGraw-Hill does not guarantee the accuracy of the information presented at these sites.

**www.mhhe.com**

*Launching the Imagination:*
*A Guide to Two-Dimensional Design*
is dedicated to Nancy Callahan.

In the beginning of my teaching career, I had the good fortune to audit the courses of two master teachers, William Itter and David Hornung. Itter's fundamentals course, derived from Joseph Albers' approach, featured assignments that were methodical, systematic, and highly analytical. Hornung's course, which focused on conceptual and visual patterns, was exuberant, synthetic, and often irreverent. Both teachers presented substantial design information brilliantly.

Based on these experiences and my own teaching, I concluded that a comprehensive approach to design requires experimentation as well as analysis, and that rambunctiousness is the natural partner to rigor. Thus, when McGraw-Hill invited me to write a design textbook, I was determined to present substantial information in the liveliest possible way.

# A COMPREHENSIVE APPROACH FOR TWENTY-FIRST-CENTURY STUDENTS

*Launching the Imagination* treats design as both a verb and a noun—as a problem-solving process as well as a well-crafted product. It challenges students to use design to explore their own ideas while encouraging them to look closely and learn from the work of other artists. The third edition retains these hallmark features of the second edition:

**Thorough coverage of 2D design.** This book covers all of the topics common to two-dimensional design courses, recognizing that artists and designers benefit from a strong shared vocabulary. This third edition has benefited from the feedback of many foundations teachers, whose suggestions are reflected in the expanded and refined discussions of elements and principles. (For instructors who would like a book that includes 3D and time design as well, a comprehensive edition is available.)

**Unique coverage of creativity and concept development.** Because contemporary foundations courses are as much about process as product, *Launching the Imagination* covers such topics as generating and developing ideas, managing time, and making the most of critiques. This material, found in Chapters Five (on cultivating creativity), Six

(on problem solving), and Seven (on critical thinking), can be assigned anytime in the course. These chapters are crafted to provide practical assistance to students in tackling design problems.

**Hundreds of full-color images.** An art textbook is only as good as the images it offers, and we have sought images that are diverse and compelling. The stylistic range found in the 250-plus images in this text represents both time-honored masterworks (such as Caravaggio's *Descent from the Cross*) and works by contemporary artists (such as Alfred Leslie's *The Killing Cycle,* which was inspired by Caravaggio's painting). There are examples from many different cultures, representing a wide range of media. Chinese and Japanese calligraphy are presented in a discussion of line, Aboriginal art illustrates earth colors, and a Persian miniature demonstrates proximity, for example. Many forms of visual culture are represented, from brochures and comic books to paintings, drawings, prints, and fiber arts.

**Conversations with practicing artists.** Guest speakers have enhanced my own courses, and I tried to re-create that experience in book form through the "Profiles" at the end of each chapter. In these interviews, students learn about working processes and career choices from a remarkable group of professionals.

## New to the Third Edition

Working with invaluable feedback from adopters of the second edition, I have expanded, reorganized, refined, and updated the presentation—all with an eye to creating a better learning experience. Significant changes to this edition include the following:

- **Stronger 2D design basics.** To provide students with an even better foundation for understanding the principles of two-dimensional design, Chapter Three from the earlier editions has been divided into two chapters. New Chapter Three, Principles of Two-Dimensional Design, describes the essentials in detail, while the new Chapter Four presents spatial systems and the illusion of motion in greater depth.

- **Enhanced coverage of creativity.** Chapter Five, Cultivating Creativity, now includes a lively description of habits of work characteristic of successful artists and designers. This section emphasizes the importance of personal responsibility and self-motivation. Chapter Six, Problem Seeking and Problem Solving, includes a new section on collaborative creativity—a pivotal skill for contemporary artists and designers.

- **Increased focus on contemporary art.** The focus on contemporary art and artists has been increased throughout. There are 40 new works by artists and designers, including Robert Stackhouse, Ann Strassman, Barbara Kruger, and Bruce Conner.

- **Close-up examination of art.** A new feature called *In Detail* gives a close-up look at an image presented earlier in the text. This gives students a better sense of the compositional and conceptual complexity of an artwork.

- **New artist profiles.** Two new profiles have been included in this edition.

  - Designer and business consultant Adam Kallish presents Design Methods, a methodical approach to problem seeking and problem solving.

  - Painter Roger Shimomura discusses the transformation of personal experience into public communication and the uses of popular culture in constructing meaning.

## FLEXIBLE FORMAT FOR ALL COURSES

To maximize flexibility, *Launching the Imagination* is available in three formats:

- A comprehensive volume.

- A split volume containing two-dimensional design plus coverage of creativity and problem solving.

- A split volume covering three-dimensional design plus coverage of creativity and problem solving.

## SUPPLEMENTS FOR STUDENTS

- **Online Learning Center (OLC)**
  The Online Learning Center, at www.mhhe.com/ stewart3e, offers resources for each chapter of the text, including chapter objectives, discussion questions, and online testing. In addition, the OLC includes links to sites that promote involvement in art and guide in conducting research on the Web.

- **MyArtStudio Available on the Online Learning Center.**
  Students who buy the Third Edition will have access to McGraw-Hill's MyArtStudio, a rich and comprehensive Web site with dozens of interactions that allow students to study and experiment with various elements and principles of art, and to view videos of art techniques and artists at work. Exercises on the Online Learning Center guide students to MyArtStudio at appropriate points in the text. MyArtStudio is adapted from the Core Concepts CD-ROM of the previous two editions. The new online format is redesigned and even easier to use. Students can watch videos about various art techniques and access interactive exercises that provide a foundation in art principles and fundamentals. All of this information is available at www.mhhe.com/ stewart3e, when you click on the MyArtStudio link. We hope that online availability will be more convenient and engaging for students.

## SUPPLEMENTS FOR INSTRUCTORS

I have worked with a remarkable team of colleagues to create an extensive online Instructor's Manual and an accompanying Web site. Advice on course construction, critique skills, and technical resources are included, along with over 50 terrific assignments. Divided into sections of Two-Dimensional Design, Three-Dimensional Design, Four-Dimensional Design, Color, Creativity, and Computer Applications, this manual provides the basic information on which the beginning teacher can build a course.

**Online Learning Center,** located at www.mhhe.com/ stewart3e, includes for instructors PowerPoint slides, chapter-related reading lists, key terms, and multiple choice quizzes. These password-protected instructor's resources also include more than 50 studio assignments, with examples, in a consistent format that makes them easy for instructors to use as is or adapt to their own purposes. To receive a password for the site, contact your local sales representative.

## ACKNOWLEDGMENTS

I would like to thank Adam Kallish for his thoughtful comments on Chapter Six, Problem Seeking and Problem solving. At McGraw-Hill, I would like to thank Production expert Jean Dal Porto, Production Editor Anne Fuzellier, Sponsoring Editor Lisa Pinto, and Marketing Manager Pamela Cooper. The artists I interviewed have been remarkably gracious and supportive. In this edition,

I would particularly like to thank Roger Shimomura, Samuel Yates, Marilyn da Silva, Adam Kallish, and Michael Remson. At Florida State University, I would like to thank Art Department chair Joseph Sanders, for his insistence that I continue to develop my own studio work while juggling a challenging new administrative job. I would also like to thank Ray Burggraf, Mark Messersmith, Lilian Garcia-Roig, Paul Rutkovsky, and graduate assistants Jeremy Waltman, David McLeish, and Judith Worley for their energy, encouragement, and sense of humor.

I am grateful for the advice of my colleagues in the United States and Canada. Their opinions and recommendations have greatly improved this textbook.

Thank you to Denise Wright and her team at Southern Editorial Publication Management, LLC, for all their hard work with our supplements program. Thanks also to Matt Kelly of Central College who updated the Instructors' Manual; Linda Vanderkolk and Grace O'Brien of Purdue University for authoring the exercises that accompany MyArtStudio.com; and Charlotte Collins of Kennesaw State University who created the instructor lecture slides.

## For the Third Edition:

Scott Betz, *Winston-Salem State University*

Denise Burge, *University of Cincinnati*

Holly Earhart, *Full Sail Real World Education*

Sarah Gjertson, *University of Denver*

Marth McLeish, *Indiana State University*

Julia Morrisroe, *University of Florida–Gainesville*

John Nettleton, *Ontario College of Art & Design*

Gayle Pendergrass, *Arkansas State University*

Renee Sandell, *George Mason University*

Kyle Trowbridge, *University of Miami*

Jeremy Waltman, *Florida State University*

Peter Winant, *George Mason University*

## For the Second Edition:

Kathleen Arkles, *College for Creative Studies*

Donald Barrie, *Seattle Central Community College*

Julie Baugnet, *St. Cloud State University*

Donna Beckis, *Fitchburg State College*

Nancy Blum-Cumming, *University of Wisconsin–Stout*

Debra K. D. Bonnello, *Lansing Community College*

Jeff Boshart, *Eastern Illinois University*

Jacquelin Boulanger, *New College of Florida*

Stephanie Bowman, *Pittsburgh State University*

Peter Brown, *Ringling School of Art*

John Carlander, *Westmont College*

Steven Cost, *Amarillo College*

Michael Croft, *University of Arizona*

Cat Crotchett, *Western Michigan University*

Claire Darley, *Art Academy of Cincinnati*

Anita M. DeAngelis, *East Tennessee State University*

Beverly Dennis

Tracy Doreen Dietzel, *Edgewood College*

Jim Doud, *American University*

Clyde L. Edwards, *Valdosta State University*

James Elniski, *School of Art Institute at Chicago*

Jane Fasse, *Edgewood College*

John Ford, *Labette Community College*

Corky Goss, *Cazenovia College*

Arlene Grossman, *Art Institute of Boston at Lesley University*

Danielle Harmon, *West Texas A&M University*

Christopher Hocking, *University of Georgia*

Carol Hodson, *Webster University*

Sara M. Hong, *University of Arizona*

Lorie Jesperson, *Lake Michigan College*

C. Ann Kittredge, *University of Maine–Presque Isle*

Deborah Krupenia, *Endicott College*

Michelle La Perriere, *Maryland Institute College of Art*

In Shile Lee, *Tompkins Cortland Community College*

Richard F. Martin, *New York Institute of Technology*

Christine McCullough, *Youngstown State University*

Julie McWilliams, *Sussex County College*

Nancy Morrow, *Kansas State University*

Byron Myrich, *Jones Junior College*

Kelly Nelson, *Longwood University*

Soon Ee Ngoh, *Mississippi State University*

Lara Nguyen, *California State University, Long Beach*

Grace O'Brien, *Purdue University*

Mark O'Grady, *Pratt Institute*

Sally Packard, *University of North Texas*

William Potter, *Herron School of Art–IUPUI*

Patsy C. Rainey, *University of Mississippi*

Gerson M. Rapaport, *New York Institute of Technology*

Gil Rocha, *Richland Community College*

Cherri Rittenhouse, *Rock Valley College*

William B. Rowe, *Ohio Northern University*

Kim Schrag, *Tompkins Courtland Community College*

Jean Sharer, *Front Range Community College*

Todd Slaughter, *Ohio State University*

Robert Smart, *Lawrence University*

Karen Spears, *Eastern Kentucky University*

Mindy Spritz, *The Art Institute of Atlanta*

Teresa Stoll, *Lake City Community College*

Katherine Stranse, *University of Arkansas–Little Rock*

Rob Tarbell, *Limestone College*

William Travis, *Rowan University*

Linda Vanderkolk, *Purdue University*

Carolynne Whitefeather, *Utica College*

Reid Wood, *Lorain County Community College*

Marilyn H. Wounded Head, *Mesa State College*

Alice Zinnes, *NYC College of Technology, CUNY*

## For the First Edition:

Scott Betz, *Weber State University*

Jeff Boshart, *Eastern Illinois University*

Peter Brown, *Ringling School of Art and Design*

Brian Cantley, *California State University, Fullerton*

Laurie Beth Clark, *University of Wisconsin, Madison*

Michael Croft, *University of Arizona*

John Fillwalk, *Ball State University*

David Fobes, *San Diego State University*

Albert Grivetti, *Clarke College*

Imi Hwangbo, *University of Louisville*

Michelle Illuminato, *Bowling Green State University*

Ann Baddeley Keister, *Grand Valley State University*

Margaret Keller, *St. Louis Community College*

Dan Lowery, *Southwestern Illinois College*

Karen Mahaffy, *University of Texas at San Antonio*

Richard Moses, *University of Illinois*

Gary Nemcosky, *Appalachian State University*

Helen Maria Nugent, *Art Institute of Chicago*

Rick Paul, *Purdue University*

Ron Saito, *California State University, Northridge*

Karen Schory, *Johnson County Community College*

Susan Slavick, *Carnegie Mellon University*

Paul Wittenbraker, *Grand Valley State University*

William Zack, *Ball State University*

part one

# Concepts and Critical Thinking

part two

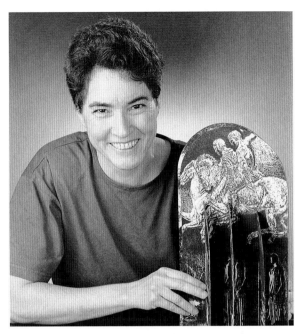

Author Mary Stewart with *Labyrinth* book.

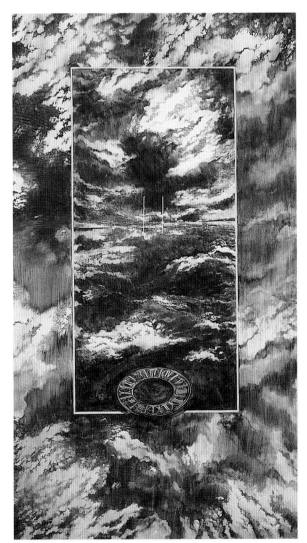

*Learning to Breathe #4, 1999.* Photocopy transfer and colored pencil, 84 × 44 in. (213.4 × 111.8 cm).

Mary Stewart is currently the Director of Foundations at Florida State University. She has received two grants from the Pennsylvania Council on the Arts and has participated in over 90 exhibitions, nationally and internationally.

From 1994–2004, Stewart worked with Greek philosophy as a primary source for her ideas. In Plato's famous dialogues, Socrates led his students through a series of conversations on the nature of beauty and the role of memory in developing knowledge. For Socrates, life was a process of self-discovery, a search for essential truths remembered from a pre-birth state. Unlike Aristotle, who argued that knowledge was derived from experience, Socrates suggested that knowledge was inherent and universal.

*Labyrinth,* shown in the top photo, is composed of 11 etchings based on cave paintings, fragments of early writing, and Greek sculpture. When collapsed, the book presents a cohesive composition; when opened, the images become fragmented, creating a sense of mystery. *Learning to Breathe,* at the bottom, is one of 12 84″ × 44″ drawings that are shown on four walls, surrounding the viewer with a series of triptychs consisting of three repeating titles: *Learning to Sink, Learning to Swim, Learning to Breathe.* As the viewer scans the room, the titles return back to the beginning, suggesting a cycle of death, transition, and birth. The size and shape of each image is intended to suggest a doorway, while photographs of train stations, clouds, gates, buildings from Hiroshima, and other ruins suggest the universal nature of memory.

about the author

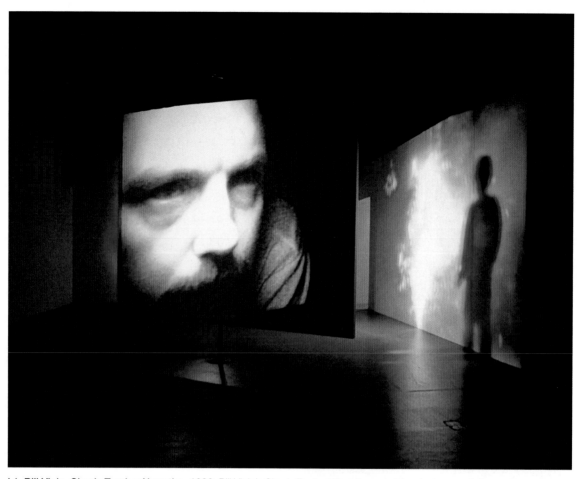

i.1 **Bill Viola, *Slowly Turning Narrative,* 1992.** Bill Viola's *Slowly Turning Narrative* consists of a large, rotating screen onto which moving images are projected. One side of the screen is a mirror, which reflects distorted images back into the room.

# BEGINNER'S MIND, OPEN MIND

You are ready to embark on a marvelous journey. New technologies and exhibition venues offer dazzling new ways to produce, perform, and publicize visual ideas. Contemporary art has expanded to include performances, earthworks and installations (i.1). Metalsmiths now use everything from plastics to precious metals to create inventive small-scale sculptures (i.2). Graphic designers develop many forms of visual communication, from shopping bags and exhibitions (i.3) to Web sites, logos, and brochures. Film and video are becoming increasingly integrated with the Internet, which promises to extend visual communication even further (i.4). The opportunities for exploration are endless (i.5). It is a great time to be studying art and design!

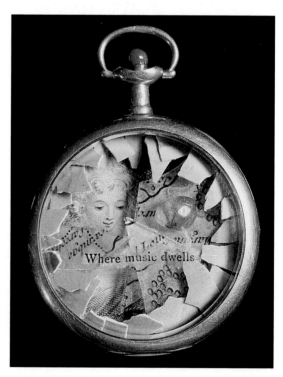

i.2 **Keith E. LoBue, *Where Music Dwells,* 1993.** A broken pocket watch can become an evocative artwork when images and words are added.

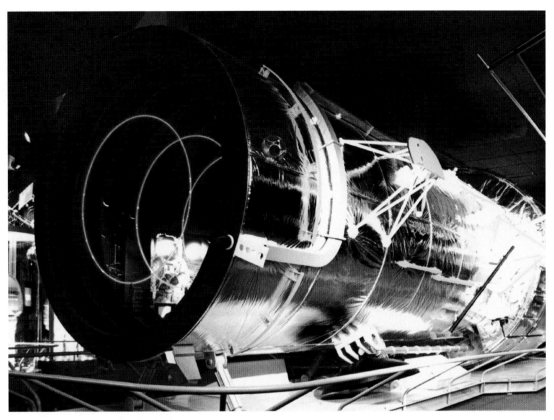

**i.3 Bill Cannan & Co., NASA's Participating Exhibit at the 1989 Paris Air Show.** To suggest the mystery of space travel and highlight individual displays, this NASA exhibition used dramatic pools of light within a mysterious dark setting.

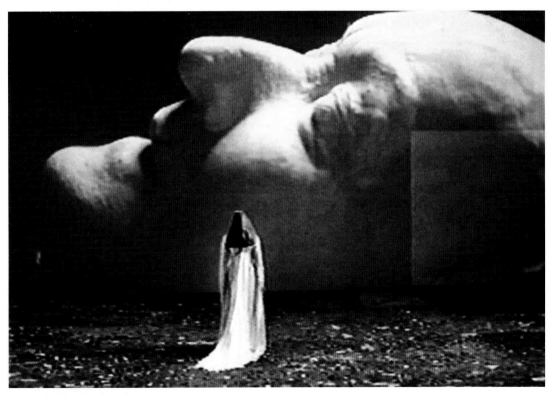

**i.4 Hans-Jürgen Syberberg, *Parsifal*, 1982.** Syberberg combined live actors with oversized projections of dreamlike landscapes in his filmic interpretation of Richard Wagner's opera.

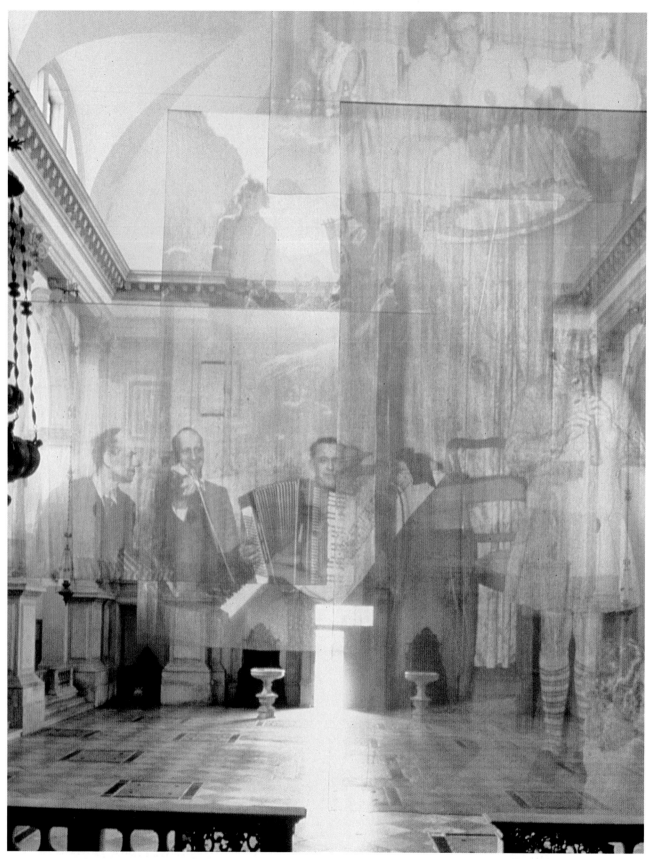

**i.5 Christian Marclay,** *Amplification,* **1995.** The photographic images in this installation shift, fuse, and divide, depending on the position of the viewer.

A journey of a thousand miles begins with one step. As a beginner, your first steps are especially important. Free of the preconceptions or habitual patterns that can paralyze more advanced students, beginners enter the learning experience with an open mind and an intense desire to explore new ideas. With no reputation to defend, they can more easily make the mistakes that are so essential to learning. Having taught students at all levels, I have found that beginners of any age are the most courageous by far. The open, unencumbered "beginner's mind" is wonderfully receptive and resilient. As a result, remarkable changes occur during your first year.

# DEFINING DESIGN

As a verb, *design* can be defined four ways:

- To plan, delineate, or define, as in designing a building
- To create a deliberate sequence of images or events, as in developing a film storyboard (i.6)
- To create a functional object, as in product design (i.7)
- To organize disparate parts into a coherent whole, as in composing a brochure

As a noun, *design* may be defined as

- A plan or pattern, such as the layout for a garden (i.8)
- An arrangement of lines, shapes, colors, and textures into an artistic whole, as in the composition of a painting or sculpture (i.9)

Design is deliberate. Rather than hope for the best and accept the result, artists and designers explore a wide range of solutions to every problem, then choose the most promising option for further development. Even when chance is used to generate ideas, choices are often made before the results are shown. Design creates a bridge between artistic intention and compositional conclusion. As painter Joseph Albers noted, "To design is to plan and to organize, to order, to relate and to control."

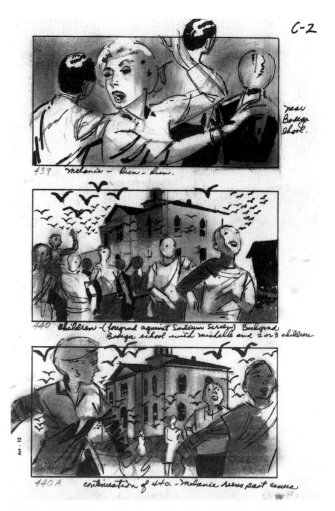

**i.6 Harold Michelson, Storyboard for Alfred Hitchcock's *The Birds.*** Storyboards are used to plan the sequence of events and compose the specific shots in a film. Alfred Hitchcock, who began his career as an artist, preplanned his films with exacting care.

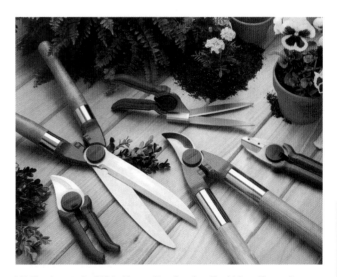

**i.7 Designworks/USA, Home Pro Garden Tool Line.** These five gardening tools are all based on the same basic combination of handle, blades, and simple pivot. Variations in proportion determine their use.

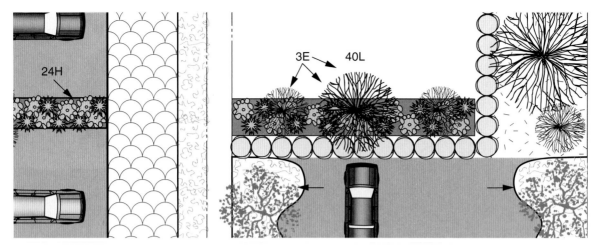

**i.8 Garden Design.** An extensive layout is generally used for planning a garden. Matching the plants to the soil conditions, setting, climate, and overall intent saves money and improves results. In this case, the design is not an artwork in itself but, rather, a plan of action.

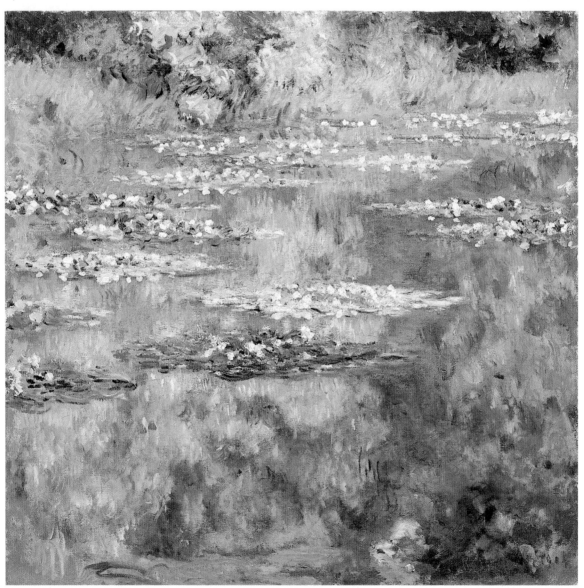

**i.9 Claude Monet,** *Waterlily Pond (Le Bassin des Nymphéas),* **1904.** Impressionist Claude Monet moved to the village of Giverny in 1883 and built an extensive water garden. The waterlilies he grew there inspired his last major series of paintings. Monet combined lines, shapes, textures, and colors to create a compelling illusion of a shimmering space.

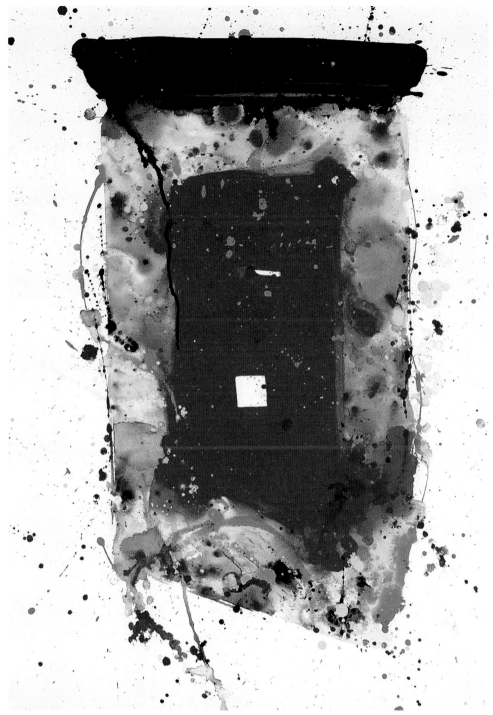

**i.10 Sam Francis, *Flash Point,* 1975.** Surrounded by explosive energy, the white square in the center of this painting provides a unifying focal point.

Two-dimensional compositions are constructed from lines, shapes, textures, values, and colors that have been arranged to create a unified whole (i.10). Lines, planes, volumes, masses, and space are the basic components of a three-dimensional composition (i.11). Time design, including video, photography, performance, kinetic sculpture, and the book arts (i.12), is based on the juxtaposition of images and events. A great idea never saved a bad painting. Art and design are visual forms of communication: without careful composition, a great idea may be lost.

Developing a wide range of solutions to every problem is the quickest way to master composition. Small, quick studies are often used to explore the

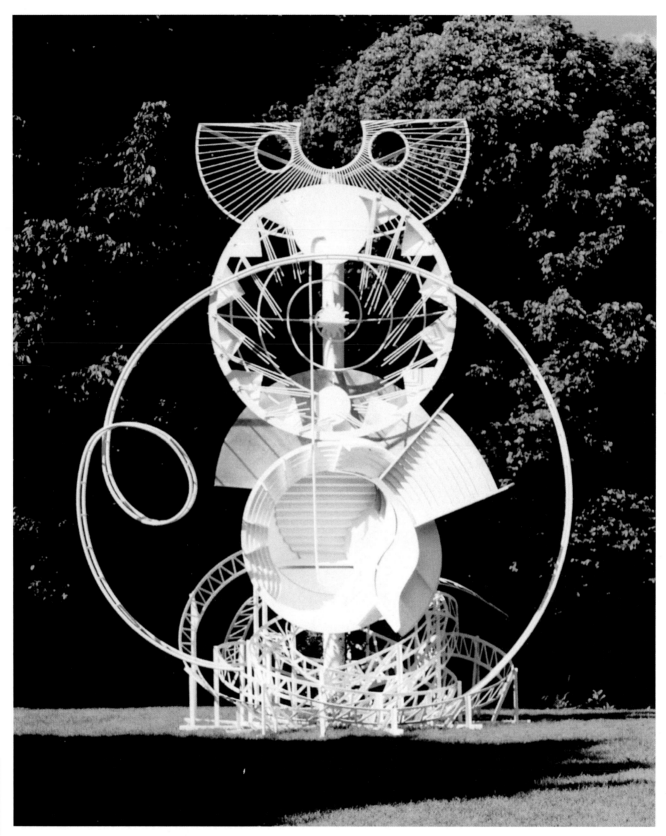

**i.11** Alice Aycock, *Tree of Life Fantasy: Synopsis of the Book of Questions Concerning the World Order and/or the Order of Worlds,* **1990–92.** Inspired by the double-helix structure of DNA and by medieval illustrations representing the entrance to paradise as a spinning hole in the sky, Aycock has combined a linear structure with a series of circular planes and a lot of open space. The resulting sculpture is as open and playful as a roller coaster.

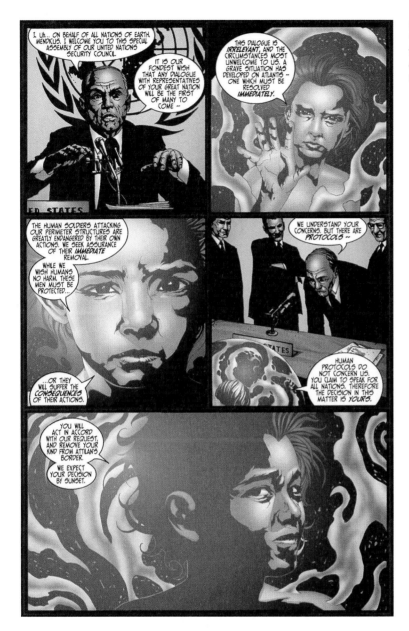

**i.12 Paul Jenkins and Jae Lee, from _Inhumans:_ "First Contact," March 1999.** Comic books, like films, rely on the development of characters, the use of "camera" angles, and the organization of multiple images.

possibilities. By translating a mental image into a rough sketch, you can immediately see whether the idea has potential. Furthermore, the best way to have a good idea is to have a lot of ideas. If you explore only one idea, you are far less likely to produce an inventive image. By selecting the best rough composition from 20 sketches, you will have a better beginning point for your final design.

In the pages that follow, the basic elements, principles, and implications of design are explored in depth. Over 600 images supply visual examples from many cultures and in all areas of art and design.

Fifteen interviews with living artists provide insight into the creative process.

Reading this book, however, is just the first step. True understanding comes through your own efforts, combined with the direction your teachers can provide. Remember that basic drawing and design courses provide the foundation on which all subsequent courses are built. You are only a college beginner once in your entire life: this is not a rehearsal. By using your time well, you really _can_ get the rocket off the launching pad.

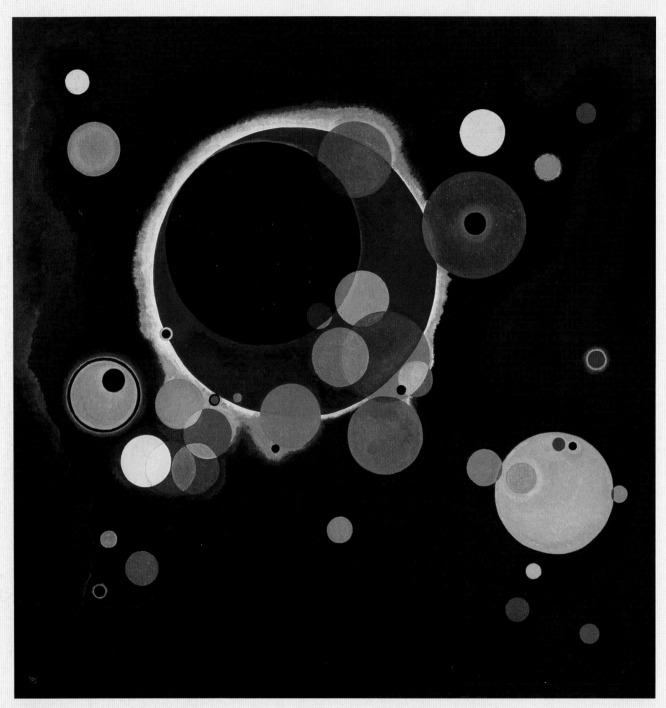

**Wassily Kandinsky,** *Several Circles,* **1926.** Oil on canvas, 55¼ × 55⅝ in. (140.3 × 140.7 cm).

# Two-Dimensional Design

The careful observation required for drawing, the understanding of color required for watercolor painting, and the craftsmanship required for metalsmithing can increase awareness of ourselves and our world. On a personal level, making art heightens our attention, engages our emotions, and provides a sense of accomplishment. Creating objects and images is engrossing and exhilarating. These personal rewards make art one of the most popular hobbies.

As art and design professionals, we must translate our personal insights into public communication. No one will pay for the production of meaningless images. The ideas and emotions a professional wishes to express must engage an audience, whether the encounter occurs in the silence of a museum or in the chaos of a city street.

This ability to communicate visually is developed through years of study plus relentless practice. Artists and designers must develop their visual awareness, create new concepts, and master various techniques. They spend hours in the studio, refining ideas and inventing alternative solutions to each visual problem. Creating the most powerful image is their compelling goal.

The elements and principles of design are the building blocks from which images are made. Line, shape, texture, and value are presented in Chapter One. Chapter Two is devoted to the characteristics and compositional impact of color. Chapter Three introduces a wide range of basic organizational strategies, known as the principles of design. These basic principles are expanded in Chapter Four, which is devoted to the illusion of space and the illusion of motion.

# Part One

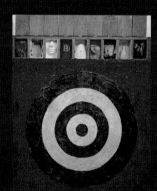

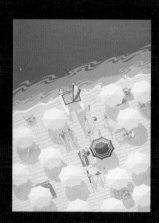

# Basic Elements

Line, shape, texture, value, and color are the basic building blocks from which two-dimensional designs are made. Just as oxygen and hydrogen are powerful both individually and when combined as $H_2O$, so these visual **elements** are powerful both independently and in combination. In this chapter, we will explore the unique characteristics of the four most basic elements and analyze their uses in art and design. Color, the most complex element, will be discussed in Chapter Two.

## LINE

### Defining Line

**Line** is one of the simplest and most versatile elements of design. Line may be defined as

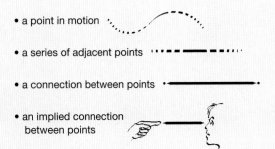

- a point in motion
- a series of adjacent points
- a connection between points
- an implied connection between points

**1.1** Despite its apparent simplicity, line can be created in many ways and can play many roles in a design.

The inherent dynamism of line is embodied in the first definition. The remaining three definitions emphasize the connective power of line. Lighter and more fluid than any of the other visual elements, line can add a special energy to a design. Simply by drawing a line, we can activate a space, define a shape, or create a compositional bridge.

### Line Quality

Each line has its own distinctive quality. This quality is largely determined by the line's orientation, direction, degree of continuity, and by the material used.

**Orientation** refers to the line's horizontal, vertical, or diagonal position. Diagonal lines and curving lines are generally the most dynamic (1.2A, 1.2D). Charged with energy, they suggest action and movement. Horizontal lines are typically the most stable, or static (1.2B). Vertical lines imply *potential* change,

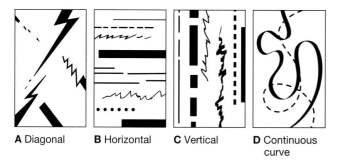

| **A** Diagonal | **B** Horizontal | **C** Vertical | **D** Continuous curve |

**1.2** Line orientation and continuity.

and can be static or dynamic, depending on the context in which they are placed (1.2C).

**Direction** refers to the implied movement of a line. Line weight is often used to accentuate direction. Generally, a swelling line suggests forward or outward movement, while a shrinking line suggests inward movement. Notice how the top and bottom diagonal lines in figure 1.2A seem to push forward as they become thicker.

**Continuity,** or linear flow, can enhance direction. As shown in figure 1.2D, a continuous line tends to generate a stronger sense of direction than a broken or jagged line.

Each material can be used to produce a range of distinctive lines. Metallic graphite can be used to produce modulating lines of varying thickness. A felt pen produces a crisp, clean, emphatic line. Charcoal and chalk are black, soft, and highly responsive to each change in pressure and direction. Brush and ink offers even wider variation in line width, continuity, and darkness. By experimenting with the range of marks each instrument can produce, we can use each material more expressively.

A strong match between line quality and the expressive intent is essential. The network of agitated lines Giacometti used in figure 1.3 suggests anxiety, while the fluid lines in figure 1.4 express movement and energy. Barnett Newman used two very different lines in *Stations of the Cross: Lema Sabachthani, The First Station* (1.5). The solid black line gains stability through its parallel position along the left edge of the painting. In contrast, the line on the right is agitated and exposed, surrounded by open space. In this painting, Newman used just two lines to express both spiritual strength and human fragility.

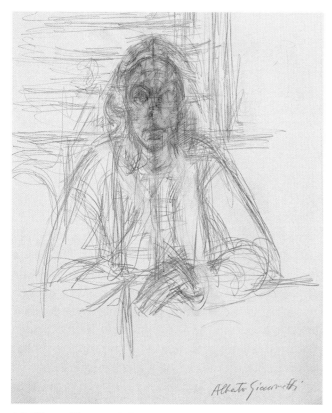

**1.3 Alberto Giacometti,** *Annette,* **1954.** Pencil on paper, 16⅜ × 11¾ in. (41.59 × 29.85 cm).

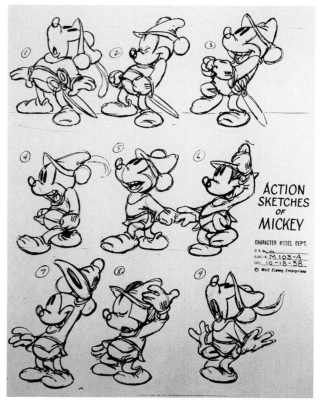

**1.4** This is an original sketch of a Walt Disney Mickey Mouse cartoon done by Walt Disney artists Frank Thomas and Ollie Johnston.

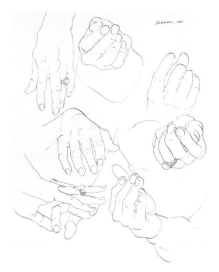

**1.6 Eleanor Dickinson, *Study of Hands,***
**1964.** Pen and ink, 13⅛ × 10⅛ in.
(34 × 26 cm).

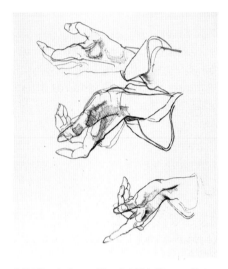

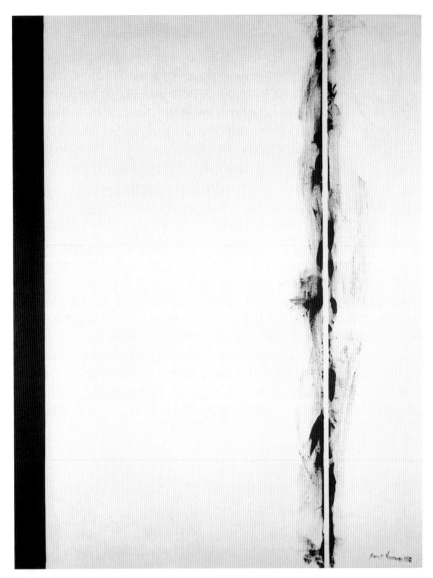

**1.5 Barnett Newman, *Stations of the Cross: Lema Sabachthani, The First Station,***
**1958.** Magna on canvas, 6 ft 5⅞ in. × 5 ft ½ in. (1.98 × 1.54 cm).

**1.7 Rico Lebrun, *Hand,* 1964.** Pen and ink.

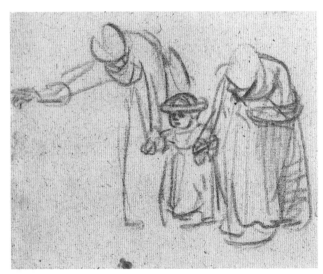

**1.8 Rembrandt van Rijn, *Two Women Helping a Child to Walk,***
**c. 1635–37.** Black chalk.

## Actual Lines

**Actual lines** can describe complex forms simply and eloquently. In figure 1.6, Eleanor Dickinson used pen and ink **contour lines** to define both the inner and outer edges of a woman's hands. Through contour drawing, the complex anatomy was distilled down to a few simple lines. Similarly, Rico Lebrun's **gesture drawing** of a hand (1.7) captures essential action rather than describing anatomical detail. We focus on what the hand is *doing* rather than on what the hand *is*. As shown in figure 1.8, Rembrandt often used economical lines to describe the spheres and cylindrical volumes from which figures are made.

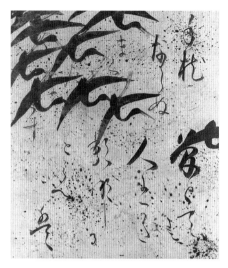

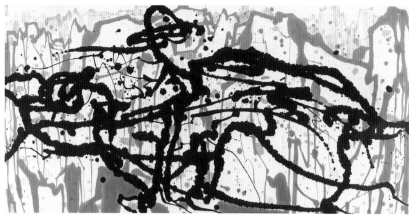

1.10 Wu Guanzhong, *Pine Spirit,* 1984. Chinese ink, color on paper, 2 ft 3⅝ in. × 5 ft 3½ in. (70 × 140 cm).

1.9 Attributed to Tawaraya Sôtatsu, calligraphy by Hon'ami Koetsu, *Flying Cranes and Poetry,* Edo period (1615–1868). Ink on gray-blue paper, gold flecked, 7⅝ × 6⅜ in. (19 × 16 cm).

Because it communicates information using basic volumes, this type of line drawing is often called a **volume summary.**

**Calligraphic lines** can add even more energy to a drawing or a design. The word *calligraphy* is derived from two Greek words: *kalus,* meaning "beautiful," and *graphein,* meaning "to write." Like handwriting, the calligraphic line is both personal and highly expressive. In figure 1.9, words and images are combined in a celebration of flight. Painter Tawaraya Sôtatsu and calligrapher Hon'ami Koetsu used variations in line weight and continuity to suggest the graceful motion of birds. This exploration of movement is pushed even further in *Pine Spirit,* by Wu Guanzhong (1.10). Fluid ink lines record the movement of the artist's hand while simultaneously creating an abstract landscape. There is a wonderful economy in each of these drawings. Like poetry, a rich story is told using minimal means.

**Organizational lines** are often used to create the loose linear "skeleton" on which a composition can be built. Ideas can be developed quickly through line, and compositional changes can be made easily. As shown in the Giacometti drawing in figure 1.3, these skeletal drawings have great energy and may be presented as artworks in themselves. In other cases, organizational lines provide the framework for elaborate compositions. When we analyze Alfred Leslie's *The Killing Cycle* (1.11), we can discern an

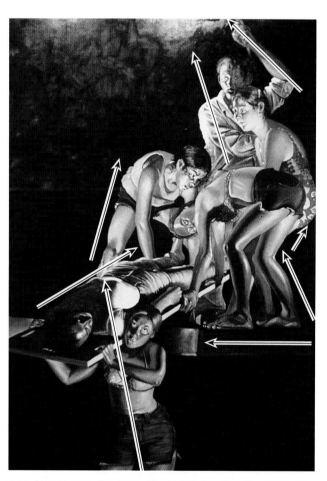

1.11 Alfred Leslie, *The Killing Cycle (#5): Loading Pier,* 1975. Oil on canvas, 9 × 6 ft (2.7 × 1.8 m).

underlying framework. A dead man on a diagonal board connects a single woman in the lower left corner to the four figures in the upper right. A horizontal line supports these four figures, while their bent arms and legs create even more diagonal lines. The diagonal lines add energy to the composition, while the horizontal line increases stability.

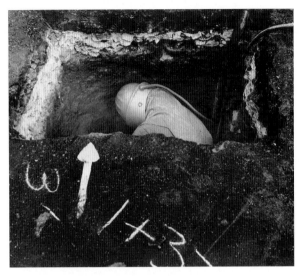

**1.12** A series of dots can create an implied line.

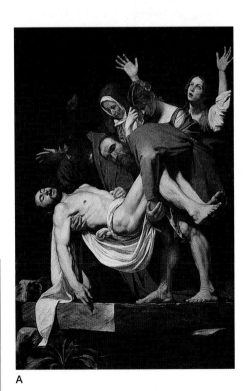

**1.13** Minor White, *Sandblaster,* San Francisco, 1949. Gelatin silver print, 10⁷⁄₁₆ × 11⁷⁄₁₆ in. (26.51 × 29.05 cm).

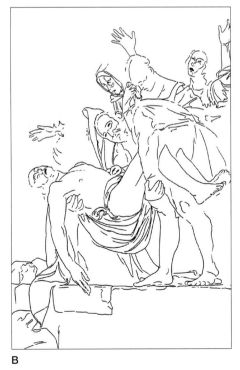

A                                    B

**1.14** Caravaggio, *The Deposition,* **1604.** Oil on canvas, 9 ft 10⅛ in. × 6 ft 7⅞ in. (3 × 2.03 m).

## Implied Lines

Lines can play a major role in a design even when they are implied rather than actually being drawn. Because **implied lines** simply *suggest* connections, the viewer must become actively involved in compositions that are constructed using this type of line.

Fortunately, we have a natural inclination to seek visual unity. Given enough clues, we will connect separate visual parts by filling in the missing pieces. The visual clues may be quite obvious. For example, we can easily link the circles in figure 1.12 to create a linear spiral. In other cases, the clues are subtle. In Minor White's *Sandblaster* (1.13), the white arrow implies a connection between the numbers in the foreground and the worker's helmet.

This inclination to connect fragmentary information is called **closure**. "Lost and found" contours require an elegant form of closure. In a "lost and found" composition, the edges of some shapes are clearly defined, while other shapes appear to merge with the background. When presented with such an image, the viewer must create a mental bridge between the resulting islands of information.

*The Killing Cycle* (1.11) is an example of a lost and found composition. The top four figures are clearly delineated, while the lower two figures begin to merge with the surrounding space. This effect is even more pronounced in Caravaggio's *The Deposition* (1.14A), the painting from which Leslie derived his inspiration. A line drawing of this image has many gaps, as details are lost in the shadows (1.14B). Used skillfully, this loss of definition becomes a strength rather than a weakness. Connections made through closure can stimulate the viewer's imagination and encourage a more personal interpretation.

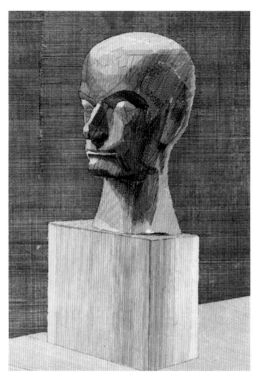

1.15 Jacques Villon, *Baudelaire,* c. 1918. Etching, printed in black, plate 16⁵⁄₁₆ × 11 in. (41.4 × 28 cm).

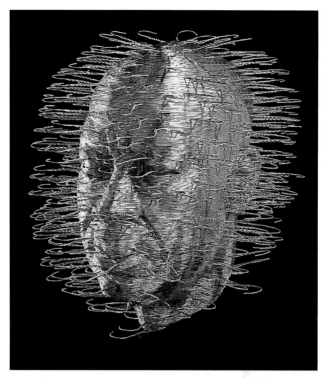

1.16 David Mach, *Eckow,* 1997. Coathangers, 2 ft 2¼ in. × 1 ft 11½ in. × 2 ft 5½ in. (67 × 60 × 75 cm).

## Linear Networks

Multiple lines can add detail to a design and create a convincing illusion of space. **Hatching** produces a range of grays through straight parallel lines. An even wider range of grays can be produced through **cross-hatching,** which creates a more complex network of lines. Jacques Villon used both hatching and cross-hatching in his portrait of poet Charles Baudelaire (1.15). The head is divided into a series of faceted planes. Hatching defines each shift in the surface of the head, while cross-hatching creates the shadows.

**Cross-contours** can create an even more powerful illusion of three-dimensionality. Often created using curving parallel lines, cross-contours "map" surface variations across shapes or objects. In figure 1.16, David Mach created a cross-contour sculpture by bending coat hangers into the shape of a human head. In two-dimensional design, we can use drawn lines to produce a similar effect.

Hatching, cross-hatching, as well as cross-contour are often combined. In *Head of a Satyr* (1.17), Michelangelo used all of these techniques to visually carve out the curves and planes of the head.

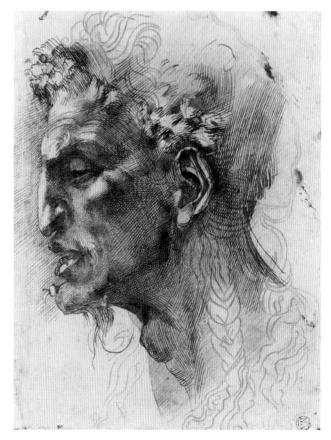

1.17 Michelangelo, *Head of a Satyr,* c. 1620–30. Pen and ink over chalk, 10⅝ × 7⅞ in. (27 × 20 cm).

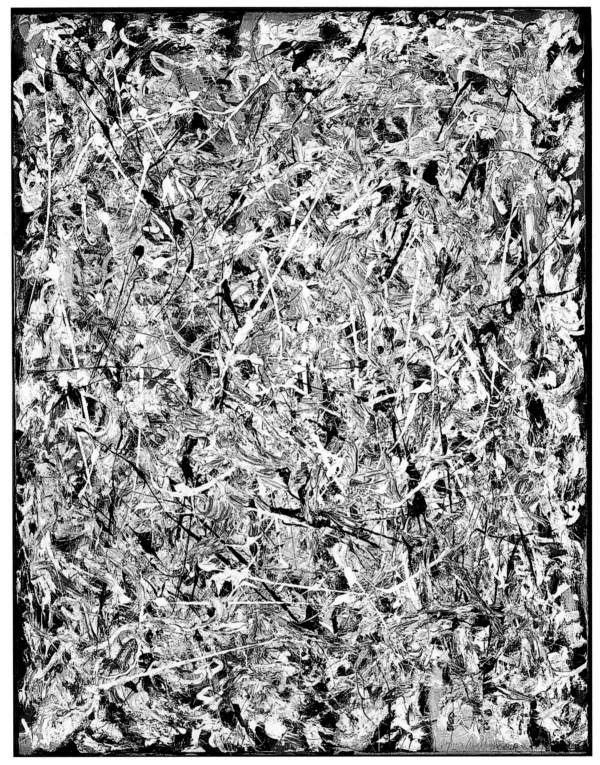

**1.18 Jackson Pollock,** *White Light,* **1954.** Oil, enamel. aluminum paint on canvas, 48¼ × 38¼ in. (122.4 × 96.9 cm).

Line networks play an equally important role in abstract and nonobjective art. Jackson Pollock dripped and spattered house paint to produce *White Light*, shown in figure 1.18. Seeking universal meaning rather than conventional representation, Pollock spontaneously generated many layers of lines on a large piece of canvas. He then trimmed the canvas, discarding the weaker sections of the design. The remaining lines seem to flow in and out of the painting. Clusters of silvery enamel form swirling, textural masses that are punctuated by explosions of red and yellow.

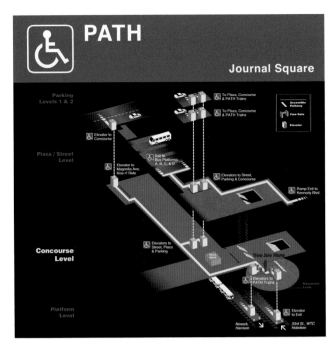

**1.19 PATH Station Maps, Louis Nelson Associates, Inc., NY.**
Graphic designer: Jennifer Stoller.

## Using Line

Line can be used to define, enclose, connect, or dissect. Line serves all of these purposes in a New York City subway map (1.19). A curved line has been combined with an angular line to define the wheelchair logo. Another line encloses this logo within a square, emphasizing its importance. Diagonal lines connect the subway entrance to the elevators, while vertical lines dissect the drawing to highlight the location of the elevators. This seemingly simple design communicates complex information clearly. Using this map, a person in a wheelchair can navigate through a busy station and catch the right train.

Careful use of the four edges of a sheet of paper can strengthen any design. In a sense, the first line we draw is actually the *fifth* line in the composition. In his *Self-Portrait* (1.20), Joel Peter Johnson used drawn lines to echo the four edges of the composition. Johnson's head breaks out of this linear boundary. As a result, the portrait appears to extend beyond the painting's edge and into the world of the viewer.

Lines can serve many purposes at once. In an advertisement for the American Institute of Graphic Arts (1.21), vertical dotted lines at the upper left and lower right highlight the speaker's schedule. A horizontal line creates a connection between the *D* and *B* in the "design to business" logo, and separates the top and bottom of the overall layout. Even

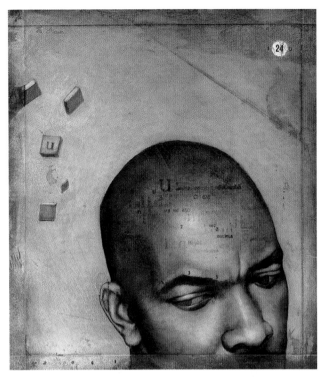

**1.20 Joel Peter Johnson, *Self-Portrait*.** Oil on board, 9 × 8 in. (22.86 × 20.32 cm).

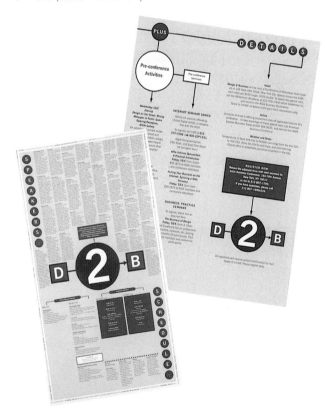

**1.21 Brochure from an American Institute of Graphic Arts Conference "Design 2 Business, October 5–6 '96 NYC."**

the columns of text can be read as vertical and horizontal lines.

Despite their apparent simplicity, lines can add structure, movement, and cohesion to all forms of two-dimensional design, from paintings to posters.

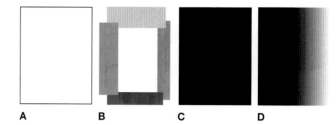

**1.22** Any form of enclosure can create a shape.

## Key Questions

- What is the dominant orientation of the lines in your design—diagonal, vertical, or horizontal? What is the expressive effect?
- What happens when lines are repeated or when lines intersect?
- How would the composition change if one or more lines were removed?
- Consider using line to direct attention to areas of particular importance.

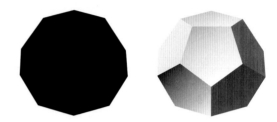

**1.23** Variations in lighting can transform a shape into an illusory volume.

# SHAPE

## Defining Shape

A **shape** is a flat, enclosed area (1.22A–D). Shapes can be created by

- Enclosing an area within a continuous line
- Surrounding an area by other shapes
- Filling an area with solid color or texture
- Filling an area with broken color or texture

A three-dimensional enclosure is called a **volume.** Thus, a square is a shape, while a cube is a volume. **Gradation,** or **shading,** can be used to make a two-dimensional shape appear three-dimensional, or volumetric. For example, in figure 1.23, a flat, angular shape becomes a faceted polyhedron when a series of gray tones is added.

Flat or gradated shapes can be used to create an arresting image. In Aaron Douglas' *Aspects of Negro Life: From Slavery Through Reconstruction* (1.24), flat shapes and transparent targets create an energetic panorama. We can almost hear

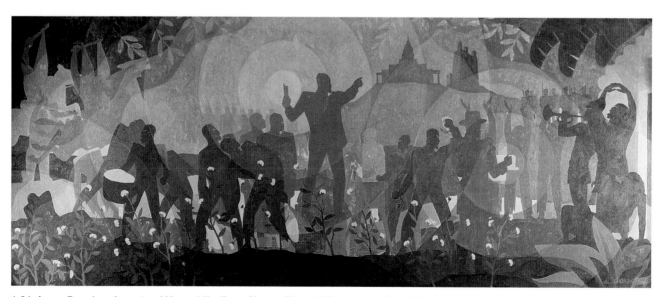

**1.24** Aaron Douglas, *Aspects of Negro Life: From Slavery Through Reconstruction,* **1934.** Oil on canvas, 5 ft × 11 ft 7 in. (1.52 × 3.5 m).

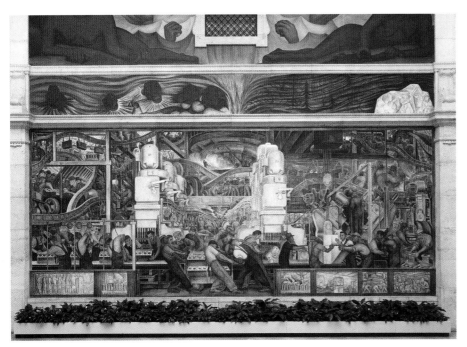

1.25 Diego M. Rivera, *Detroit Industry, North Wall*, 1932–33. Fresco, 17 ft 8½ in. × 45 ft (5.4 × 13.7 m).

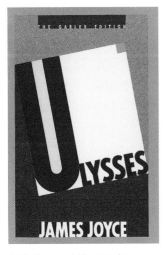

1.26 Cover of *Ulysses,* by James Joyce, 1986. Designer: Carin Goldberg.

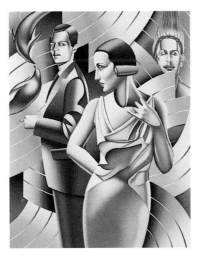

1.27 Cover image from *The Penguin Pool Murder,* a Hildegarde Withers Mystery, by Stuart Palmer. Art Director & Designer: Krystyna Skalski, Illustrator: John Jinks.

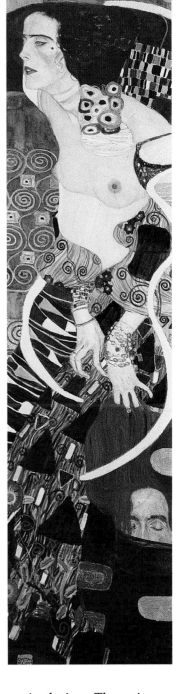

1.28 Gustav Klimt, *Salomé,* 1909. Oil on canvas, 70⅛ × 18⅛ in. (178 × 46 cm).

the speaker in the center and feel the movement of the crowd. In Rivera's *Detroit Industry* (1.25), a combination of size variation and shading suggest volume and increase the illusion of space. One-point perspective (which will be discussed at length in Chapter Four) has been used to increase visual depth even further.

Graphic designers are equally aware of the power of both flat and gradated shapes. In a cover for *Ulysses* (1.26), Carin Goldberg used crisp, simple shapes to create a dramatic design. The primary colors of red, yellow, and blue, combined with the slanted title block, immediately attract attention. Krystyna Skalski and John Jinks used a very different approach for their cover for a mystery novel (1.27). Gradation now suggests a light source and helps create the illusion of space.

Gustav Klimt combined flat and volumetric shapes to create *Salomé* (1.28). In this horrific tale from the biblical New Testament, John the Baptist has been imprisoned for his criticism of the royal family. Salomé, the king's niece, performs a stunning dance and the delighted king grants her a single wish. In revenge, Salomé asks for John's head. The tall, vertical shape of the painting is similar to the size and shape of a standing viewer. Flat patterns and color surround the volumetric figures, while two curving lines add a sinuous energy to the center of the design.

## Types of Shape

The size and shape of a soccer field are very different from the size and shape of a tennis court. In both cases, the playing area defines the game to be played. It is impossible to play soccer on a tennis court or to play tennis on a soccer field.

Similarly, the outer edge of a two-dimensional design provides the playing field for our compositional games. The long, horizontal rectangles used by Douglas and Rivera create an expansive panorama,

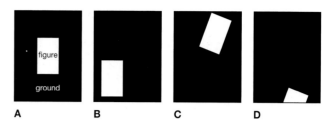

**1.29** Various figure/ground relationships.

while the vertical rectangle used for Salomé compresses the sordid drama into a narrow, claustrophobic column. Thus, creating a dialogue between compositional shapes and the surrounding format is our first area of concern.

### Figure and Ground, Positive and Negative

As shown in figure 1.29A, a shape that is distinguished from the background is called a **positive shape,** or **figure.** The area around a positive shape is called the **negative shape,** or **ground.** Depending on its location relative to the ground, the figure can become dynamic or static, leaden or buoyant (1.29B–D).

In traditional paintings such as Caravaggio's *The Deposition,* the entire composition is treated like a window into an imaginary world. To increase this illusion, the canvas texture is sanded down before the paint is applied, and heavy brushstrokes are kept at a minimum. We are invited to see *into* the painting, rather than focusing on its surface.

When a shaped format is used, we become more aware of the artwork's physicality. The 9-foot-tall teacup in Elizabeth Murray's *Just in Time* (1.30) is monumental in size and loaded with implication. The painted shapes connect directly to the shaped edge, emphasizing the crack running down the center of the composition. This is no ordinary teacup. For Murray, this crack in everyday reality invites us to enter an alternative world.

When the figure and ground are equally well designed, every square inch of the composition becomes supercharged. In Bill Brandt's photograph (1.31), the brightly lit arm, face, and breast dramatically divide

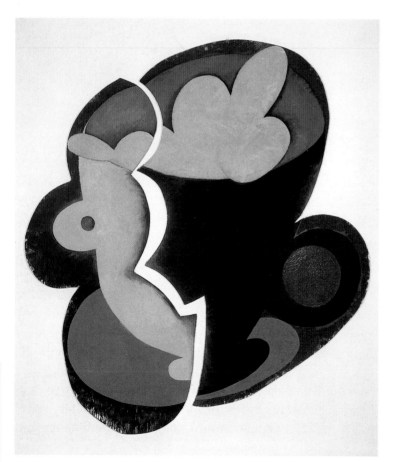

**1.30 Elizabeth Murray,** *Just in Time,* **1981.** Oil on canvas in two sections, 106 × 97 in. (269.24 × 246.38 cm).

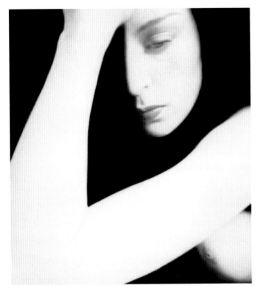

1.31 Bill Brandt, *Nude*, 1952. Gelatin silver print.

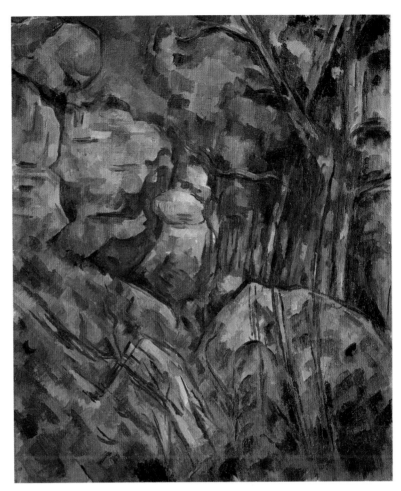

1.32 Paul Cézanne, *Rocks Near the Caves above the Chateau Noir,* 1904. Oil on canvas, 21.3 × 25.6 in. (54 × 65 cm).

the black ground, creating three strong, triangular shapes. These triangles energize the design and heighten our awareness of the compositional edge.

An ambiguous or shifting relationship between figure and ground can add surprising energy and power to a design. In Paul Cézanne's *Rocks Near the Caves above the Chateau Noir* (1.32), the trees and cliffs begin to break apart, creating a shifting pattern of planes and spaces. Completed just one year before Einstein published his special theory of relativity, this painting served as a springboard into Cubism.

Figure/ground reversal pushes this effect even further. **Figure/ground reversal** occurs when first the positive then the negative shapes command our attention. As shown in a fragment from *Metamorphosis II* (1.33), M. C. Escher was a master of figure/ground reversal. The organic shapes on the left become an interlocking mass of black and white lizards. The lizards then evolve into a network of hexagons. Combined with the figure/ground reversal, this type of metamorphosis animates the entire 13-foot-long composition.

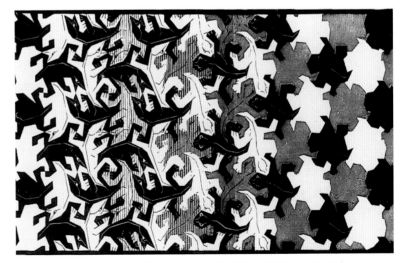

1.33 M. C. Escher, part of *Metamorphosis II,* 1939–40. Woodcut in black, green, and brown, printed from twenty blocks on three combined sheets, 7½ × 153⅜ in. (19 × 390 cm).

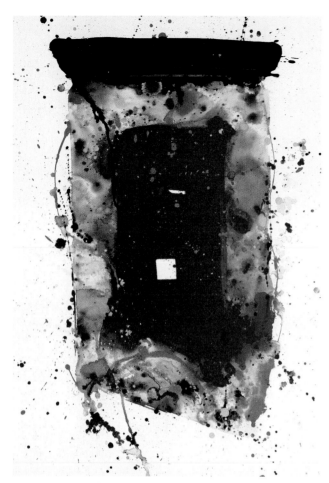

1.34 Sam Francis, *Flash Point*, 1975. Acrylic on paper, 32¼ × 22⅞ in. (82 × 59 cm).

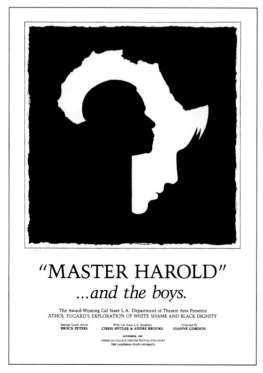

1.35 David McNutt, *"Master Harold" . . . and the Boys,* 1985. Poster.

Figure/ground reversal requires a carefully balanced dialogue between opposing forces. Escher generally achieved this balance by using light and dark shapes of similar size. In figure 1.34, Sam Francis achieved a similar balance between a very small white square and a much larger red rectangle. The crisp boundary and central location strengthen the square. Despite its small size, it holds its own against the larger mass of swirling red paint.

Graphic designers often use figure/ground reversal to create multiple interpretations from minimal shapes. In figure 1.35, David McNutt used a single white shape on a black ground to create the head of a master and a servant within the outline of Africa. Used to advertise a South African play, the poster immediately communicates a dramatic human relationship within a specific cultural context.

### Rectilinear and Curvilinear Shapes

**Rectilinear shapes** are composed from straight lines and angular corners. **Curvilinear shapes** are dominated by curves and flowing edges. Simple rectilinear shapes, such as squares and rectangles, are generally cooperative. When placed within a rectangular format, they easily connect to other shapes and can run parallel to the compositional edge (1.36A). Curvilinear shapes, especially circles, are generally less cooperative. They retain their individuality even when they are partially concealed by other shapes (1.36B).

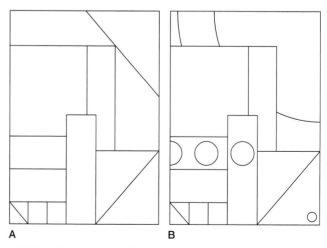

A          B

1.36 **Rectilinear and curvilinear shapes.** Rectilinear shapes can easily be fit together to create a unified design. Curvilinear shapes tend to be more individualistic.

Aubrey Beardsley (1.37) combined rectilinear and curvilinear shapes to create another interpretation of the Salomé story, described on pages 11–12. Using an internal boundary line, he emphasized the composition's rectangular shape. Within this boundary, curving black and white shapes create a series of complex visual relationships. A bubble pattern dominates the upper left corner. In the upper right corner, Salomé clutches Saint John's head. Extending from the head down to the flower, a white line follows the transformation of the dead saint's blood into a living plant. This line creates a conceptual and compositional connection between the top and bottom edges.

A very different combination of rectilinear and curvilinear shapes activates Robert Rauschenberg's *Brace* (1.38). The central image of three baseball players is surrounded by layered rectangles to the right, left, and bottom. A solid line extends from the catcher to the top edge. Vigorous brushstrokes add power to the painting. Occupying only a small fraction of the composition and surrounded by vigorously painted shapes, the circle *still* dominates the design: we *have* to keep our eyes on the ball!

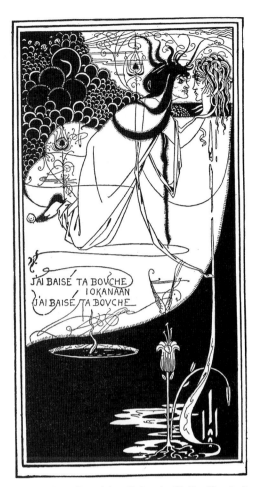

**1.37 Aubrey Beardsley,** *Salomé with the Head of John the Baptist,* **1894.** Line block print, 11 × 6 in. (27.9 × 15.2 cm).

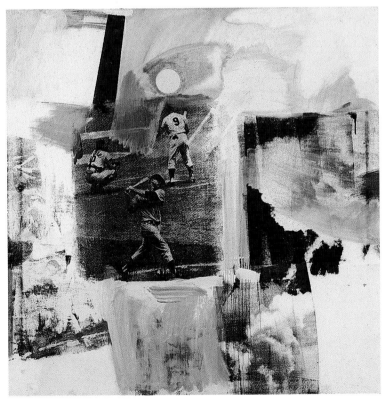

**1.38 Robert Rauschenberg,** *Brace,* **1962.** Oil and silkscreen on canvas, 60 × 60 in. (152.4 × 152.4 cm).

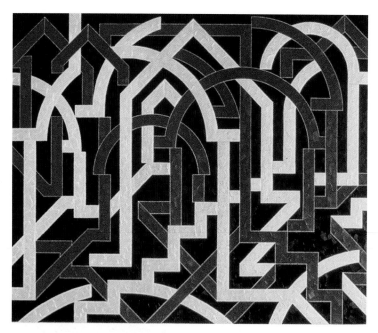

1.39 Valerie Jaudon, *Tallahatchee*, 1984. Oil and gold leaf on canvas, 6 ft 8 in. × 8 ft (2 × 2.4 m).

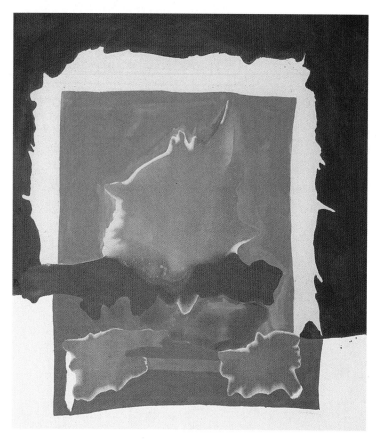

1.40 Helen Frankenthaler, *Interior Landscape*, 1964. Acrylic on canvas, 8 ft 8⅞ in. × 7 ft 8⅝ in. (266 × 235 cm).

### *Geometric and Organic Shapes*

**Geometric shapes** are distinguished by their crisp precise edges and mathematically consistent curves. They dominate the technological world of architecture and industry, and they appear in nature as crystalline structures and growth patterns, such as the spiral. In Valerie Jaudon's *Tallahatchee* (1.39), geometric shapes provide a clarity, harmony, and universality comparable to a musical composition. **Organic shapes** are more commonly found in the natural world of plants and animals, sea and sky. As shown in Frankenthaler's *Interior Landscape* (1.40), organic shapes can add unpredictable energy, even when the composition as a whole is based on rectangular shapes.

## Degrees of Representation

**Nonobjective shapes,** such as circles, rectangles, and squares, are **pure forms.** Pure forms are shapes created without direct reference to reality. Artists often use pure form to embody elusive emotions or express universal meaning. For example, in *Several Circles* (1.41), Wassily Kandinsky sought to express his complex spiritual feelings. For him, the simple circular shapes were as poignant and expressive as music.

**Representational shapes** are derived from specific subject matter and strongly based on direct observation. Most photographs are representational and highly descriptive. For example, in Ansel Adams' *Monolith, The Face of Half Dome, Yosemite Valley* (1.42), each variation in the cliff's surface is clearly defined.

Between these two extremes, **abstract shapes** are derived from visual reality but are distilled or transformed, reducing their resemblance to the original source. In *Seventh Sister* (1.43), Robert Moskowitz deleted surface details from the rocky mountain. His abstracted cliff is a general representation of a vertical surface rather than a descriptive painting of a specific cliff.

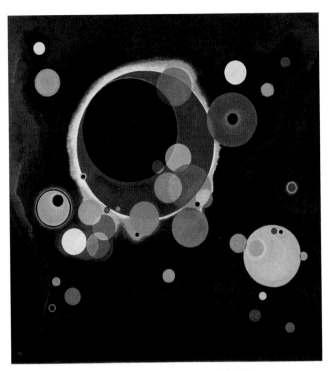

**1.41** Wassily Kandinsky, *Several Circles,* **1926.** Oil on canvas, 55¼ × 55⅜ in. (140.3 × 140.7 cm).

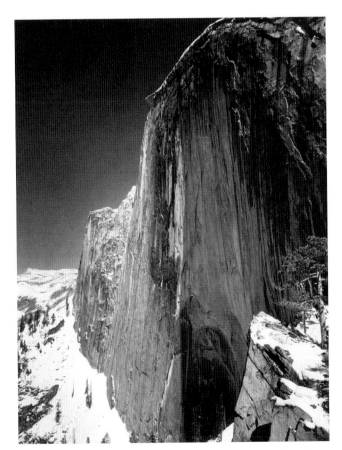

**1.42** Ansel Adams, *Monolith, The Face of Half Dome, Yosemite Valley.* Photograph.

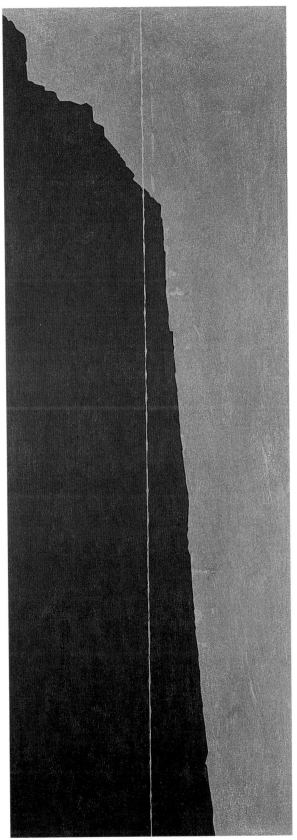

**1.43** Robert Moskowitz, *Seventh Sister,* **1982.** Oil on canvas, 108 × 39 in. (274.3 × 99 cm).

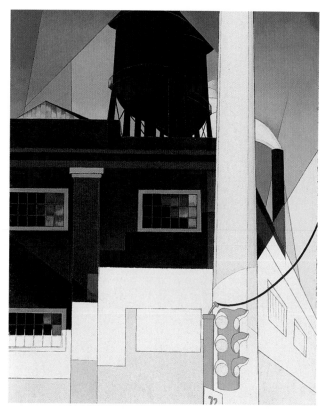

**1.44** Charles Demuth, *. . . And the Home of the Brave,* **1931.** Oil on composition board, 29½ × 23⅜ in. (74.8 × 59.7 cm).

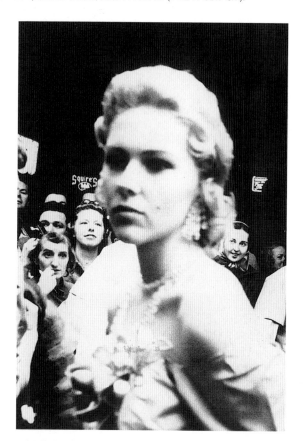

**1.45** Robert Frank, *Movie Premiere, Hollywood,* from *The Americans,* **1955–56.** Gelatin silver photograph, 12½ × 8⅜ in. (31.75 × 21.27 cm).

Reference to reality is a traditional way to increase meaning in an artwork. Drawing on their experience in the physical world, viewers can connect to the illusion of reality presented in the painting. In a nonobjective image, lines, shapes, textures, and colors must generate all of the meaning. Because there is no explicit subject matter, some viewers find it more difficult to understand such images.

When working abstractly, the artist can combine the power of association with the power of pure form. Charles Demuth's *. . . And the Home of the Brave* (1.44) demonstrates the power of abstraction. A factory has been turned into a series of lines and geometric shapes. Variations on red, white, and blue add a symbolic connection to the American flag. Painted during a period of nationwide unemployment, the factory is dark and forbidding. The ironic title (which is based on a line from the American national anthem) adds a subtle political statement.

## Degrees of Definition

**Definition** is the degree to which a shape is distinguished from both the ground area and the positive shapes within the design. **High definition** creates strong contrast between shapes and tends to increase clarity and immediacy of communication. For this reason, the diagrams used in this book generally feature black figures on a white ground. **Low-definition** shapes, including soft-edged shapes, gradations, and transparencies, can increase the complexity of the design and encourage multiple interpretations.

Definition is an inherent aspect of photography. In addition to variations in focus, the photographer can choose finer-grained film and slick paper to create a crisper image and coarser-grained film and textured paper to create a softer image.

Variations in photographic definition can substantially affect meaning. We normally expect to see high definition in the foreground and low definition in the background. In *Movie Premiere, Hollywood* (1.45), Robert Frank reversed this expectation. He focused on the faces of the worshiping crowd rather than the somber actress, trapped by her fans. As a result, the photograph challenges our clichéd image of a glamorous celebrity and suggests the darker side of fame.

Definition also plays an important role in drawing. Many media, including graphite and charcoal, can be used to create strong, clear lines as well as soft, fuzzy shapes. In Sidney Goodman's *Man Waiting* (1.46), charcoal was used to create a mysterious figure in a threatening space. The darker, more clearly defined shapes in the upper torso seem to push toward us, while the legs, hips, and chair dissolve into the background. Similarly, in Juan Muñoz's *Raincoat Drawing* (1.47), simple white lines define a boundary and suggest an interior space. The shading used in the staircase increases the illusion of space. Encouraged to fill in the details, the viewer becomes actively involved in both drawings.

## Key Questions

- Variations in definition can increase the illusion of space. Will your design benefit from greater depth?
- Definition can also direct the viewer's attention to specific areas in the design. How can definition enhance meaning in your design?

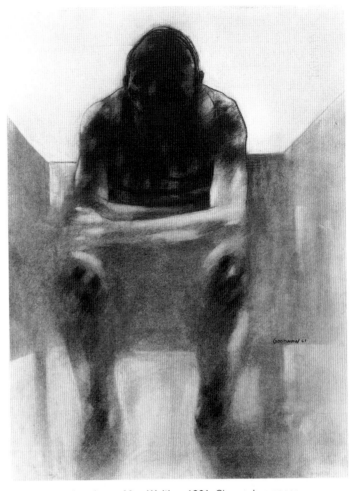

**1.46 Sidney Goodman, *Man Waiting*, 1961.** Charcoal on paper, 25⅝ × 19⅛ in. (65.1 × 48.7 cm).

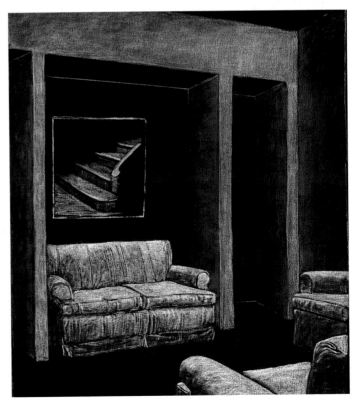

**1.47 Juan Muñoz, *Raincoat Drawing*, 1992–93.** Mixed media on fabric, 49³⁄₁₆ × 40⅛ in. (124.94 × 101.92 cm).

The
average high
induced
by cocaine
lasts
thirty
minutes.

The
average death
induced
by cocaine
lasts
slightly
longer.

Citizens Against Cocaine Abuse

**1.48 Ad by Citizens Against Cocaine Abuse: "The average high induced by cocaine lasts thirty minutes. The average death induced by cocaine lasts slightly longer."** Art Director & Designer: Gary Goldsmith, Copywriter: Neal Gomberg, Agency: Goldsmith/Jeffrey, Client: Citizens Against Cocaine Abuse.

## Using Shape

Simple shapes are often used when clear, direct communication is needed. Gary Goldsmith used just two shapes in an ad for an antidrug campaign (1.48). The text on the left reads "The average high induced by cocaine lasts thirty minutes." The text in the black shape on the right reads "The average death induced by cocaine lasts slightly longer." When these two sentences are compositionally combined, the narrow white band and the large black rectangle suggest the division between life and death.

More complex shapes are often used when the message is subtle or contradictory. **Collage** is one method for creating such complex shapes. Constructed from visual fragments initially designed for another purpose, a collage combines two kinds of shapes: the shape of each piece of cut paper and the shapes of the information printed on the paper.

In Bearden's *The Dove* (1.49A), the outer edges of each cut fragment create a lively pattern of curvilinear and rectilinear shapes. A second set of shapes is created by the lines and textures printed on these photographic fragments. A linear diagram of this artwork demonstrates the complexity of the resulting composition (1.49B). Combining his perceptions of contemporary Harlem with childhood memories, Bearden used this interplay of the cut edges and printed textures to create a pattern of shifting shapes.

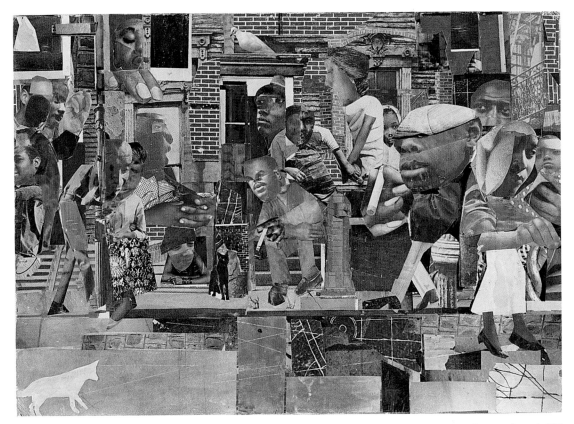

**1.49A Romare Bearden, *The Dove,* 1964.** Cut-and-pasted paper, gouache, pencil, and colored pencil on cardboard. 13⅜ × 18¾ in. (34 × 47.5 cm).

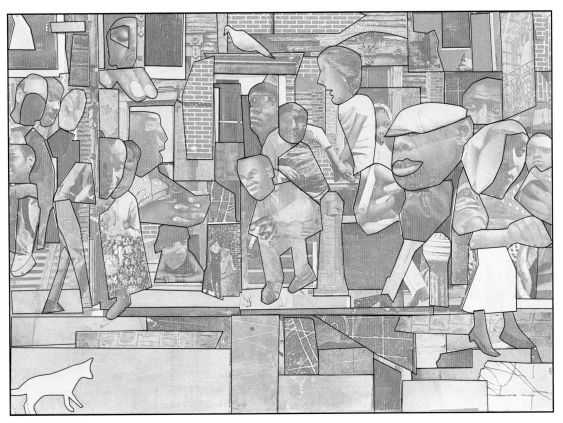

**1.49B Romare Bearden (compositional diagram).** Printed and cut shapes work together to create a complex composition.

**1.50** Jasper Johns, *Target with Plaster Casts*, **1955.** Encaustic and collage on canvas with objects, 51 × 44 × 2½ in. (129.5 × 111.8 × 6.4 cm).

In *Target with Plaster Casts* (1.50), Jasper Johns combined simple shapes with sculptural objects to create an equally complex composition. A series of concentric circles creates a clearly defined target at the center of the painting. Nine sculptural fragments of a human figure line the upper edge—an ear, a hand, a mouth, and so forth. To add further complexity, scraps of newspaper were embedded in the colored wax from which the painting was constructed. Equally attracted to the representational body parts above and the symbolic target below, we must reconcile two very different forms of visual information.

## Key Questions

- Experiment with rectilinear, curvilinear, geometric, and organic shapes. Which shape type will best express your idea?
- What happens when you combine flat, solid shapes with gradated shapes? Or fuse negative and positive?
- Representational, nonobjective, and abstract approaches are discussed in this section. Which approach will best express your idea?

# TEXTURE

The surface quality of a two-dimensional shape or a three-dimensional volume is called **texture.** Texture can create a bridge between two- and three-dimensional design. It engages our sense of touch as well as our vision, and it can enhance the visual surface and conceptual substance of a design.

## Types of Texture

**Physical texture** creates actual variations in a surface. The woven texture of canvas, the bumpy texture of thickly applied paint, and the rough texture of wood grain are common examples. **Visual texture** is an illusion. It can be created using multiple marks or through a descriptive simulation of physical texture. **Invented texture** is one form of visual texture. Using invented texture, the artist or designer can activate a surface using shapes that have no direct reference to perceptual reality.

Bruce Conner used textures from many sources to construct his paper collage *Psychedelicatessen Owner* (1.51). Floral patterns, visual gemstones, and cross-contours were combined to create a witty and improbable portrait.

## Creating Texture

When creating any type of texture, we must take two basic factors into account.

First, every material has its own inherent textural quality. As shown in figure 1.46, charcoal is characteristically soft and rich, while a linocut, such as Beardsley's *Salomé* (see figure 1.37) creates crisp, distinct edges. It is difficult to create soft, atmospheric textures using linocut or crisp textures using charcoal.

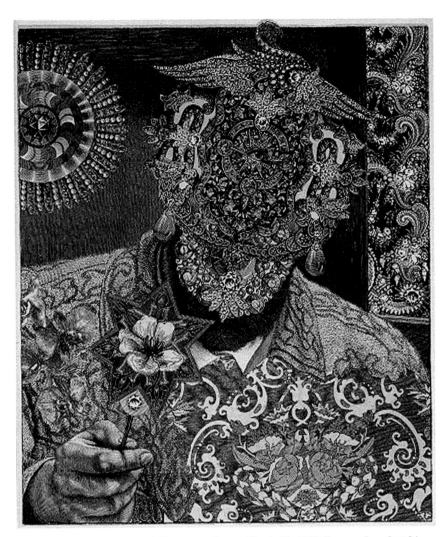

1.51 Bruce Conner, *Psychedelicatessen Owner,* March 31, 1990. Paper collage 8 × 6 in.

Second, the support surface contributes its own texture. This surface may be smooth, as with most photographs, or quite bumpy, as with the canvas and embedded collage Jasper Johns used for his *Target* (see figure 1.50, page 22). Thus, work with texture requires a heightened sensitivity to both the support surface and the materials used to create the design.

## Texture and Space

Visual texture is created whenever lines, dots, or other shapes are repeated. Variations in the size, density, and orientation of these marks can produce different

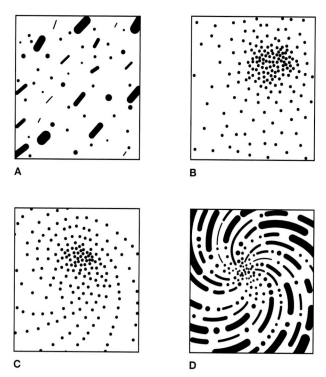

A

B

C

D

**1.52** Examples of textural size, density, and orientation.

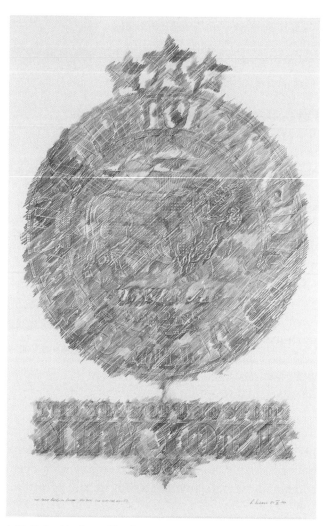

**1.54** Robert Indiana, *The Great American Dream: New York,* **1966.** Colored pencil rubbing on paper, 39½ × 26 in. (100.33 × 66.04 cm).

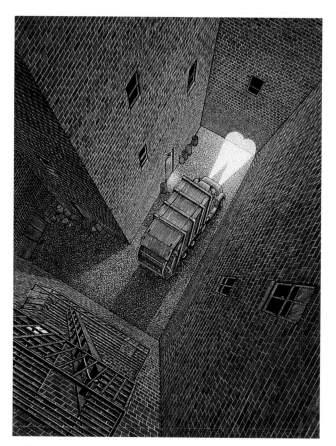

**1.53** Douglas Smith, *No Turning,* **1986.** Scratchboard and watercolor, 11¼ × 15 in. (29.2 × 38.1 cm).

spatial effects. Larger and darker marks tend to advance outward (1.52A). Finer marks, tightly packed, tend to pull us inward (1.52B). In figure 1.52C, the marks have been organized into a loose spiral. The overall impact is strongest when size, density, and orientation are combined, as in figure 1.52D.

In figure 1.53, Douglas Smith combined texture and linear perspective to produce a dramatic illusion of space. The lines of mortar between the bricks all point toward the truck in the center, while the bricks themselves diminish in size as the distance increases. The truck at the bottom of the wall of bricks seems to be trapped in a claustrophobic space.

By contrast, Robert Indiana's *The Great American Dream* (1.54) is spatially shallow. Indiana constructed a three-dimensional model of a coin or medallion from layers of cardboard. He then laid his drawing paper on top of the construction and made a rubbing, using colored pencils. This seemingly simple composition can be interpreted in at least three ways. First, creating a design through rubbing can remind us of the coin rubbings we may have made as children. Second, in many cultures, rubbing coins evokes wealth or good luck. Finally, the rubbing itself creates the *illusion* of the coin or medallion, not the reality. Perhaps the Great American Dream is an illusion, ready to dissolve into economic disarray.

Both spatial and flat textures can be created using letters, numbers, or words. Variations in the size, density, and orientation can strongly affect the meaning of these verbal textures. In figure 1.55, African-American painter Glenn Ligon repeatedly wrote, "I feel most colored when I am thrown against a sharp white background" on a gallery wall. As the density of the words increases, the words begin to fuse together, creating variations in the visual texture while reducing verbal clarity.

1.55 Glenn Ligon, Untitled *(I feel most colored when I am thrown against a sharp white background)*, 1990. Oilstick and gesso on wood, 6 ft 6 in. × 30 in. (2 m × 76.2 cm).

## Key Questions

- How many ways can texture be created?
- How can texture be used to increase the illusion of space?
- What happens to your design when solid shapes and textured shapes are combined?

## Trompe L'Oeil

Taken to an extreme, visual texture can so resemble reality that a deception occurs. This effect is called **trompe l'oeil,** from a French term meaning "to fool the eye." Trompe l'oeil can become a simple exercise in technical virtuosity or can significantly alter our perception of reality. By simulating architectural

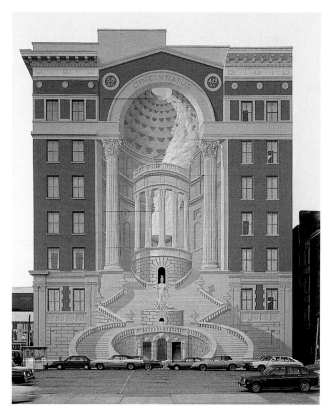

1.56 Richard Haas, *trompe l'oeil* mural on Brotherhood Building, Cincinnati, OH.

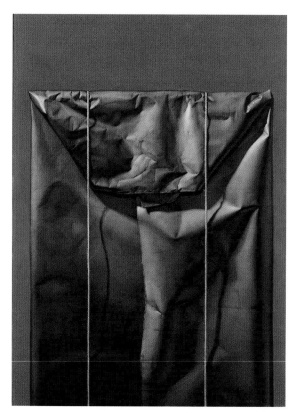

1.57 Claudio Bravo, Detail of *Package,* 1969. Charcoal, pastel, and sanguine chalk, 30⅞ × 22½ in. (78.42 × 57.15 cm).

details, Richard Haas created an amazing dialogue between illusion and reality in figure 1.56. This wall-sized trompe l'oeil painting actually appears to expand architectural space.

## Combining Physical and Visual Texture

Each material has a distinctive physical texture, and each drawing method creates a distinctive visual texture. By combining physical and visual textures, we can unify a composition and add another layer of conceptual and compositional energy.

Blended graphite, pastel, or charcoal creates the smooth surface often favored for highly representational images. Claudio Bravo developed the visual textures in *Package* (1.57) using pastel and charcoal. By carefully drawing every fold, he created a convincing simulation of a three-dimensional object.

Cross-hatching creates a more active visual texture. Dugald Stermer's portrait of mathematician Bertrand Russell (1.58) is constructed from a network of vigorous lines. The bumpy texture of the paper adds more energy to this lively drawing.

Albrecht Dürer's engraving of a horse (1.59) is even more highly textured. Each line in this image was carefully carved into a thin sheet of copper, then filled with ink and printed on an etching press. The resulting lines are slightly raised, or embossed. Thus, the cross-hatching creates a distinctive visual texture, while the embossed ink adds a subtle physical texture.

Physical and visual textures are combined in *Wayland's Song (with Wing)* (1.60). In this myth, a metalsmith named Wayland is captured by the King of Sweden, then crippled and forced to create treasures on demand. In revenge, he murders the king's sons and makes drinking cups from their skulls. He then flees, using wings fashioned from metal sheets. By adding straw and a lead wing to the photographic base image, Anselm Kiefer was able to combine the illusionistic qualities of painting with the physical immediacy of sculpture.

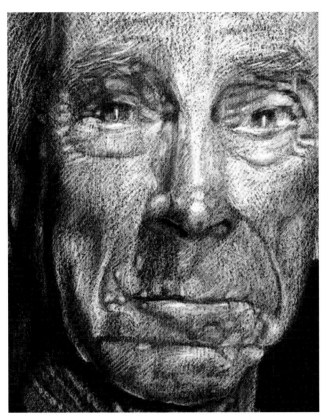

1.58 Dugald Stermer, Portrait of *Bertrand Russell, for the New York Times Book Review,* 2002. Colored pencil.

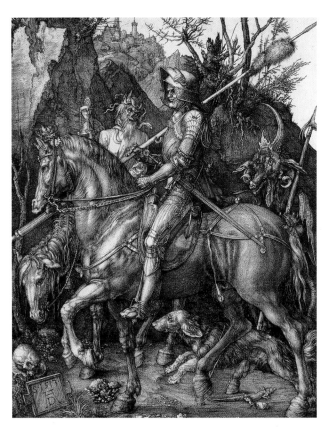

1.59 Albrecht Dürer, *The Knight, Death and the Devil,* 1513. Engraving, 11 × 14 in. (28 × 36 cm).

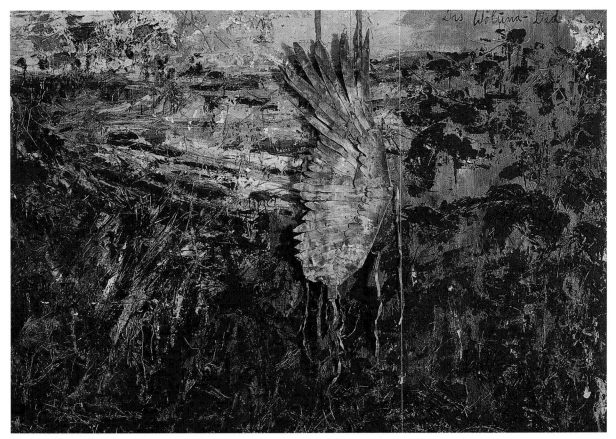

1.60 Anselm Kiefer, *Wayland's Song (with Wing),* 1982. Oil, emulsion, straw, and photograph with lead wing, 110¼ × 149⅝ in. (280 × 380 cm).

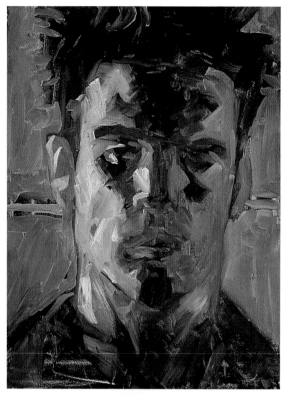

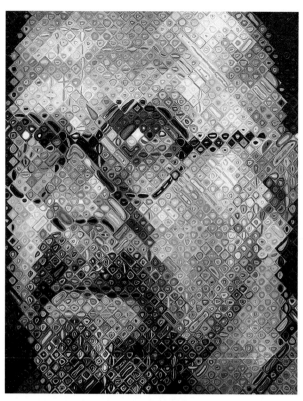

**1.61** Benjamin Marra, *Self-Portrait*, 1998. Oil, 8½ × 11 in. (21.6 × 28 cm).

**1.62** Chuck Close, *Self-Portrait,* 1997. Oil on canvas, 8 ft 6 in. × 7 ft (2.59 × 2.13 m).

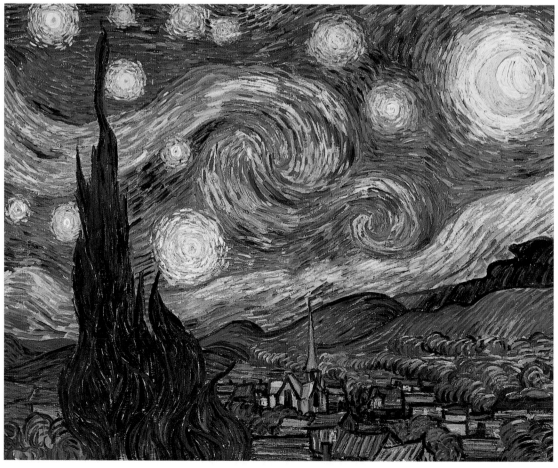

**1.63** Vincent Van Gogh, *The Starry Night*, 1889. Oil on canvas, 29 × 36½ in. (73.7 × 92.1 cm).

## Marks and Meanings

Every mark we make can add or subtract from the composition as a whole. When the texture is random or inappropriate, the composition becomes cluttered and confused. On the other hand, deliberate use of texture can enhance the illusion of space and increase compositional unity.

For example, each brushstroke in Benjamin Marra's *Self-Portrait* (1.61) describes a different facet of the face. Just as a sculptor carves out a portrait in plaster, so Marra used bold brushstrokes to carve out this portrait in paint. There are no random marks. Using both visual and physical texture, Marra increased the painting's immediacy and dimensionality.

Chuck Close's *Self-Portrait* (1.62) offers a very different interpretation of the head. Working from a photograph, Close methodically reduced the face to a series of squares within a grid. He then painted circles, diamonds, and other simple shapes inside each square. The grid provides structure, while the loosely painted interior shapes create an unexpected invented texture.

In Van Gogh's *Starry Night* (1.63), the texture of oil paint serves three distinct purposes. First, it creates a physical texture, suggesting the actual texture of the trees in the foreground. Second, it brings great energy to every painted shape: we feel the wind; we become mesmerized by the glowing whirlpools of light. Finally, we become connected to the artist himself. Van Gogh's hand is clearly evident in every brushstroke he made.

## Key Questions

- What physical textures can be created by your materials?
- What visual textures can be created by your materials?
- Can the marks you make enhance the spatial illusion or increase compositional unity?

# VALUE

**Value** refers to the relative lightness or darkness of a surface. The word *relative* is significant. The lightness or darkness of a shape is largely determined by its surroundings. For example, on a white surface, a gray square seems heavy and imposing (1.64A). The same gray square has less visual weight and seems luminous when it is surrounded by a black ground (1.64B). A **value scale** further demonstrates the importance of context (1.65). The solid gray line appears luminous when it is placed on a black background. As it crosses over the middle grays and into the white area, it seems to darken.

## Contrast

Both communication and expression are affected by **contrast,** or the amount of difference in values. High contrast tends to increase clarity and improve readability (1.66). Low contrast is often used for shapes of secondary importance or when the message is subtle.

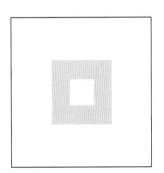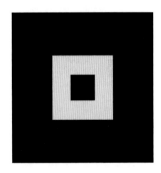

**1.64** Relative value.

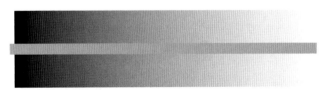

**1.65** Value scale.

| In Xanadu did Kubla Khan | In Xanadu did Kubla Khan |
| A stately pleasure dome decree: | A stately pleasure dome decree: |
| Where Alph, the sacred river, ran | Where Alph, the sacred river, ran |
| Through caverns measureless to man | Through caverns measureless to man |
| Down to a sunless sea | Down to a sunless sea |

**1.66** Contrast affects readability.

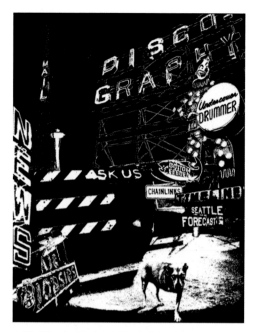

**1.67 Alice in Chains, "Dog's Breath" Website.** Sony Music Creative Services, Santa Monica, CA. Graphic Interface Designer: Mary Maurer.

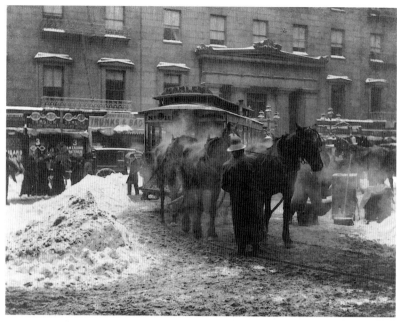

**1.68 Alfred Stieglitz, *The Terminal,* c. 1892.** Chloride print, 3½ × 4½ in. (8.8 × 11.3 cm).

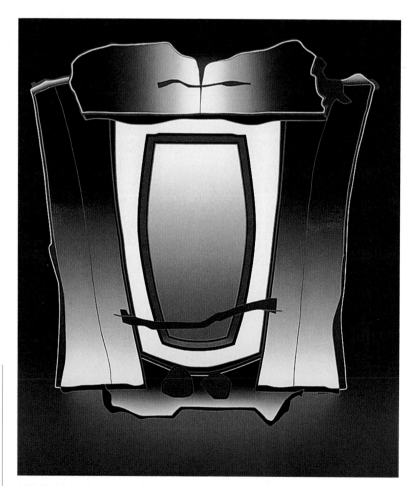

**1.69 Deborah Remington, *Capra,* 1974.** Oil on canvas, 6 ft 4 in. × 5 ft 7 in. (1.93 × 1.7 m).

Photographers are especially aware of the importance of contrast. By using a filter or changing the print paper, they can quickly modify contrast. High contrast gives the *Alice in Chains* Website (1.67) a gritty immediacy. Each word and each shape are clearly defined and confrontational. The city in Stieglitz's photograph (1.68) is quieter and more atmospheric. This low-contrast photograph invites the viewer into a preindustrial world of horses and carriages.

As demonstrated by Deborah Remington's *Capra* (1.69), value gradation can suggest a light source, create a sense of volume, or enhance the illusion of space.

## Value Distribution

**Value distribution** refers to the proportion and arrangement of lights and darks in a composition. Careful use of value distribution can increase emotional impact. A composition that is 80 percent black simply has a different "feel" than a composition that is 80 percent white.

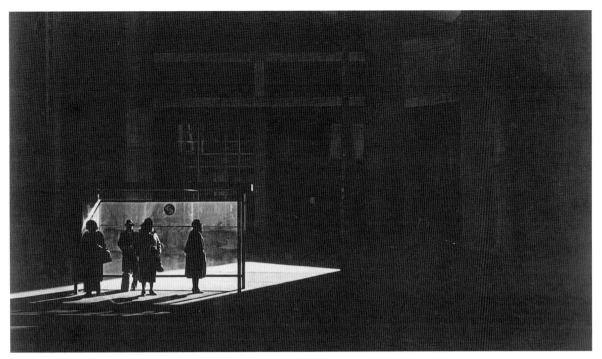

**1.70 Ray K. Metzker,** *Philadelphia,* **1963.** Gelatin silver print on paper, 6⅛ × 8¾ in. (15.4 × 22.3 cm).

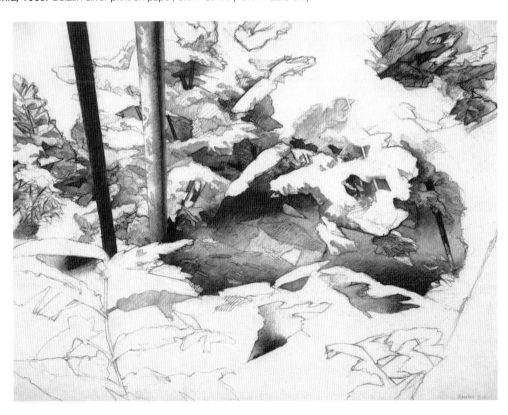

**1.71 Conley Harris,** *Doubles/Triples, Italy.* Charcoal drawing, 23 × 30 in. (58.42 × 76.2 cm).

Darker values are often used to create a sense of mystery or increase dramatic tension. For example, Ray K. Metzker's *Philadelphia* (1.70) is dominated by dark values. Surrounded by somber buildings in a silent city, the commuters huddle together under the brightly lit bus shelter like actors in a play.

Lighter values tend to suggest openness, optimism, and clarity. For example, lighter values dominate the bottom and right edges of Conley Harris' landscape (1.71), creating an expansive effect. The darker values at the center of the composition then pull us inward.

## Value and Volume

When a full range of values is used, a two-dimensional shape can seem three-dimensional, or **volumetric**. Figure 1.72 shows the transformation of a circle into a sphere. We begin with a simple outline, then add the **attached shadows,** or values that directly define the basic form. Addition of a **cast shadow** in the third image grounds the sphere. In the fourth drawing, the separation between the shadow and the sphere creates a floating effect.

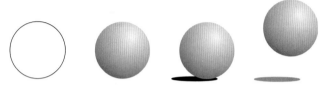

**1.72** From shape to volume through use of lighting.

This illusion of space is so convincing that objects can appear to extend out from a two-dimensional surface. The earliest oil painters often used **grisaille,** or a gray underpainting, to create this illusion of space. Color was then added, using transparent glazes or layers of paint. A detail from van Eyck's *Ghent Altarpiece* (1.73) shows both the grisaille painting and the full-color painting. The two statues in the center were painted using a range of grays, while color has been added to the kneeling figures on the right and left. Variations in value give all of the figures a remarkable dimensionality.

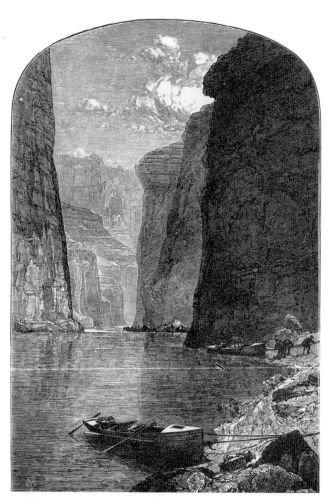

**1.74 Thomas Moran, *Noon-Day Rest in Marble Canyon*, from *Exploration of the Colorado River of the West*, by J. W. Powell, 1875.** Wood engraving after an original sketch by Thomas Moran, 6½ × 4⅜ in. (16.5 × 11 cm).

## Value and Space

When combined in a composition, very dark, crisp shapes tend to advance spatially, while gray, blurry shapes tend to recede. For example, in Thomas Moran's *Noon-Day Rest in Marble Canyon* (1.74), the dark values in the foreground gradually fade until the cliffs in the background become gray and indistinct. This effect, called **atmospheric perspective,** is one of the simplest ways to create the illusion of space.

**Chiaroscuro** (literally, "light-dark") is another way to create the illusion of space. A primary light source is used to create six or more values. A dark background is added to increase contrast. In *Judith and Her Maidservant with the Head of Holofernes*

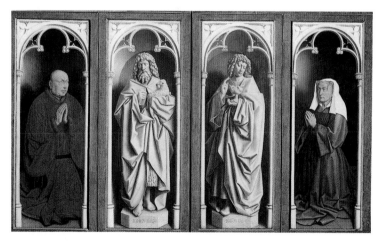

**1.73 Jan van Eyck, The *Ghent Altarpiece* (closed), completed 1432.** Oil on panel, approx. 11 ft 6 in. × 7 ft 7 in. (3.5 × 2.33 m).

by Artemesia Gentileschi, (1.75), the highlighted areas are clearly delineated, while darker areas seem to dissolve into the background. The resulting image is as dramatic as a theatrical stage.

## Value and Lighting

Filmmakers and set designers are especially aware of the expressive uses of value. Working with a wide range of lights, including sharply defined spotlights and more diffused floodlights, they can increase or decrease the illusion of space, emphasize an object or an action, and influence our emotional response to a character.

Four common forms of lighting are shown in figure 1.76. As described by Herbert Zettl in *Sight, Sound, Motion: Applied Media Aesthetics*, a key light is the primary source of illumination. Placing this light at a 45-degree angle can enhance the illusion of space. Addition of a backlight separates the actor from the background and adds definition. When a fill light is added, the contrast between light and dark becomes less harsh, and the actor may appear less formidable. In theatrical performances, powerful side lighting is often used to increase drama while enhancing dimensionality.

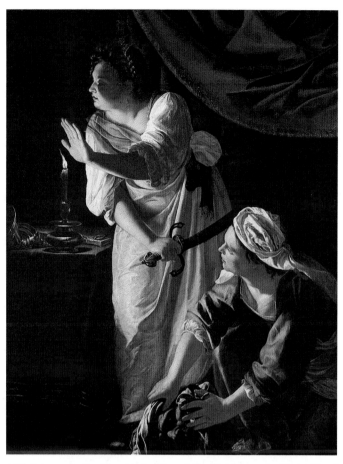

1.75 Artemesia Gentileschi, *Judith and Her Maidservant with the Head of Holofernes*, c. 1625. Oil on canvas, 72½ × 54¾ in. (1.84 × 1.42 m).

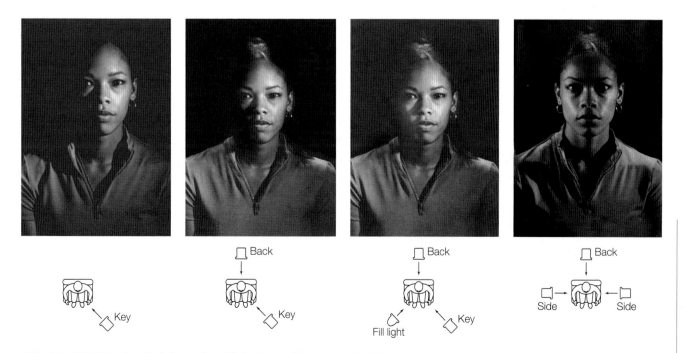

1.76 John Veltri, Lighting Techniques from *Sight, Sound, Motion: Applied Media Aesthetics*, 3rd ed., by Herbert Zettl, 1999.

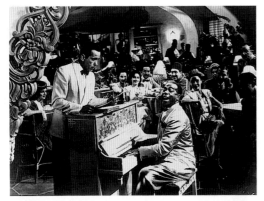

1.77A

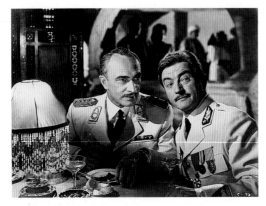

1.77B

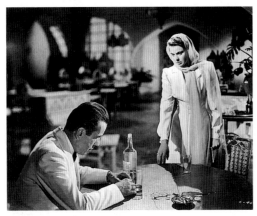

1.77C

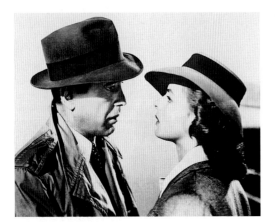

1.77D

All of these aspects of lighting are used expressively in the film *Casablanca*, directed by Michael Curtiz. The lighting is fairly dark when we first enter Rick's Cafe Americain, the saloon where most of the action occurs. In this dark and mysterious place, a man will be shot, a seduction will be thwarted, and a romance will be rekindled. The piano player, Sam, and the audience members closest to the stage are brightly lit as he sings an optimistic song (1.77A). The two villains in the film, Major Strasser and Captain Renault, are often strongly side-lit (1.77B), which makes them appear more formidable and enhances the texture in their faces. By contrast, much softer light is used for the face of the heroine, Ilsa, who is emotionally and politically fragile.

Indeed, value and lighting is used to accentuate Ilsa's emotions throughout the film. When she tries to explain to Rick the reason she had left him in Paris two years earlier, Ilsa wears a pure white dress and enters the darkened saloon like a virginal beam of light (1.77C). Later, when she visits Rick in his apartment, shadows cover her face, accentuating her conflicted emotions as she tries to decide whether to remain with her husband, Victor, whom she idealizes, or return to Rick, whom she loves. In the final scene at the airport, diffused lighting again emphasizes Ilsa's vulnerability (1.77D). She and Victor disappear into the foggy night, escaping from Casablanca, while Rick and a reformed Captain Renault stroll away together to join the Foreign Legion.

## Key Questions

- What is the advantage of a wide value range? What is the advantage of a narrow value range? Which works best in your design?

- What happens when you invert the values — that is, the black areas become white and the white areas become black?

- Would your design benefit from a stronger illusion of space? If so, how can value be used to increase the illusion of space?

# SUMMARY

- The elements of two-dimensional design are line, shape, texture, value, and color.

- Lines can contain, define, dissect, and connect. Line networks can be created using hatching, cross-hatching, and cross-contours.

- A shape is created whenever an area is enclosed. The figure is the primary shape, while the ground, or negative shape, provides the surrounding context.

- When figure and ground shapes are equally strong, figure/ground reversal can occur.

- There are many types of shapes, including rectilinear, curvilinear, geometric, organic, representational, nonobjective, and abstract. When gradated, shapes can appear three-dimensional.

- Texture is the visual or physical surface of a shape. Visual texture can be created through multiple marks, while actual variations in the surface create physical texture.

- Relative lightness or darkness in an artwork is called value. Value can be used to create the illusion of space, suggest volume, shift compositional balance, and heighten emotion.

# KEYWORDS

| | | | |
|---|---|---|---|
| abstract shape | cross-hatching | invented texture | shape |
| actual line | curvilinear shape | line | texture |
| atmospheric perspective | definition | low-definition | trompe l'oeil |
| attached shadow | direction | negative shape (ground) | value |
| calligraphic line | elements | nonobjective shape | value distribution |
| cast shadow | figure/ground reversal | organic shape | value scale |
| chiaroscuro | geometric shape | organizational line | visual texture |
| closure | gesture drawing | orientation | volume |
| collage | gradation (shading) | physical texture | volume summary |
| continuity | grisaille | positive shape (figure) | volumetric |
| contour line | hatching | pure form | |
| contrast | high-definition | rectilinear shape | |
| cross-contour | implied line | representational shape | |

# IN DETAIL

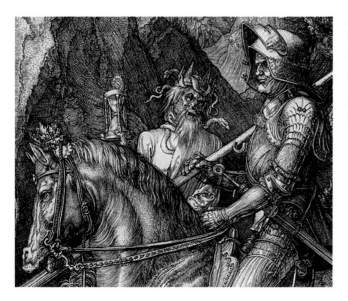

An engraving is created by cutting intricate networks of lines into a sheet of metal using a sharp tool known as a burin. Ink is pressed into these lines and the surface metal is wiped clean. The plate is then positioned face up on a printing press and dampened paper is positioned over the plate. Both are cranked through the press at high pressure, transferring the ink to the paper and creating a slight embossment. Denser and deeper networks create darker areas in the design, while cross-contour lines define surface variations in fur, armor, and clothing.

# Profile:

## Phillia Yi, Printmaker

Energy and Expression Using
Woodcut on a Large Scale

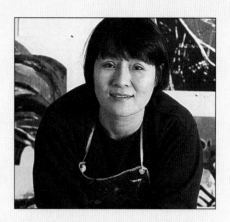

Phillia Changhi Yi has revitalized the ancient process of woodcut through her large-scale prints. Drawing directly on luan plywood, Yi cuts away the negative shapes and inks the raised positive shapes to create abstract images that vigorously combine line, color, texture, and movement. Yi has over 20 solo shows and numerous international group shows to her credit. She lectures widely and has taught workshops at Manhattan Graphics Center, Women's Studio Workshop, and the Southern Graphics Council Conference.

**MS:** The energy in all of your images is impressive. What is its source?

**PY:** Conflict is my primary source, conceptually and compositionally. As a woman from Korea living in the United States, I find myself caught between cultures. This isolates me in an interesting way and gives me a unique perspective. My work reflects the day-to-day dilemmas and tension of my multicultural experience.

Crisis moments often trigger ideas, but historic events are never treated literally. I combine abstract imagery with representational elements in my prints. Both flat and illusory space is created, suggesting an altered sense of time and scale. Static forms are juxtaposed with fluid shapes, and both warm and cool colors are used in opaque and translucent layers. This activates the psychological space and creates a complex, highly charged composition.

**MS:** Many members of your family are doctors. How did you become an artist?

**PY:** Getting the right encouragement at the right time gave me the confidence to pursue art. All of my five siblings are talented, I think, but choosing an art career seemed too risky. My father encouraged me to study graphic design, but I found that printmaking was my real passion. My mentor, Professor Romas Viesulas at Tyler School of Art, said that I had the commitment and ability for a career in art. His confidence gave me confidence.

**MS:** How do you develop your images?

**PY:** I begin with a month of drawing, usually in charcoal, on 29" × 41" sheets of printmaking paper. In the drawings, I work out my images and ideas. Social and political themes dominate. For example, the beating of Rodney King by members of the Los Angeles Police Department and the subsequent burning of Koreatown inspired *Dance.*

*The Other Side,* shown here, deals with the power of women, who must prevail in a world dominated by men. The whole composition is based on the intersection between these two forces, near the center of the print. In a sense, the large black shape represents the unconscious, while the curving red shape suggests that which is conscious, palpable, and real. I am interested in the uneasy alliance or balance between complex life forces, rather than a simple battle between adversaries. Each corner is treated differently, adding more variety and energy to the print.

**MS:** The size of this piece is extraordinary. Using eight panels, you have created a print that is 12 feet long!

**PY:** When I was studying printmaking at SUNY–New Paltz, I was surrounded by printmakers. The size of the press, acid trays, rollers, and other equipment seemed to limit the size of the print. When I went to Tyler in Philadelphia, my roommate, who was a painter, introduced me to her friends. Some were completing a 5' × 7' painting a day! I realized that the small size and slow process of printmaking had historically given it a "second-class" status. I was determined to overcome this perception, so I developed a working method that is forceful, spontaneous, and direct. There is still a great deal of deliberation, but the cutting and printing processes are relatively fast.

MS: Some artists work very methodically over a long period of time, while others work in short, intensive bursts. What is your approach?

PY: I adapt my method to my situation. I have obligations as a teacher, a mother, and an administrator, so summer is my only solid block of work time. A regular schedule is best for me. At the beginning of the summer, I go to the studio for a few hours each day. I soon increase this to about 6 hours a day for drawing. When I am cutting the blocks and printing, I often work for 8 to 10 hours a day. I am very consistent.

MS: What is the best work method for your students?

PY: Success is primarily based on commitment.

I would say that art-making is about 5 percent talent and inspiration and 95 percent hard work. A professional or a serious student continues to work despite obstacles. It is important for students to explore ideas and make mistakes: that is the best way to learn.

MS: What is the purpose of your artwork?

PY: Art is expression, not explanation. Artists must be attentive, noticing every detail of experience. Art both reflects and influences society and culture. In that sense, I feel that artists have a responsibility to their generation, not just to create objects of beauty but to create objects of truth—whether they are beautiful or not. My ideas come from my daily life and my personal experience, both good and bad. The most important characteristic is my belief that art should be expressed in terms of human experience. My work is essentially optimistic: I embrace all that the world has to offer.

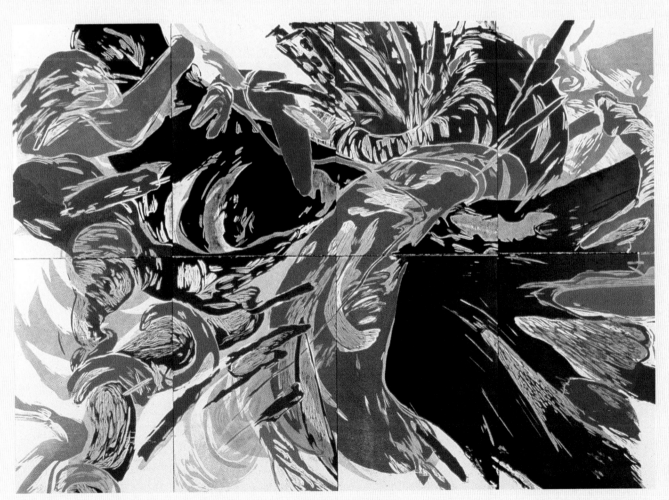

Phillia Changhi Yi, *The Other Side*, 1993. Color woodcut, 84 × 120 in. (213 × 305 cm).

# chapter two

# The Element of Color

Color immediately attracts attention. When presented with a collection of bottles filled with liquid in various colors, very young children will group the objects by color rather than by size or shape. An interior designer may use rose-red walls in a restaurant to increase emotional warmth, while using light blue walls in a day-care center to encourage calm. Bright yellow and magenta red add pizzazz to an eye-catching poster in figure 2.1. Designed to call attention to the disparity in the number of exhibitions granted to male and female artists, this poster had to compete with other posters displayed on walls throughout New York City. Color is both the most elusive and most emotionally complex design element. By harnessing its power, we can substantially expand our compositional capabilities.

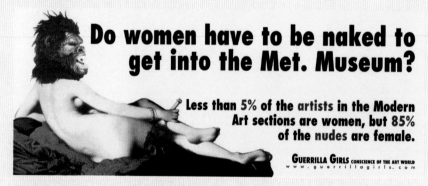

2.1 Guerrilla Girls, "Do women have to be naked to get into the Met. Museum? Less than 5% of the artists in the Modern Art sections are women, but 85% of the nudes are female," 1989. Poster, 11 × 28 in. (27.9 × 71.1 cm).

## COLOR THEORY

**Color theory** is the art and science of color interaction and effects. In *The Art of Color*,[1] Johannes Itten lists the following approaches to color theory:

- The physicist studies electromagnetic wavelengths in order to measure and classify color.

- The chemist, working with the molecular structure of dyes and pigments, seeks to produce highly permanent colors and excellent paint consistency.

- The physiologist investigates the effects of color and light on our eyes and brain.

- The psychologist studies the expressive effects of color on our mind and spirit.

An artist combines all these areas of knowledge. Like the physicist, the artist uses color wavelengths to create various effects. Like the chemist, the artist must be aware of the safety and permanence of dyes and pigments. When using color to create the illusion of space, the artist puts into practice theories developed by the physiologist. And both communication and expression are strongly affected by the psychological effects of color.

## COLOR PHYSICS

Two major color systems are used in art and design. **Additive color** is created using beams of light (2.2A). Red, green, and blue, the familiar RGB on a computer screen, are the primary colors in this system. Many additional colors can be mixed from these primaries. **Subtractive color** is created when white light is reflected off a pigmented or dyed surface (2.2B). The subtractive primaries are blue, red, and yellow.

This book was printed using cyan blue, magenta red, and yellow, the transparent primaries (or **process colors**) commonly used in mass production. Figure 2.3 provides an example of process printing. As viewers, we optically combine thousands of cyan, magenta, and yellow dots to create a coherent image. Black (abbreviated as *K* in the CMYK printing system) was then added to enhance detail and increase contrast (2.4A–G).

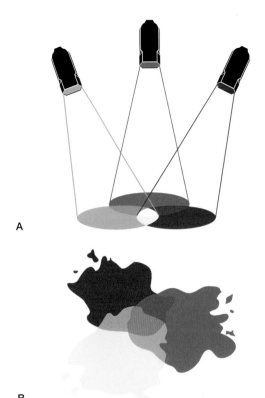

A

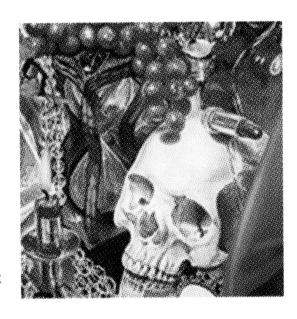

B

**2.2 A.** Light primaries and their additive mixtures.
**B.** Pigment primaries and their subtractive mixtures.

**2.3** Color printing detail of *Wheel of Fortune*, showing dot pattern used in CMYK printing.

**A** Yellow  **B** Magenta  **C** Yellow and magenta  **D** Cyan  **E** Yellow, magenta, and cyan  **F** Black  **G** Full color printing

**2.4A–G** Color separation in CMYK printing. Dots of yellow, magenta, cyan, and black are layered to create a full-color image.

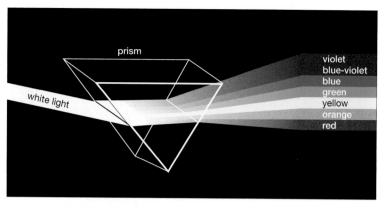

**2.5** When white light passes through a prism, the spectrum becomes visible.

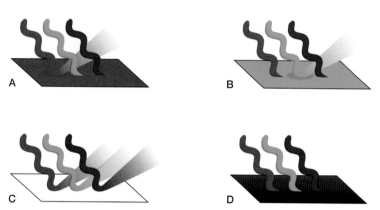

**2.6** We see color when the primaries of light are reflected off a colored surface. A red surface absorbs the green and blue wavelengths, while reflecting the red. All wavelengths are reflected by a white surface. All wavelengths are absorbed by a black surface.

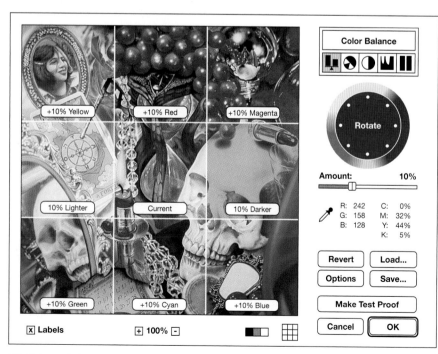

**2.7** Color variations using a computer.

## Color and Light

When white light passes through a prism, it is refracted, or bent. This creates a wide spectrum of hues, which is dominated by red, orange, yellow, green, blue, blue-violet, and violet (2.5). Each hue, or separate color, is defined by a specific electromagnetic wavelength, with red as the longest and violet as the shortest. When white light hits a colored surface, some wavelengths are reflected, while other wavelengths are absorbed. As shown in figure 2.6A, a red surface reflects the red wavelengths while absorbing the blue and green wavelengths. Similarly, a green surface reflects the green wavelengths while absorbing the red and blue (2.6B). All wavelengths are reflected off a white surface (2.6C); all wavelengths are absorbed by a black surface (2.6D). Color reflection and absorption are rarely total. As a result, we can often see hints of various colors within a dominant color.

## Using Additive Color

Lighting designers, videographers, and Website artists use additive color extensively. Beams of red, green, and blue light are used to create a full-color video projection. The mixture of adjacent beams creates cyan, magenta, and yellow, which are the secondary colors in the additive system. When all three beams are combined, white light results.

We can quickly and easily create variations in additive color on a computer. In figure 2.7, the current color choice is shown in the center. Variations are shown in the eight surrounding squares. Even a 10 percent increase in a given color produces a very different result.

Our perception of additive color is influenced by

- The intensity (or wattage) of the projected light.
- The light source, from incandescent light and fluorescent light to daylight.
- The surface quality of the illuminated object. Projected light behaves very differently on transparent, translucent, and textured surfaces.
- The ambient (overall amount of) light in the environment.

Because the variables are subtle and complex, effective work with additive color requires great skill.

## Using Subtractive Color

Painters, printmakers, and illustrators use subtractive color in various forms, including acrylics, oils, pastels, and inks. Each pigment or dye used in the manufacture of such materials is chemically unique. Quinacridone red and pthalocyanide blue are transparent and intense. The cadmiums and earth colors are generally opaque. **Color overtones** complicate matters further. Color theorist David Hornung defines an overtone as "a secondary hue bias in a primary color." For example, alizarin crimson is a red with violet overtones, while scarlet is a red with orange overtones. To create a wider range of mixtures, artists and designers often use a six-hue palette, including two reds, two yellows, and two blues, plus **achromatic** black and white, which have no hue. Since many foundation color projects are done using paint, ink, or colored paper, the remainder of this chapter will focus on subtractive color.

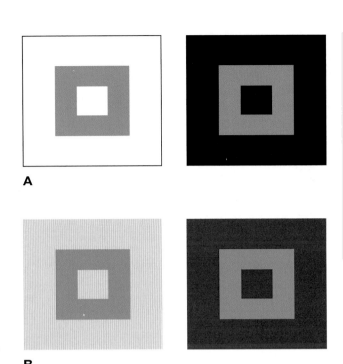

**A**

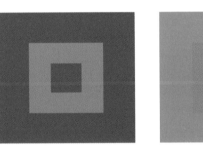

**B**

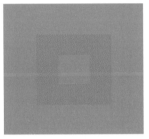

**C**

**2.8** Examples of simultaneous contrast. Light/dark contrast is shown in figure A, a complementary reaction is shown in figure B, and subtle variations are shown in figure C. The blue-green square is the same color in all examples, but appears different due to the surrounding colors.

# COLOR INTERACTION

**Color interaction** refers to the way colors influence one another.

Colors are never seen in isolation. The blue sheet of paper we examine in an art supply store reminds us of the blue of the sky, the ocean, or the fabrics in a clothing store. Lighting also affects our perceptions. Incandescent light creates a warm orange glow, while standard fluorescent lights produce a bluish ambiance. And, when our blue paper is added to a design, it is profoundly affected by the surrounding colors.

This effect is called **simultaneous contrast.** Three principles of simultaneous contrast are shown in figure 2.8A–C. Light/dark contrast is shown in the first pair of images. A blue-green square appears much lighter when it is placed on a black background. A complementary reaction is shown in the second pair. The same blue-green square appears to glow when it is surrounded by red rather than a neutral gray. In the third example, the same blue-green square appears almost green when it is surrounded by solid blue, yet it appears almost blue when surrounded by green.

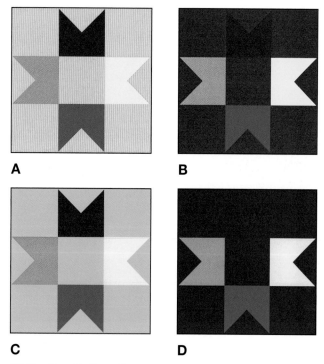

A                    B

C                    D

**2.9 The Bezold effect.** Changing a single color alters the entire design.

The **Bezold effect** demonstrates the profound influence of color interaction. Color theorist Wilhelm Bezold (1837–1907) realized that change in a single color can substantially alter our perception of an entire pattern. In figure 2.9A–D, changing the background color from gray to red adds an electric energy to the design. A light green background accentuates the darker shapes while diminishing the brightness of the orange shape. A dark violet background creates a strong contrast in value and pushes the orange and yellow shapes forward. The compositional impact can be substantial, even when the amount of changed color is small.

Color interaction becomes especially dramatic when complementary colors, such as red-orange and blue-green, are used in a composition. In the human eye, two types of cells, known as rods and cones, are arranged in layers on the retina. These cells serve as photoreceptors. The rods record lightness and darkness, while the cones are used to distinguish the hues, such as red and blue. According to **opponent theory,** the cones can register only one color in a complementary pair at a time. Constant shifting between the opposing colors creates a visual overload at the edges of the shapes, resulting in an electric glow. In *Inner Lhamo Waterfall* (2.10), Pat Steir used this effect to suggest the majesty and mystery of the falling water.

A similar characteristic of human vision can be used to create an **afterimage.** If we stare at a red square for 30 seconds (2.11), then stare at a white sheet of paper, a blue or green shape will seem to appear. This is due to fatigue in the cones, the color sensors in our eyes. Overloaded by the intense red, our eyes revert to the blue and green cones, creating the afterimage.

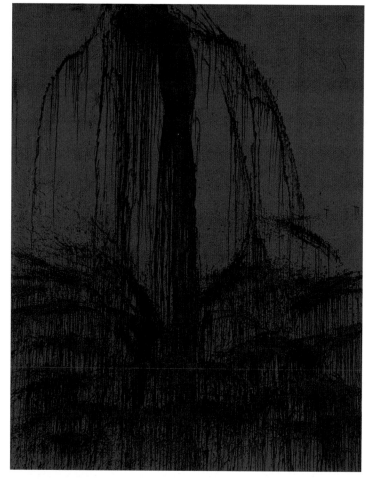

**2.10 Pat Steir,** *Inner Lhamo Waterfall,* **1992.** Oil on canvas, 114 × 90¼ in. (289.6 × 229.2 cm).

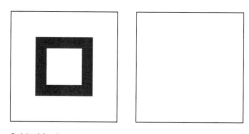

**2.11** Afterimage exercise.

# DEFINING COLOR

## Hue

The **hue,** or name of a color, is determined by its wavelength. Red, blue, green, yellow, and so forth are all hues.

Physicists, painters, and philosophers have devised numerous systems to organize hues. Johannes Itten's 12-step color wheel (2.12) is a clear and simple example. Red, blue, and yellow **primary colors** are in the center. These colors can be mixed to produce many other colors. The **secondary colors** of green, orange, and violet follow. These colors are mixed from adjacent primaries. A circular spectrum of **tertiary colors** completes the wheel. The mixture of a secondary color and the adjacent primary color creates a tertiary color.

The Munsell color wheel (2.13) more accurately identifies cyan blue, magenta red, and yellow as the primaries, while the three-dimensional Munsell color tree (2.14) provides examples of changes in color value and intensity as well as hue.

Artists often use a wide range of hues to capture the richness of reality. In *Wheel of Fortune* (2.15), Audrey Flack used a full spectrum of hues to define a collection of symbolic objects in meticulous detail. The makeup and mirrors symbolize vanity; the candles, hourglass, and skull suggest the passage of time; the grapes suggest passion. Reds, blues, and yellows dominate the painting. Hints of orange, violet, and green complete the spectrum.

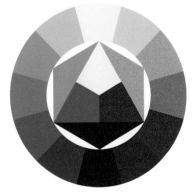

**2.12** The 12-step Itten color wheel.

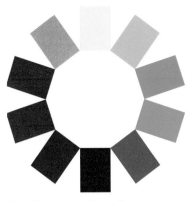

**2.13** The 10-step Munsell color wheel.

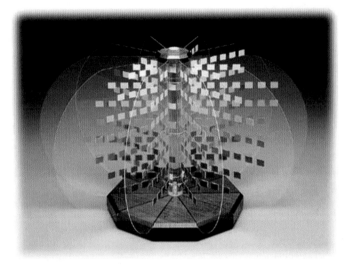

**2.14 Munsell color tree, 1972.** Clear plastic chart, 10½ × 12 in. (26.7 × 30.5 cm); base size 12 in. (30.5 cm) diameter; center pole size 12⅝ in. (32.1 cm) high; chip size ¾ × 1⅜ in. (1.9 × 3.5 cm).

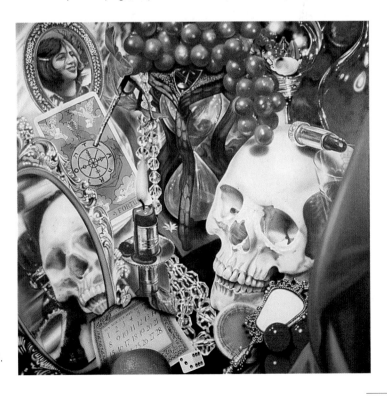

**2.15 Audrey Flack, *Wheel of Fortune,* 1977–78.** Oil over acrylic on canvas, 8 × 8 ft. (2.44 × 2.44 m)

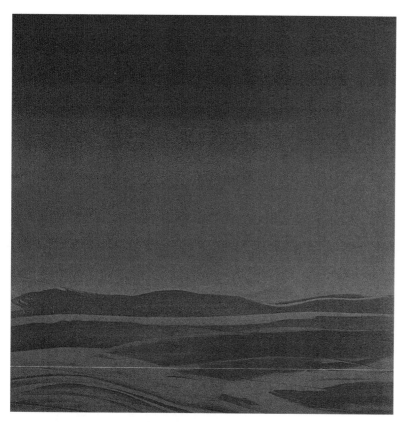

2.16 Robert Lazuka, *Thoughts of Summer*, 1999. 21 × 21 in. (53 × 53 cm).

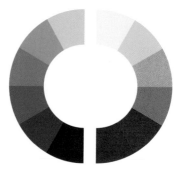

2.17 Separation of the color wheel by temperature.

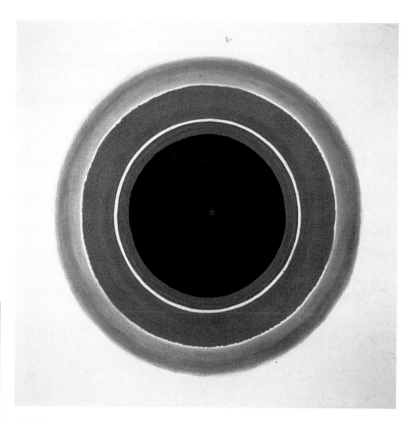

2.18 Kenneth Noland, *A Warm Sound in a Gray Field*, 1961. 6 ft 10½ in. × 6 ft 9 in. (2.1 × 2.06 m).

A limited number of hues can be equally effective. *Thoughts of Summer* (2.16) was composed using a narrow range of solid and gradated reds. The blocks of color shimmer with energy, suggesting the oppressive heat of a summer day. Using a limited palette, Robert Lazuka created a quiet yet hypnotic image.

Temperature is an especially important aspect of hue. **Temperature** refers to the heat a color generates, both physically and psychologically. Try laying six colored squares of equal value on fresh snow on a sunny day. By the end of the day, the warm-colored oranges, reds, and violets will sink into the melting snow, while the blue and green squares will remain closer to the surface. Figure 2.17 shows a simple division of the color wheel by temperature.

Color temperature can help create the illusion of space. Under most circumstances, warm colors advance, while cool colors recede. This effect is demonstrated very clearly in Kenneth Noland's *A Warm Sound in a Gray Field* (2.18). The red ring with its yellow halo pushes toward us, while the blue-black circle pulls us inward. The small red dot in the center of the composition

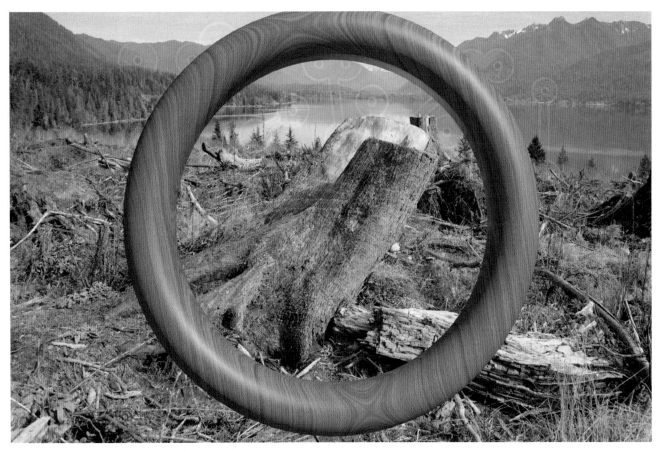

2.19 MANUAL (Suzanne Bloom and Ed Hill), *Quinault,* from *A Constructed Forest,* 1993. Chromogenic print, 24 × 36 in. (61 × 91.4 cm).

further activates the void by creating another advancing shape. In *Quinault* (2.19), Suzanne Bloom and Ed Hill used a similar combination of warm and cool colors to create a very different illusion of space. A warm brown ring dominates the image, targeting the tree stump in the center. The cool blue lake and mountains recede into the background.

## Value

**Value** refers to the relative lightness or darkness of a color. By removing hue from the equation, we can create a simple value scale (2.20A) that shifts from white to black through a series of grays. As shown in figure 2.20B, hues such as violet, blue, and green are inherently darker in value than pure yellow or orange. Translation of color into value is shown in the final column. Despite the wide variety of hues, all the colors in 2.20C have nearly the same value.

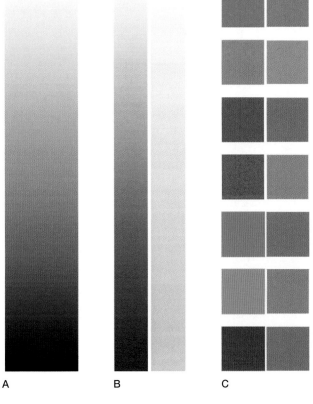

A    B    C

**2.20** Value scales.

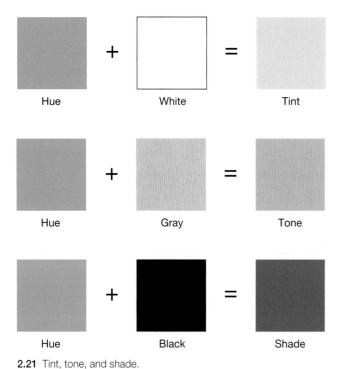

Hue + White = Tint

Hue + Gray = Tone

Hue + Black = Shade

**2.21** Tint, tone, and shade.

Three basic variations in value are shown in figure 2.21. When white is added to a hue, the resulting **tint** will be lighter in value. The addition of gray produces a **tone.** The addition of black creates a darker **shade.** One of the simplest ways to unify a design is to limit the colors used to the tints, tones, and shades of a single hue.

Using a full range of values, we can create a very convincing representation of reality. In *Vision* (2.22), Nicora Gangi transformed a simple still life into a dramatic drawing. A bright light in the background pushes the dark foreground vessels toward us. The limited value range in David Hockney's *Mist* (2.23) is equally effective. The gray-green palm trees dissolve into the peach-colored fog as quietly as a whisper.

By making a black-and-white photocopy, we can easily check the range of values in a design. The photocopied image will be quite

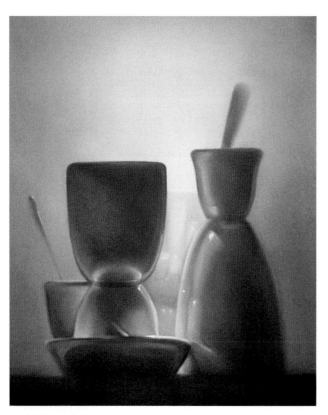

**2.22 Nicora Gangi,** *Vision,* **1994.** Pastel, 10 × 14 in. (25 × 36 cm).

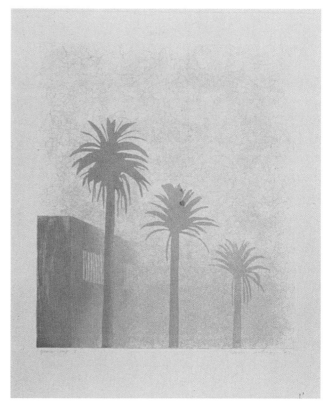

**2.23 David Hockney,** *Mist,* **1973.** From The Weather Series. Lithograph in 5 colors, edition 98, 37 × 32 in. (93.9 × 81.2 cm).

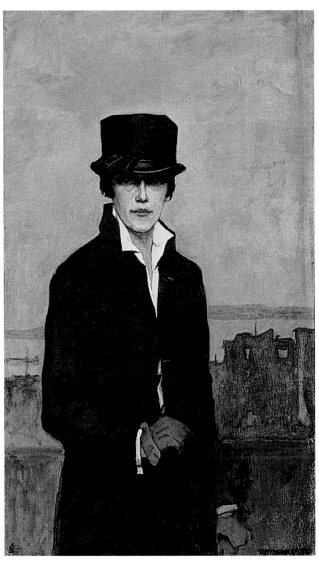

2.24 Romaine Brooks, *Self-Portrait*, 1923. Oil on canvas, 46¼ × 26⅞ in. (117.5 × 68.3 cm).

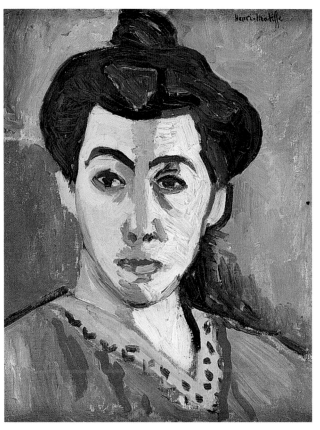

2.25 Henri Matisse, *Green Stripe (Madame Matisse)*, 1905. Oil on canvas, 16 × 12¾ in. (40.6 × 32.4 cm).

readable when the value range is broad. When a very narrow range of values is used, the photocopy will produce a solid black or gray image.

Value is the dominant force in some paintings, while hue is a dominant force in others. Each approach has a distinctive emotional effect. Romaine Brooks' *Self-Portrait* (2.24) is essentially a value painting. Blacks, whites and grays dominate the image. Her eyes are concealed by the brim of her hat and the shadow it casts. Patches of red on the woman's lips and coat add just a touch of color. She is wary and reserved. Value, rather than hue, is the appropriate choice for this image.

In contrast, hue dominates Henri Matisse's *Green Stripe* (2.25). Surrounded by large blocks of red, green and violet, the woman seems bold and self-confident. The avocado-green dividing line separates blocks of pink on the right and lime-green on the left half of her face, suggesting warmer and cooler aspects of her personality. Even her eyes and hair are painted in blue-black adding yet more color to this expressive portrait.

# Intensity

**Intensity, saturation,** and **chroma** all refer to the purity of a color. The primary colors are the most intense. This intensity generally diminishes when colors are mixed.

Figure 2.26A–C presents three intensity scales. Column A shows the most intense primary and secondary colors. Column B demonstrates the loss of intensity when black is added. In column C, two complementary colors are mixed, producing a range of elegant, low-intensity colors.

High-intensity colors are often used to maximize impact. Grace Hartigan's *City Life* (2.27) explodes with energy, as a full palette of blues, reds, and yellows dance across the canvas. In the background, a blue and orange striped awning vibrates with complementary color. Dark blocks of violet in the lower left corner and blue in the lower right compress the warm reds, oranges and yellows at the center of the composition, adding yet more energy. The entire scene is highly abstracted. Our understanding of both space and movement are based on the use of color rather than on photographic representation.

A combination of high- and low-intensity colors can be especially effective. Arshile Gorky combined primary hues and subtle earth colors in *The Liver Is the Cock's Comb* (2.28). Grays, tans, and browns cover more than half of the surface. Surrounded by these low-intensity colors, the brilliant yellow and red shapes seem to pulsate with energy. Like variations in the volume and tempo in an interesting piece of music, the interplay between subdued and intense colors adds complexity to the composition.

Gorky's masterful understanding of how the eye reads and responds to color gives his paintings their unusual vibrancy and sense of animation. There is a wider range in his application of muted color than in Hartigan's work, but the impact is comparable. In both cases, the viewer is drawn into and moves throughout the painting because of the use of color.

**2.26** Intensity scales.

A   B   C

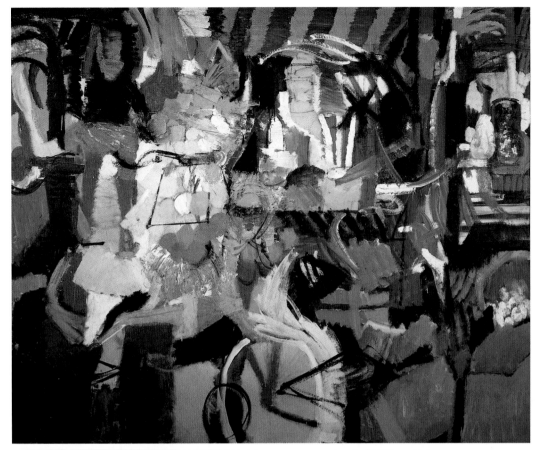

**2.27  Grace Hartigan,** *City Life,* **1956.** Oil on canvas, 81 × 98½ in. (205.7 × 250.2 cm).

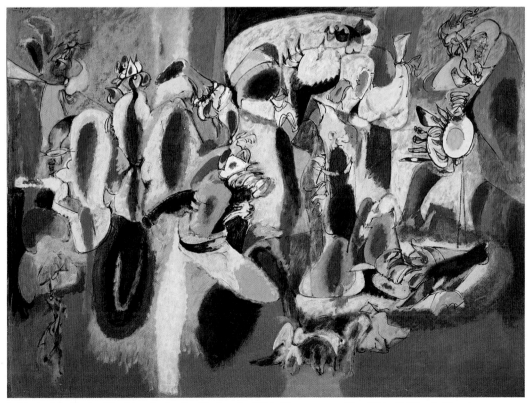

**2.28  Arshile Gorky,** *The Liver Is the Cock's Comb,* **1944.** Oil on canvas, 72 × 98 in. (1.86 × 2.49 cm).

# COLOR SCHEMES

Relationships among colors are critical to the success or failure of a design, and many theories of **color harmony** have been developed to help artists, architects, and designers make good choices. A basic color wheel can help illustrate five common approaches.

## Monochromatic

Variations on a single hue are used in a **monochromatic** color scheme (2.29). The advantage of this system is a high level of unity: all the colors are strongly related. Boredom, due to the lack of variety, is a potential disadvantage. In *Tracers–Side Order* (2.30), Guy Goodwin used various textures, patterns, and words to add interest to the monochromatic image.

## Analogous

Adjacent colors on the color wheel are used in an **analogous** color scheme (2.31). As with monochromatic harmony, a high degree of unity is ensured, but the wider range of hues offers greater variety and can increase interest.

Blues and a surprising variety of greens activate the *Chromatics Place Setting* shown in figure 2.32.

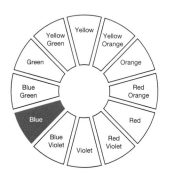

**2.29** Monochromatic color system.

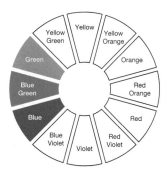

**2.31** Analogous color system.

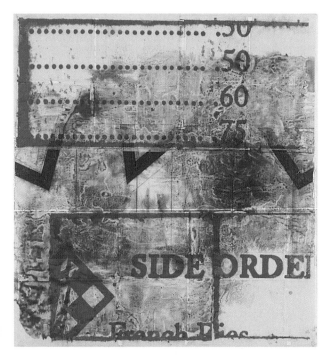

**2.30 Guy Goodwin,** *Tracers–Side Order,* **1999.** Resin, polyurethane, ink on polycarbonate, 51 × 54 × 4 in. (130 × 137 × 10 cm).

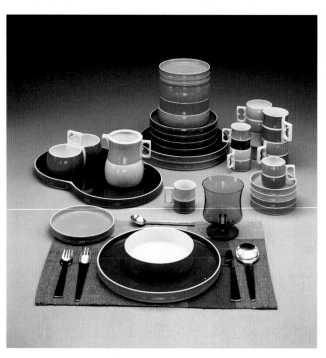

**2.32 Gerald Gulotta, shape designer; Jack Prince, pattern designer.** *Chromatics Place Settings,* **1970.**

## Complementary

The palette dramatically expands in a **complementary** color scheme (2.33). Complementary colors are opposites on the traditional color wheel. When mixed together, they can lower intensity and produce a wide range of browns. When paired in a composition, complementary colors become ideal partners. Each increases the power of the other.

Bacon's *Four Studies for a Self-Portrait* (2.34) is dominated by the complements of red and green. The design is unified by browns, including the reddish brown filling the background. Vigorous slashes of pure green and red add visual energy and create the illusion of movement.

Each complementary pair has its own distinctive strengths. Violet and yellow provide the widest value range, while orange and blue provide the widest range of variations in temperature. Red and green are closest in value and create extreme agitation when placed side by side. By mixing two complements plus black and white, we can create a range of colors that begins to suggest the power of a full spectrum.

## Split Complementary

An even wider range of possibilities is offered by the **split complementary** color scheme (2.35). Rather than pair colors that are in opposite positions on the color wheel, the artist completes the scheme using the two colors on either side of one of the complements. Georgia O'Keeffe's *Jack in the Pulpit No. V* (2.36) is dominated by rich greens and violets, with accents of yellow at the top of the composition and a vertical line of red just to the left of the center.

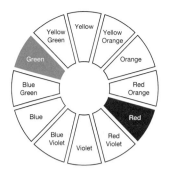

**2.33** Complementary color system.

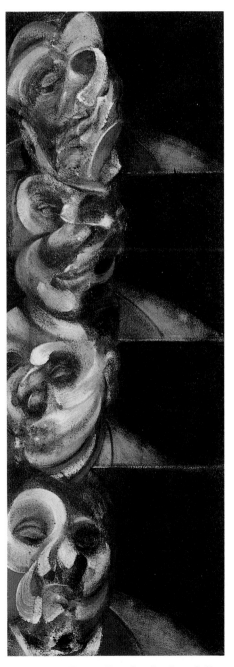

**2.34 Francis Bacon, *Four Studies for a Self-Portrait*, 1967.** Oil on canvas, 36 × 13 in. (91.5 × 33 cm).

## Key Questions

- Which will work better in your design, a limited or a wide range of hues?
- What proportion of warm and cool colors best communicates your idea?
- What happens when you combine low-intensity colors with high-intensity colors?

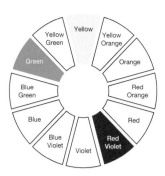

**2.35** Split complementary system.

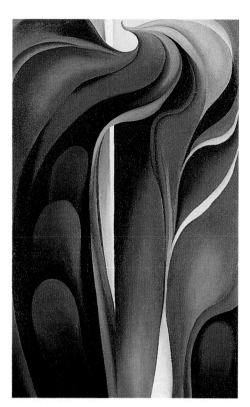

**2.36** Georgia O'Keeffe, *Jack in the Pulpit No. V*, 1930. Oil on canvas, 48 × 30 in. (122 × 76 cm).

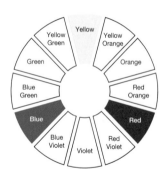

**2.37** Triadic system.

**2.38** Joel Katz Design Associates, Cover of *Philadelphia Architecture: A Guide to the City*, 2nd ed., 1984.

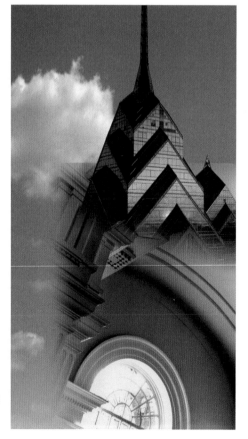

## Triadic

The **triadic** color scheme pushes the choices even farther apart, so that they are now located in a triangular position, equally spaced around the wheel (2.37). This scheme is often used when variety and a strong impact are essential. In a cover for *Philadelphia Architecture* (2.38), variations on red, blue, and yellow bring energy to the design, while the dark gray values provide detail.

## Chromatic Grays and Earth Colors

While the basic color wheel can help us identify many kinds of relationships, two important types of colors are not included: chromatic grays and earth colors. A **chromatic gray** is made from a mixture of various hues, rather than a simple blend of black and white. The result is both subtle and vibrant. In *The Magpie* (2.39), the grays vary widely, from the purples and blue-grays in the shadows to the golden-gray light in the foreground and the silvery grays for the snow-covered trees. This is not a dark, sullen winter day. Through the use of chromatic grays, Claude Monet makes the warm light and transparent shadows sparkle in the crisp air.

**Earth colors,** including raw sienna and burnt sienna, raw and burnt umber, and yellow ochre, are made generally from pigments found in soil. Often warm in temperature, when used together they create a type of analogous harmony. For example, browns, oranges, and tans accentuate the gestural energy and organic shapes in *Bush Cabbage Dreaming at Ngarlu* (2.40), by Australian artists

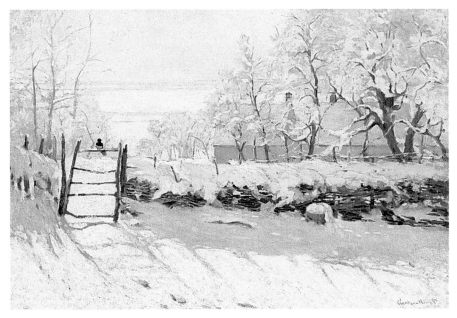

**2.39 Claude Monet, *The Magpie*, 1869.** Oil on canvas, 35 × 51 in. (89 × 130 cm).

Cookie Stewart Japaljarri, Alma Nungarrayi Granites, and Robin Japanangka Granites. This acrylic painting was inspired by traditional aboriginal artworks, which are literally made from earth colors. When used alone, earth colors can unify even the most agitated composition. When used in combination with high-intensity colors, they can provide an elegant balance between subdued and louder, more overt colors.

## Using Disharmony

Selecting the right colors can make the difference between a visual disaster and a visual delight. As a result, color harmony is the subject of endless books offering advice to artists, architects, and surface pattern designers. Monochromatic, analogous, complementary, split complementary, and triadic systems are traditional forms of color harmony.

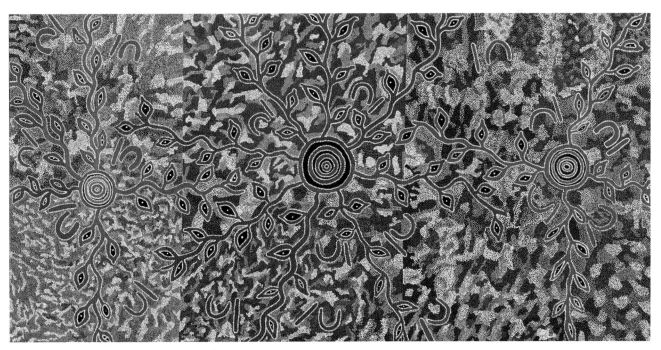

**2.40 Cookie Stewart Japaljarri, Alma Nungarrayi Granites, and Robin Japanangka Granites; *Bush Cabbage Dreaming at Ngarlu*; Yuendumn, Central Australia, 1986.** Acrylic on canvas, 47½ × 93½ in. (120.5 × 237.5 cm).

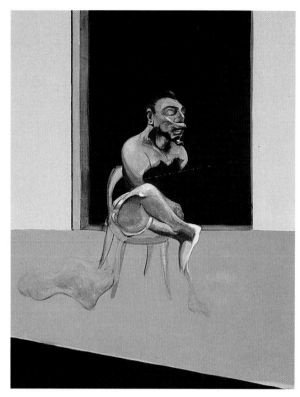

**2.41 Francis Bacon, *Triptych*, 1972.** Oil on canvas, one of three panels, each 78 × 58 in. (198.1 × 147.3 cm).

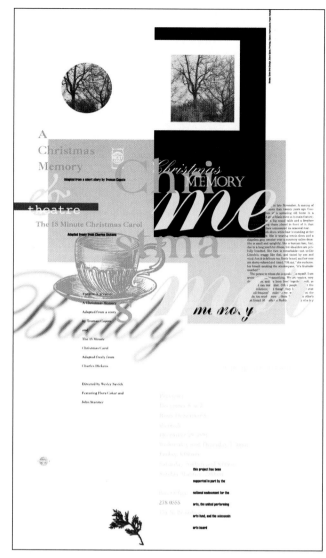

**2.42 Steve Quinn, *A Christmas Memory*, 1991.** Photoshop, 11 × 17 in. (27.94 × 43.18 cm).

However, cultural definitions of harmony are as changeable as popular music. In a search for eye-catching images, designers in all fields invent new color combinations each year. For example, the pink, gray, and black prized by designers in one year may seem passé in the next. Consequently, definitions and uses of color harmony are actually quite fluid.

Furthermore, when skillfully used, color **disharmony** can be as effective as color harmony. Disharmony is often used when the subject matter is disturbing or when an unusual visual approach is needed. In figure 2.41, Francis Bacon used pinks, grays, greens, and blacks to produce a painting that is as disturbing as it is beautiful. The colors in the body suggest disease, while the blocks of black, green, and gray create a room that is bleak and disorienting. Using a similar pink, gray, and black plus yellow-orange, Steve Quinn created a gentle evocation of memory in his Christmas poster (2.42). Here, the words and images shift back and forth in space, as fluid as a dream. As these examples demonstrate, the degree and type of harmony used must depend on the ideas behind the image and on the visual context in which an image will appear.

## Key Questions

- What are the advantages of each of the traditional color schemes?
- When a limited palette is used, how can a few colors produce the greatest impact? When a full palette is used, how can the colors become unified?
- What happens when your composition is dominated by earth colors or chromatic grays? How does it change when an intense color is added?
- Which is more suitable for the idea you want to express: traditional color harmony or some form of disharmony?

# COMPOSING WITH COLOR

**Composition** may be defined as the combination of multiple parts into a harmonious whole. The effect of color on composition is profound. Color can shift visual balance, create a focal point, influence our emotions, and expand communication. In this section, we will consider four major compositional effects of color.

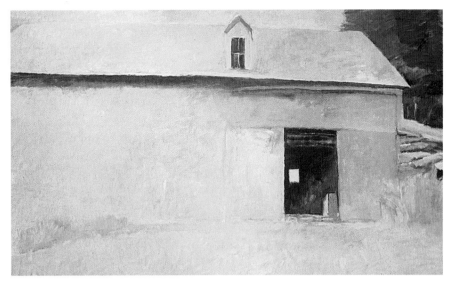

2.43  Wolf Kahn, *The Yellow Square,* 1981. Oil on canvas, 44 × 72 in. (112 × 183 cm).

## Creating the Illusion of Space

Pictorial space is like a balloon. When we "push" on one side, the other side appears to bulge outward. Through our color choices, we can cause various areas in a composition to expand or contract visually. In most cases, cool, low-intensity colors tend to recede, while warm, high-intensity colors tend to advance. In Wolf Kahn's *The Yellow Square* (2.43), the greens and violets defining the exterior of the barn gently pull the viewer into the painting, while the blazing yellow window inside the barn pushes out as forcefully as the beacon in a lighthouse.

This effect can play an even more important role in nonobjective paintings. As described by painter Hans Hofmann, the "push and pull" of color can be a major source of energy in a nonobjective composition. For example, a large block of intense red dominates Hofmann's *Magnum Opus* (2.44). The blue rectangle at the left side pulls us inward, while the crisp yellow shape on the right pushes outward.

2.44  Hans Hofmann, *Magnum Opus,* 1962. Oil on canvas, 84⅛ × 78⅛ in. (213 × 198 cm).

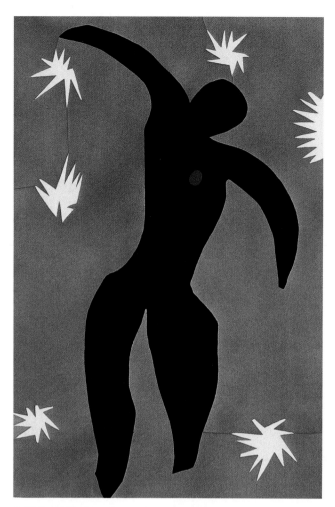

**2.45 Henri Matisse, *Icarus*, from *Jazz* series, 1947.** Gouache on paper, cut and pasted, 17⅛ × 13⅜ in. (43.6 × 34 cm).

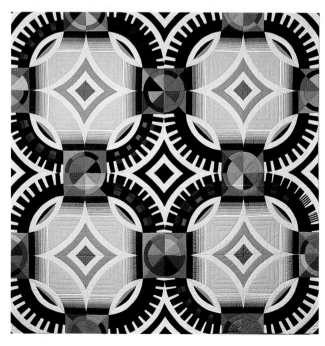

**2.46 Nancy Crow, *Double Mexican Wedding Rings 1*, © 1988.** Hand quilted by Marie Moore. 72 × 72 in. (183 × 183 cm).

## Weight and Balance

The effect of color on visual weight and balance is equally dramatic. In *Icarus* (2.45), Henri Matisse visually tells the story of the boy who flew too close to the sun, melting his wax wings and plunging into the ocean. The black body "falls" into the blue background, while a red heart seems to pull the figure upward, away from death. Six bursts of yellow surround the figure. Equally suggestive of the stars above the boy and of light shimmering on the water below, these simple shapes add energy to the composition and meaning to the myth.

## Distribution and Proportion

Through careful distribution, even the most disharmonious colors can work together beautifully. Four rectilinear gray shapes dominate Nancy Crow's *Double Mexican Wedding Rings 1* (2.46). Gradated values extend outward, creating a subtle glow. Twelve small multi-colored squares accentuate the edges of the four large squares and frame up the composition as a whole. In most compositions, the earth colors, chromatic grays, and high-intensity reds, blues, and yellows would clash. In this composition, an even distribution of colors creates a unified composition.

Proportional distribution is another way to harmonize seemingly incompatible colors. Willem de Kooning's *Door to the River* (2.47) is dominated by a large mass of brilliant yellow. Five patches of blue-gray provide a subordinate **accent color.**

## Key Questions

- How much space is needed in your composition, and how can color increase the illusion of space?
- How can color shift the visual balance in your composition?
- Can color shift or enhance the emphasis in your composition?

Vigorous strokes of olive and grays create essential connections between major compositional shapes, adding both energy and unity to the design.

## Color as Emphasis

Graphic designers often use color to emphasize critical information in a composition. The subway map in figure 2.48 provides a good example. Cooler areas of gray, green, and blue, placed on a black background, provide basic structural information. The bright yellow lines show the path through the subway. Red, which is used at only one point in the diagram, clearly locates the viewer on the map.

Color can also be used to create a focal point. A small red astronomical observatory dominates Vernon Fisher's *Objects in a Field* (2.49). Located just above the center of the painting, it commands our attention while echoing the curved shape of the white parachute in the foreground.

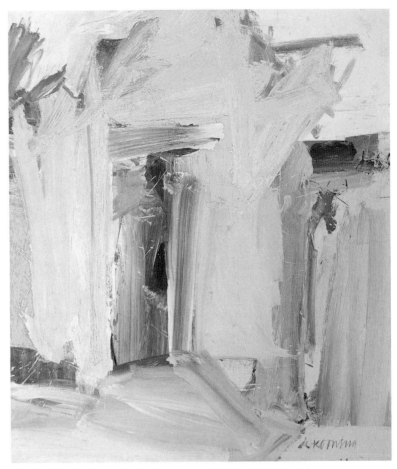

2.47 Willem de Kooning, *Door to the River*, 1960. Oil on canvas, 80 × 70 in. (203.2 × 177.8 cm).

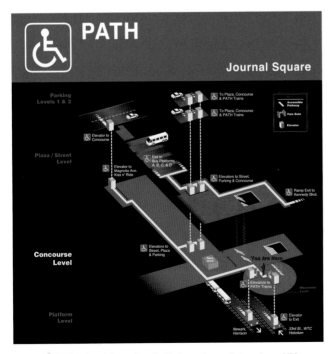

2.48 PATH Station Maps, Louis Nelson Associates, Inc., NY. Graphic designer: Jennifer Stoller.

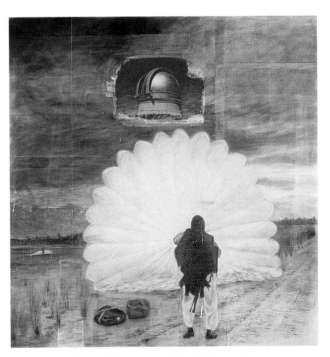

2.49 Vernon Fisher, *Objects in a Field,* 1986. Acrylic on canvas, 8 × 8 ft (2.4 × 2.4 m).

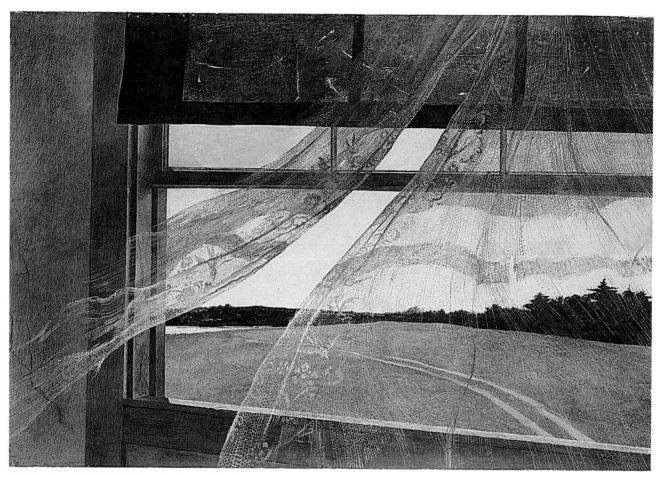

**2.50 Andrew Wyeth, *Wind from the Sea*, 1947.** Tempera on masonite, 18½ × 27½ in. (47 × 69.9 cm).

# COLOR, EMOTION, AND EXPRESSION

Colors are never emotionally neutral. The subtle browns and greens in Andrew Wyeth's *Wind from the Sea* (2.50) suggest the sepia color of a nineteenth-century photograph and evoke the slow pace and serenity of a countryside at rest. Richard Diebenkorn's *Interior with Book* (2.51), painted just 12 years later, provides a very different interpretation of a similar interior scene. The intense yellows and oranges in the background push toward us, while the solid blocks of blue pull inward, flattening the image. The tension and power thus generated create a California landscape that is a world apart from Wyeth's New England. The color in Sandy Skoglund's *Radioactive Cats* (2.52) creates yet another interpretation of an interior space. The gray walls, furniture, and clothing suggest a world that is lifeless and coated in ash. In contrast, the lime-green cats glow with an inquisitive energy that may be toxic!

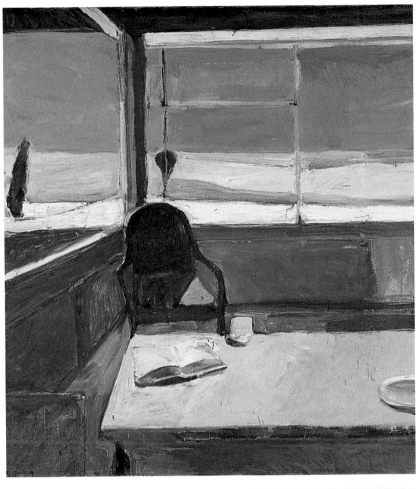

**2.51 Richard Diebenkorn, *Interior with Book*, 1959.** Oil on canvas, 70 × 64 in. (178 × 163 cm).

**2.52 Sandy Skoglund, *Radioactive Cats*, 1980.** Cibachrome print, 30 × 40 in. (76.2 × 101.6 cm).

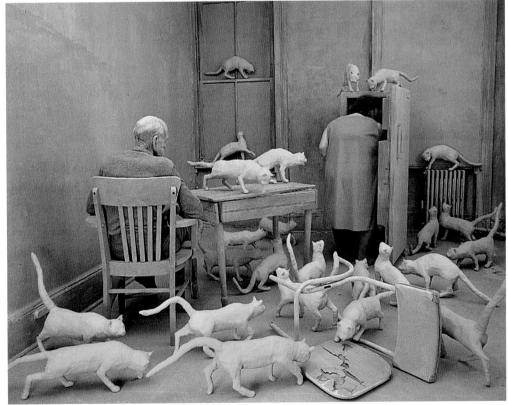

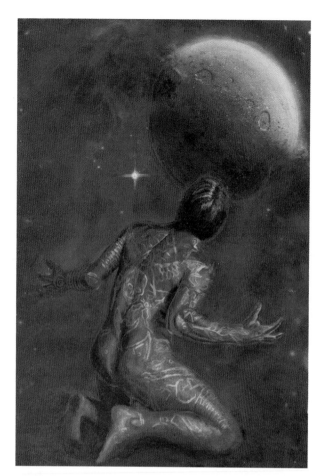

2.53 Joseph Spadaford, *Illustrated Man*, 1998. Acrylic.

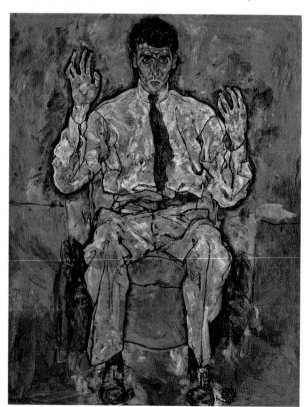

2.54 Egon Schiele, *Portrait of Paris von Gütersloh*, 1918.
Oil on canvas, 55¼ × 43¼ in. (140.3 × 109.8 cm).

## Color Keys

A dominant color, or **color key,** can heighten psychological as well as compositional impact. The blues that dominate Joe Spadaford's *Illustrated Man* (2.53) suggest both magic and melancholy. Based on Ray Bradbury's collection of stories by the same name, Spadaford had to suggest the torment of a man whose tattoos come to life at night. At the other extreme, in Egon Schiele's *Portrait of Paris von Gütersloh* (2.54), the flaming orange around and within the figure places the anxious man in an emotional electric chair. Designers also use color keys. Blood red dominates Chaz Maviyane-Davis' *Our Fear Is Their Best Weapon* (2.55). The soldier's face is tightly cropped, highlighting his fierce red eyes. The powerful slogan, presented in faded black letters, is almost consumed by the red background. As the text says, the voice of the people will be lost if fear is allowed to prevail. In these three cases, color was used to heighten emotion rather than represent reality.

## Symbolic Color

Colors are often assigned symbolic meaning. These meanings may vary widely from culture to culture. In *The Primary Colors,* Alexander Theroux writes:

> [Blue] is the symbol of baby boys in America, mourning in Borneo, tribulation to the American Indian and the direction South in Tibet. Blue indicates mercy in the Kabbalah and carbon monoxide in gas canisters. Chinese emperors wore blue to worship the sky. To Egyptians it represented virtue, faith, and truth. The color was worn by slaves in Gaul. It was the color of the sixth level of the Temple of Nebuchadnezzar II, devoted to the planet Mercury. In Jerusalem a blue hand painted on a door gives protection . . . and in East Africa, blue beads represent fertility.[2]

In Hopi culture, colors symbolize spatial location and geographic direction. The Kachina doll in figure 2.56 represents Butterfly Maiden, a benevolent spirit. Red represents a southerly direction; white, the east or northeast; blue or green, the west.

Symbolic color also plays a major role in *Flag* (2.57) by Jasper Johns. Part of a series of images based on the American flag, this print presents a reversal of the usual colors at the top. If we stare at

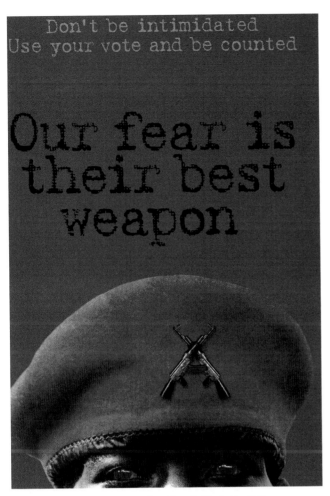

**2.55 Chaz Maviyane-Davis,** *Our Fear Is Their Best Weapon,* **2002.** Offset poster.

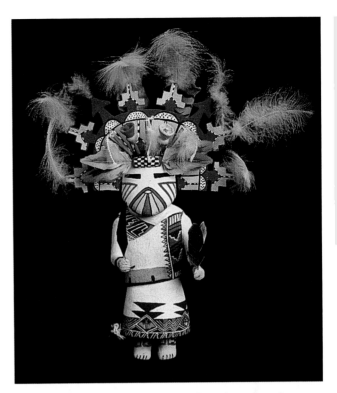

**2.56 Butterfly Maiden, Hopi Kachina.** Carved cottonwood, 13½ in. (35 cm).

this flag, then shift our attention to a white sheet of paper, we will once again see the familiar red, white, and blue. In this painting, an afterimage was used to suggest the contradictory nature of patriotism.

## Key Questions

- Will deeper space strengthen your composition? If so, what colors might you choose?
- Will a shift in coloristic balance improve your design?
- Will a dominant color key increase the emotional impact of your design?
- Considering the ideas you want to express, which is more effective: an even distribution of color or focused use, as a way to emphasize a particular shape or word?

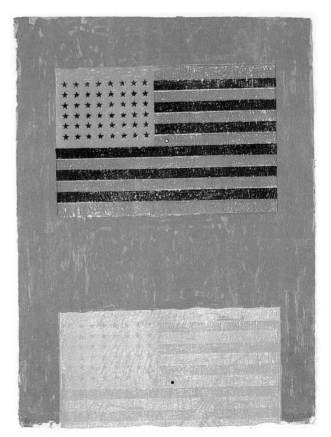

**2.57 Jasper Johns,** *Flag,* **1968.** Lithograph, printed in color, composition: 34⅝ × 25⅞ in. (87.9 × 65.7 cm).

## Expressive Color

Color and value each have unique strengths. A group of self-portraits by Käthe Kollwitz demonstrates three possibilities. The black-and-white value study on cream-colored paper (2.58) has a simple eloquence, while a more developed value drawing (2.59) adds drama and definition to the figure. The last portrait (2.60) places the warm figure against the cool background and makes her seem more accessible.

Color can increase the power of a given shape, shift compositional weight, and create a focal point. It can enhance the illusion of space, suggest volume, and heighten emotion. Well used, color is one of the most expressive elements of art and design.

**2.58  Käthe Kollwitz, *Self-Portrait in Profile, Facing Left, I*, 1889.** Lithograph, 5⅞ × 5⅞ in. (15 × 15 cm).

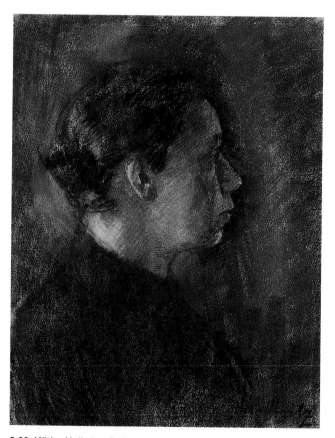

**2.60  Käthe Kollwitz, *Selbstbildnis im Profil Nach Rechts*, c. 1900.** Pastel on laid paper, 19 × 14⅜ in. (46.8 × 36.5 cm).

**2.59  Käthe Kollwitz, *Selbstbildnis und Aktstudien (Self-portrait and Nude Studies)*, 1900.** Pencil, dark gray ink wash, with white and yellowish highlights, on heavy brown paper, 11 × 17½ in. (27.8 × 44.5 cm).

# SUMMARY

- Color immediately attracts attention. Its emotional and physiological impact strengthens communication and heightens expression.

- Red, green, and blue are the additive color primaries. Blue, red, and yellow are the subtractive color primaries.

- The three basic qualities of color are hue (the name of the color), value (its lightness or darkness), and intensity (its purity).

- Using a monochromatic, analogous, complementary, split complementary, or triadic color scheme can increase harmony in your design.

- The level of color harmony must match the expressive intent. In the right context, disharmony can be more expressive than harmony.

- In a composition, color can enhance the illusion of space, shift visual weight and balance, and help emphasize compositional details.

- Distribution and proportion can help unify disharmonious colors.

- Colors are never emotionally neutral. A dominant color key can heighten psychological impact, while a symbolic color provides a cultural reference.

# KEYWORDS

accent color
achromatic
additive color
afterimage
analogous
Bezold effect
chroma
chromatic gray
color harmony

color interaction
color key
color overtone
color theory
complementary
composition
disharmony
earth colors
hue

intensity
monochromatic
opponent theory
primary colors
process colors
saturation
secondary colors
shade
simultaneous contrast

split complementary
subtractive color
temperature
tertiary colors
tint
tone
triadic
value

# IN DETAIL

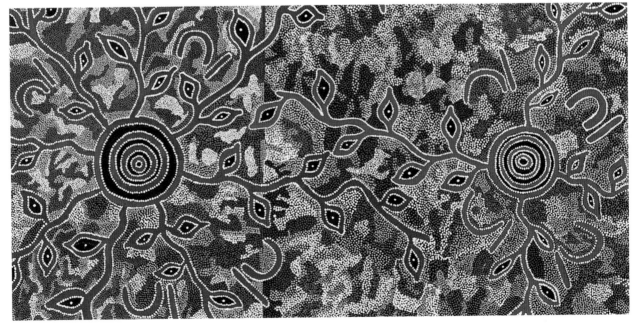

Multiple dots of paint serve two major purposes in this composition. First, the textures they create produce a vibrant energy. Second, they form a map of a mythical and actual Australian landscape. Seemingly random, each dot is actually highly purposeful.

# Profile:

## Ann Baddeley Keister, Fiber Artist

### Color, Construction, and Communication: Designing a Tapestry

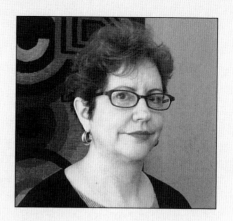

Ann Baddeley Keister is a nationally renowned fiber artist. Her work has been exhibited both nationally and internationally and is in many private and corporate collections, including The Vanguard Group, The Discovery Channel, and the Indianapolis Museum of Art.

**MS:** When I look at your work, I am impressed by the very deliberate use of design in these complex narrative tapestries. These images could be painted or done on a computer so much more quickly. What is the advantage of weaving? What attracted you to fiber arts?

**AK:** My undergraduate degree actually was a general degree in design, which allowed me to explore a number of different craft and fine art media, including textiles. The University of Kansas has a great fiber facility, and since I had learned how to knit and sew at the age of seven, the materials of textile art just felt natural and familiar to me. I love making the structure through the repetitive action of weaving. And I'm attracted to the pliability of the material. For me, metals are too unforgiving, clay is too messy—fiber, as a material, just feels "right" to me. I feel that there is a strong symbiosis between the images that I am interested in making and the material from which those images are constructed. One seems to feed off of the other.

**MS:** Designer Paul Rand said, "Art is an idea that has found its perfect form. Design is the means by which this is realized." And it is often said that art is about expression, while design is about communication. Is your work both art and design?

**AK:** Yes, and it is also craft and decoration. Contemporary fiber arts is such a diverse field. I love pure pattern AND I love storytelling. I love looking at beautiful colors, and want to offer the viewer a visual feast through my work!

**MS:** What is your usual work process?

**AK:** Many of my projects begin with a commission.

I determine the client's requirements and puzzle over possible solutions. With *Memory*, during a walk along the Grand River, I saw a historical marker describing the late nineteenth-century flood. I began to think about this terrible storm that washed away bridges and created piles of logs careening through the city. I immediately realized that this event could provide my image.

I made a number of pencil sketches, exploring compositional possibilities. I then developed these sketches in color, using the Adobe Illustrator. I have an extensive knowledge of color theory and this actually gives me the freedom to choose my colors very intuitively. I am using a lot of blue in this piece, since it is one of the school's colors, and I have a lot of discordant colors, which seem appropriate for such a devastating event.

A full-size, 6′ × 10′ computer print comes next. I match colors from my collection of approximately 200 colors of wool yarns. One strand on the loom is made up of six strands of yarn. I use a lot of optical mixing to create very subtle gradations. Finally, I weave the piece. The most useful thing I learned from my teachers is this: DO YOUR WORK! There is no substitute for action. Weaving is slow and simply has to be done consistently. During my summer work time, I am in the studio from about 9 to 6 an average of five or six days a week. Since weaving is an activity that makes demands on the body and the concentration, I do take breaks in my daily work with forays into the garden or other household chores. This is one reason that I find working at home so satisfying. My domestic interests in cooking, the garden, and my home often find their way into the imagery in my work as well.

**MS:** What are your criteria for excellence?

**AK:** I seek unity between concept and composition. Each of the formal elements: line, shape, texture, and color — is essential. There is almost always a dynamic sense of space in my work, which makes the tapestry read well in an architectural setting. I seek an inseparable connection between imagery, technique, and material.

**MS:** Do you have any advice for my students?

**AK:** Take this time to be inventive. Try out many possibilities. If you don't like an image, don't do it! Invent another way to solve the problem. The joy you bring to the creative process will be apparent in the final design.

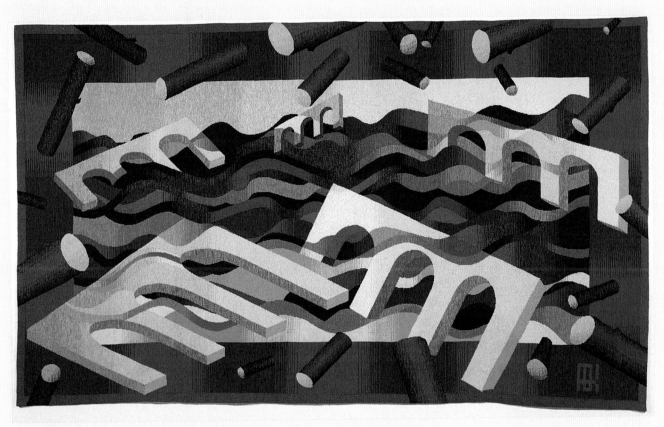

Ann Baddeley Keister, *Memory*, 2000. Wool tapestry, 6 × 10 ft (1.83 × 3.1 m).

# Principles of Two-Dimensional Design

Imagine yourself practicing jump shots on a deserted basketball court. By focusing all of your attention on the basket, you can master the sequence of moves needed to score. Now, imagine yourself playing in a high-paced game. You are now surrounded by skillful and cooperative teammates. The skills you practiced alone become heightened as you take passes and make shots. The complexities increase and the stakes rise when 10 players fill the court.

Developing a rich complex composition can be equally exhilarating. **Composition** can be defined as "the combination of multiple parts into a unified whole."[1] In a well-composed design, line, shape, texture, value, and color work together, as a team. As one element becomes dominant, another element becomes subordinate. A dialogue is created between positive and negative shapes, and opposing forces add vitality rather than creating confusion.

We will begin this chapter with a discussion of unity and variety, the basis on which all design is built. We will then define and discuss balance, scale, proportion, rhythm, and emphasis. Connections between concept and composition will be emphasized throughout.

## UNITY AND VARIETY

**Unity** can be defined as similarity, oneness, togetherness, or cohesion. **Variety** can be defined as difference. Unity and variety are the cornerstones of composition. When they are combined effectively, we can create compositions that are both cohesive and lively.

Mark Riedy used three major strategies to unify figure 3.1. First, all of the major shapes are organized diagonally, from the lower left to the upper right. A series of parallel lines in the sand and sea emphasizes this diagonal structure. The cast shadows then create another diagonal pattern, running from the upper left to lower right. Second, the top third of the painting is filled with the blue water, while the beach fills the bottom two-thirds. This proportional relationship has been used since antiquity to create a dynamic form of balance. Third, one shape is repeated 19 times, creating the graceful collection of umbrellas. Repetition in any form tends to increase unity.

A sailboat, 9 groups of bathers, and especially the single red umbrella add variety. The red umbrella breaks the pattern set by the 18 white umbrellas. The resulting focal point attracts our attention to a particular spot on the beach. As we begin to notice the number of people clustered around this umbrella,

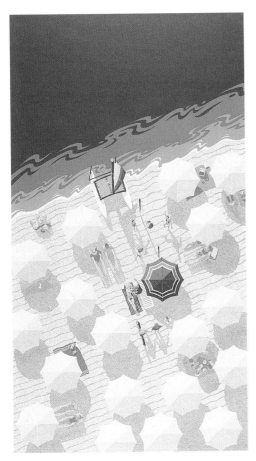

**3.1 Mark Riedy, *Day at the Beach*, 1988.** Acrylic airbrush.

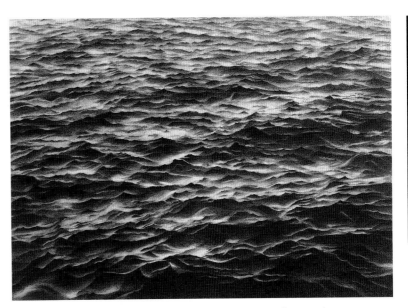

**3.2 Vija Celmins, *Untitled (Ocean)*, 1969.** Graphite on acrylic ground on paper, 14 × 18 in. (35.6 × 45.7 cm).

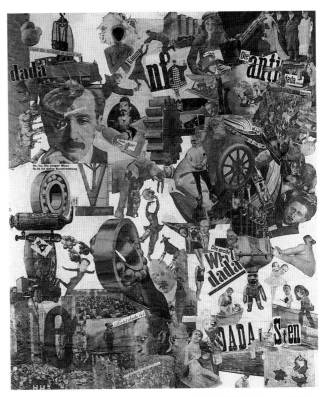

**3.3 Hannah Höch, *Cut with a Kitchen Knife*, 1919.** Collage, 44⅞ × 35½ in. (114 × 90 cm).

we are pulled into the painting and the miniature world it represents. One small red circle dramatically changes our visual and emotional response to the entire painting.

We face a new compositional challenge with each design we make. There are no simple formulas: each idea has its own expressive requirements. For example, in figure 3.2, Vija Celmins used a highly unified drawing to create a quiet, contemplative image. The size and shape of the waves are the only variations. At the other extreme, Hannah Höch's *Cut with a Kitchen Knife* (3.3) is crowded with conflicting images and fragmentary words. Created shortly after the end of World War I, this collage reflects the tumultuous economic and political conditions in postwar Germany. Celmins used a highly unified pattern of waves to suggest the ocean's hypnotic power, while Hoch used a collection of conflicting images to suggest chaos. Using very different approaches, each artist created an appropriate composition for the concept she wished to convey.

Excessive unity can be monotonous, while excessive variety can be chaotic. In the following section, we will analyze these and other unifying forces in depth, consider ways to increase variety, and explore ways to create a partnership between the two.

# Gestalt: Theory and Application

Artists and designers use many strategies to create compelling compositions. **Gestalt** psychology offers a fascinating analysis of these strategies. According to this theory, visual information is understood holistically before it is examined separately. We first scan the entire puzzle, then analyze the specific parts. An image composed of units that are unrelated in size, style, orientation, and color appears chaotic and unresolved. The implications of Gestalt are complex, and many books have been written on the subject. In this brief introduction, we will focus on six essential aspects.

## Grouping

When presented with a collection of separate visual units, we immediately try to create order and make connections. **Grouping** is one of the first steps in this process. We generally group visual units by location, orientation, shape, and color. For example, the units in figure 3.4A form two distinct group despite their dissimilarity in shape. Orientation creates group cohesion in figure 3.4B. The diagonal placement of the various elements creates unity despite the

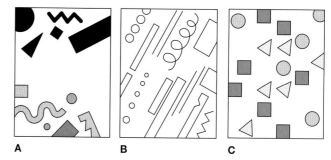

**3.4A–C** Examples of grouping by location, orientation, and shape.

variations in shape. Grouping by shape is shown in figure 3.4C. We mentally organize this set of units by shape in spite of their similarity in size and value.

*Rama and Laskshmana Bound by Arrow-Snakes* (3.5) demonstrates the compositional and conceptual power of grouping. We first see the complete composition. Multiple groups of humans and animals fill the long, horizontal rectangle. Next, we may notice that the composition is divided into three sections, each dominated by a distinctive background color. Blue and gray dominate the section on the left; red and orange dominate the section on the right. A yellow background fills

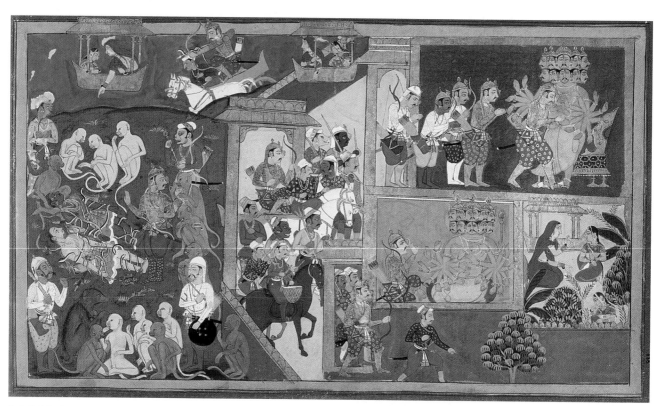

**3.5** Sahibdin and workshop, *Rama and Laskshmana Bound by Arrow-Snakes,* from the *Ramayana,* Mewar, c. 1650–52. Opaque watercolor on paper, 9 × 15¼ in. (22.86 × 38.42 cm).

the center. Within these major groups, we can discern further subdivisions, including the two clusters of monkeys on the right, the four compositional boxes on the left, and the throng of horsemen in the center.

Like a comic book, this painting tells a complex story of prophecy, magical transformation, imprisonment, and escape. It begins in the rose-colored box on the right, as Indrajit devises a defense against Rama and Laskshmana, who are about to attack the palace. On the left, Indrajit's arrows turn into writhing snakes, binding the attackers. Indrajit's triumphal march dominates the center of the composition. By grouping the various events, the artist was able to present complex visual information effectively.

## Containment

As we can see from figure 3.5, groups are most easily created when visual units are placed inside a container. **Containment** is a unifying force created by the outer edge of a composition or by a boundary within a composition. A container encourages us to seek connections among visual units and adds definition to the negative space around each positive shape. In figure 3.6A, a random collection of shapes becomes more unified when a simple boundary is added (3.6B). Any shift in the location of this boundary creates a new set of relationships. A vertical rectangle is often used when a rising or sinking movement is needed, while a horizontal format can create an expansive effect (3.6C). The circular container in figure 3.6D draws our attention to both the center and to the outer edges of the composition.

Larry Moore's illustration in figure 3.7 uses containment in an especially inventive way. Three containers are used in this composition. The edge of the drawing provides the first container; the curtains provide the second; and the face itself provides the third container. A wide variety of corporate logos cover the face. Logos must attract the viewer's attention, regardless of the context in which they are placed, and each of these logos was originally designed as a distinct visual unit. In this composition, however, the individualistic logos become a cooperative team. The connections created by the three levels of containment are stronger than the separations created by the individualistic logos.

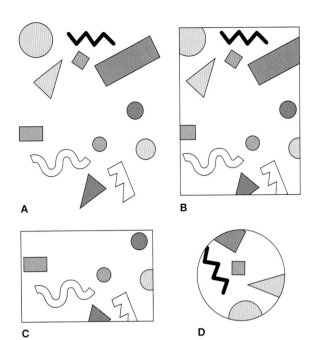

**3.6A–D** A container of any kind helps unify disparate visual units.

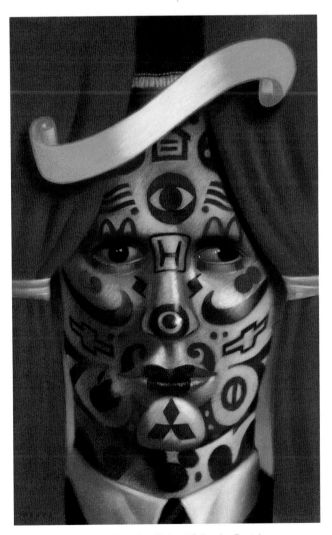

**3.7 Larry Moore, for Creative Club of Orlando.** Pastel on paper, 10 × 15 in. (25.4 × 38.1 cm).

## Repetition

**Repetition** occurs when we use the same visual element or effect over and over. By leafing through Chapter One, we can find many examples of unity through repetition. Kandinsky's *Several Circles* (page xxiv) is unified by shape. The repeated circles create a cohesive design despite the wide range of colors used. Repeated textures unify many works, including the Villon portrait on page 7, the Durer engraving on page 27, and the Moran landscape on page 32.

In Aaron Macsai's *Panels of Movement* (3.8), similar lines, shapes, textures, and colors were used in each of the 10 panels from which the bracelet was constructed. A spiral shape, an undulating line, a sphere, and at least one triangular shape appear in each of the panels. Despite their variations in size, texture, and location, these repeated shapes create a strong connection from panel to panel.

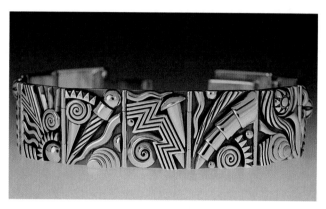

**3.8 Aaron Macsai,** *Panels of Movement.* Bracelet, 18K gold, sterling, copper, ⅞ × 7 in. (2 × 18 cm).

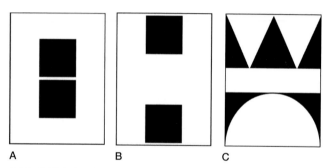

**3.9A–C** Variations in proximity.

A    B    C

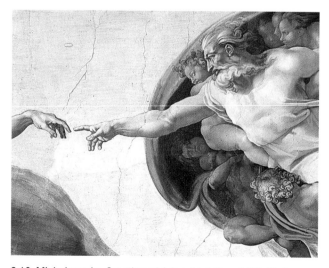

**3.10 Michelangelo,** *Creation of Adam* (detail), c. 1510. Sistine Chapel, Rome.

## Proximity

In design, the distance between visual elements is called **proximity.** As shown in figure 3.9A, close proximity helps increase unity. More distant shapes read as separate events (3.9B). **Fusion** occurs when shapes or volumes are placed so close together that they share common edges. When shapes of similar color and texture fuse, new negative shapes can be created as the surrounding area becomes more clearly defined (3.9C).

Careful use of proximity can create visual tension, adding energy to the design. A detail from Michelangelo's *Creation of Adam* (3.10) demonstrates the expressive power of visual tension. Jehovah's hand, on the right, nearly touches Adam's hand, on the left. As we gaze at the ceiling of the Sistine Chapel, less than 6 inches of space separate the two. In this cosmology, all of human history begins when the spark of life jumps this gap. If the hands had been placed too far apart or too close together, the spark that animates both the man and the painting would have been lost.

## Continuity

**Continuity** may be defined as a fluid connection among compositional parts. This connection can be actual or implied. With actual continuity, each shape touches an adjoining shape. With implied continuity, we mentally make the connections.

Skillful use of continuity can add visual movement to a design. **Movement** creates deliberate visual pathways and helps direct the viewer's attention to areas of particular interest. In Frank Stella's *Lac Laronge IV* (3.11), curving lines and shapes flow from one circle to the next, creating actual continuity. Color distribution creates implied continuity, which enhances this visual flow. The upward curve of blue in the upper left corner is echoed by a quarter turn of blue in the lower right corner. The downward curve of reds in the lower left corner is echoed by a quarter turn of scarlet in the upper right corner. The hints of olive and brown add a further spin to the wheel.

Movement can play an equally important role in a representational design. In Géricault's *Raft of the Medusa* (3.12A), a pattern of diagonal lines (3.12B) directs our attention to a single **focal point,** or primary point of interest. The arms and legs of the sailors, the floorboards of the raft, and even the angle of the sail all lead us toward the rescue ship in the upper right corner. This dramatic use of movement greatly increases the emotional power of this historical painting. One hundred forty-nine survivors from a sinking ship began a desperate journey on the raft. When rescued two weeks later, only 15 had survived. The pattern of bodies and extended arms pulls us irresistibly toward the sailor at the front of the raft, whose very life depends on the attention he can attract.

### Closure

**Closure** refers to the mind's inclination to connect fragmentary information to produce a completed form. In figure 3.13, thousands

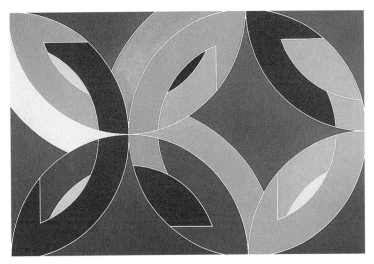

3.11 Frank Stella, *Lac Laronge IV,* 1969. Acrylic polymer on canvas, 9 ft ⅛ in. × 13 ft 6 in. (2.75 × 3.11 m).

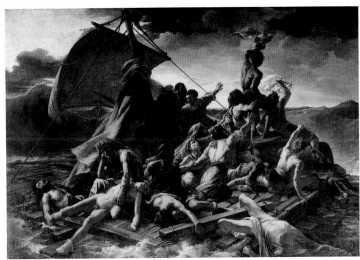

3.12A Théodore Géricault, *Raft of the Medusa,* 1818–19. Oil on canvas, 16 ft 1 in. × 23 ft 6 in. (4.9 × 7.2 m).

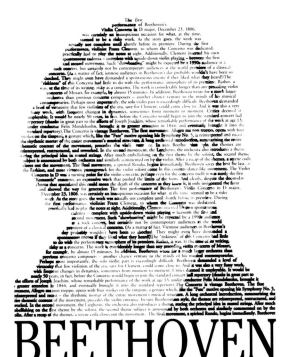

3.13 Because of closure, hundreds of separate shapes can be combined to create a face.

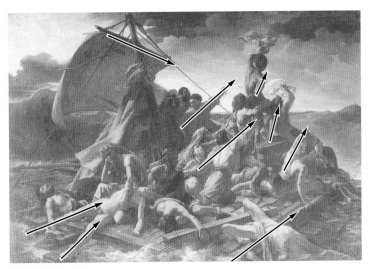

3.12B Diagram of *Raft of the Medusa,* showing eye movement toward focal point.

of letters have been connected to form words, and hundreds of words have been connected to create a portrait of composer Ludwig van Beethoven.

Closure makes it possible to communicate using implication. Freed of the necessity to provide every detail, the artist or designer can convey an idea through suggestion, rather than description. When the viewer completes the image in his or her mind, it is often more memorable than an explicit image.

### Combining Gestalt Principles

Artists and designers often combine all of the principles of Gestalt in a single composition. In figure 3.14, closure and containment help us read the disoriented words at the top of the composition. Proximity then helps us connect these words to the doll's face that fills the bottom half of the design. In *Turn of the Screw*, a play by Henry James, two children turn the tables on their governess, with devastating results. The turning text and frightened face convey both the title and the feeling perfectly.

## Patterns and Grids

A **pattern** is created when any visual element is systematically repeated over an extended area. Many patterns are based on a module, or basic visual unit. In a sly reference to the mass production of culture, Andy Warhol used the *Mona Lisa* as a module in figure 3.15. A **grid** is created through a series of intersecting lines in Figure 3.16A–C. Both can be used to create containment, increase continuity, strengthen proximity, and encourage closure. As a result, patterns and grids tend to increase compositional unity.

Patterns are often used to decorate walls, books, or fabrics. In his *Canterbury Tales* (3.17), designer

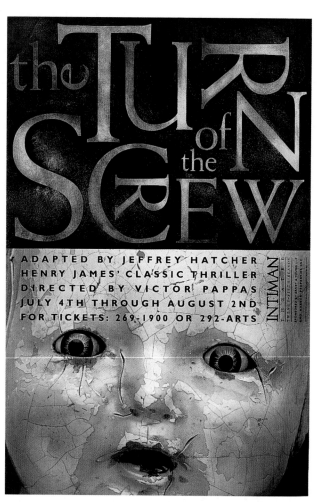

3.14 Cyclone Design, *Turn of the Screw.* Theater poster.

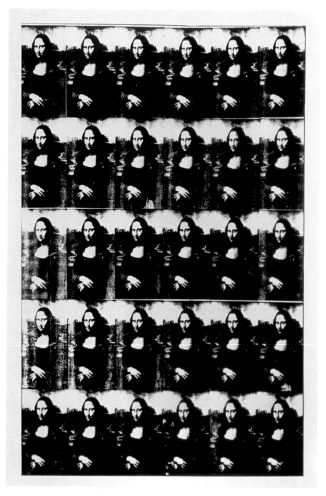

3.15 Andy Warhol, *30 Are Better than One*, 1964. Silkscreen ink and synthetic polymer paint on canvas, 110 × 82 in.

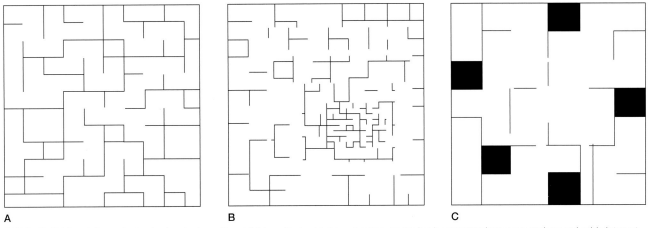

**A**　　　　　　　　　　**B**　　　　　　　　　　**C**

**3.16A–C** Grid variations. A simple checkerboard is a highly unified grid. Any variation on the basic structure increases variety and adds interest.

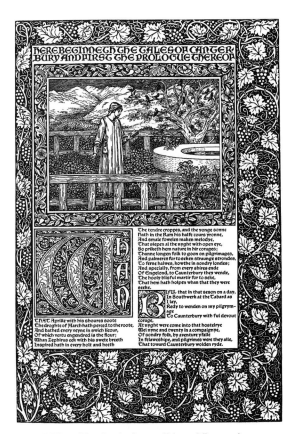

**3.17** William Morris, designer; Edward Burne-Jones, illustrator. Illustrated page from *The Canterbury Tales,* 1896.

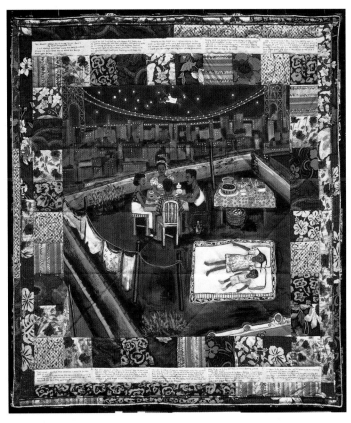

**3.18** Faith Ringgold, *Tar Beach,* 1988. Acrylic on canvas, fabric border, 74 × 69 in. (187.96 × 175.26 cm).

William Morris used complex floral patterns to create multiple borders and backgrounds. Curvilinear patterns of grapevines, flowers, and oak leaves fill the borders. The flowing text at the top of the page echoes these curving shapes and creates an additional pattern. There are even more patterns in the main drawing. The standing man is surrounded by two distinct leaf patterns, and a linear pattern suggests wood grain.

Multiple fragments of visual information can also be unified through pattern. In *Tar Beach* (3.18), Faith Ringgold used a pattern of repeating squares to organize blocks of printed fabric into a distinctive border. Based on Ringgold's own memories of sleeping on an apartment roof during hot weather, this pattern refers to the quilt depicted in the painting and to the magical expanse of buildings and lights visible from the rooftop.

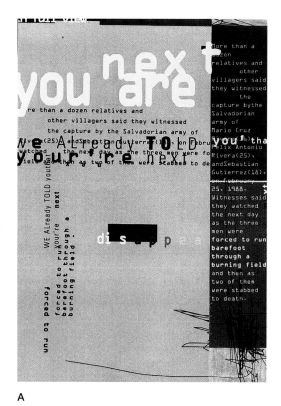

A

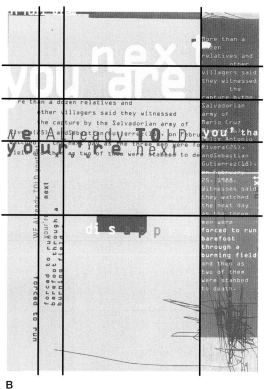

B

3.19A Joan Dobkin. Informational leaflet for Amnesty International, 1991.

3.19B Diagram of Amnesty leaflet, showing organizational structure.

Compositional grids are most commonly created using vertical and horizontal lines. The unifying power of a grid is so great that even the most disparate information gains cohesion when a grid is used. In Dobkin's *Amnesty International leaflet* (3.19A), commercial and handmade letterforms tell the story of political repression and governmental terror in El Salvador. Disoriented words and menacing phrases convey the helplessness and fear of the victims. Fragments of sentences appear and disappear unexpectedly. An underlying grid, shown in figure 3.19B, brings just the right amount of order to this poignant design.

## Key Questions

- What strategies have you used to unify your composition?
- What gives your composition variety?
- Is the balance between unity and variety appropriate for the ideas you want to express?
- What would happen if your composition were constructed using a pattern or grid?

# BALANCE

In design, **balance** refers to the distribution of weight or force within a composition. Negative and positive shapes can work together to create an equilibrium among compositional units, regardless of their size, weight, or shape.

## Weight and Gravity

**Visual weight** can be defined in two ways. First, *weight* refers to the inclination of shapes to float or sink. Second, *weight* can refer to the relative importance of a visual element within a design.

The compositional forces that most influence visual weight are size, value, type of shape, texture, location, and orientation. The context in which a visual unit is placed strongly affects each of these forces. For example, when a shape is placed on a neutral white ground, darker values and vigorous textures generally increase its visual weight. As noted in Chapter One, circles tend to stand out when placed in a rectangular format, while squares fit together easily. Location within the format also affects visual weight. Shapes that appear to extend beyond the upper edge tend to rise, while shapes that appear to extend below the bottom appear to sink.

The vertical, horizontal, or diagonal orientation of a line or shape also affects visual weight. Try this simple experiment. Which is the most dynamic and which is the most stable position for the box in figure 3.20? Most viewers find positions A and B the most stable. In these positions, the box is at rest, with the vertical and horizontal edges reconfirming the stability we experience when objects are at rest in the real world. By contrast, position C and position D place the box in a dynamic position, halfway between standing and falling. A composition that is dominated by diagonals tends to be visually dynamic, while a composition that is dominated by horizontals tends to be more stable, or static.

Bernice Abbott's photograph of New York skyscrapers (3.21) demonstrates the power of orientation.

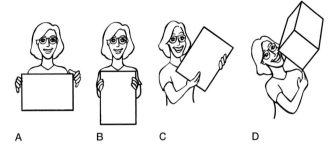

**3.20A–D** Which box is the most static? Which is the most dynamic?

Using dramatic vertical shapes within a tall vertical format, she captured the soaring energy of Wall Street within a small image.

Even the most abstract design is governed by gravity. In figure 3.22, a rectangle filled with

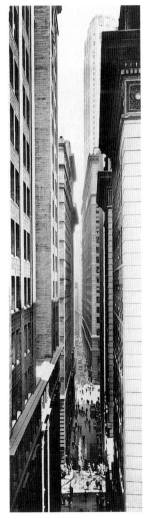

3.21 Bernice Abbott, *Exchange Place*, New York, 1934. Photograph.

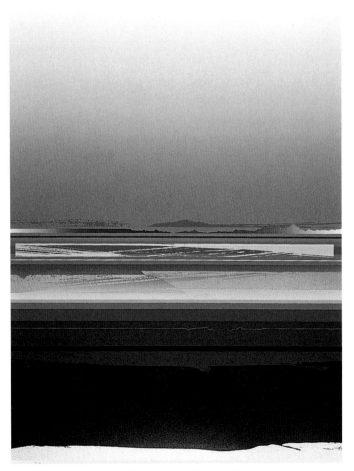

3.22 Tetsurō Sawada, *Brilliant Scape (Blue)*,1985. Silkscreen, 22⅞ × 15¾ in. (58 × 40 cm).

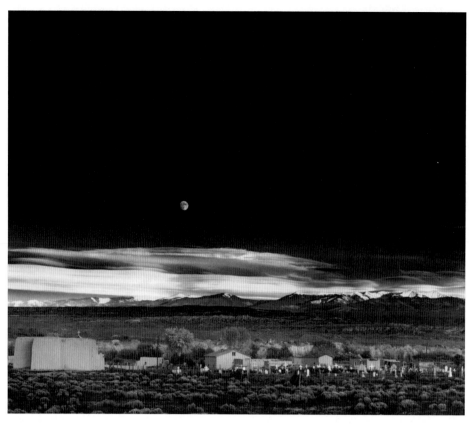

**3.23** Ansel Adams, *Moonrise, Hernandez, New Mexico*, **1941.** Photograph.

horizontal lines suggests the stability and tranquility of a landscape. Image stability would have increased if a horizontal format had been used. Instead, by using a vertical orientation and devoting the upper half to a gradated blue shape, Tetsurō Sawada combined the serenity of a landscape with the expansive feel of the soaring sky.

**Visual weight** can also refer to the relative importance of a visual element within a design. In *Moonrise, Hernandez, New Mexico, 1941* (3.23), Ansel Adams combined balance, gravity, and movement to create an image that is both tranquil and dramatic. A squarish format dominated by horizontal lines provides stability. The quiet village sinks to the bottom of the design. The tiny moon, positioned just to the right of compositional center, pulls us into the velvety black sky at the top half of the image. As the focal point for the image, the moon has the most visual weight in this photograph.

## Symmetrical Balance

**Symmetrical balance** occurs when shapes are mirrored on either side of an axis, as in a composition that is vertically divided down the center (3.24A). A shift in this axis (3.24B) creates symmetry between the top and bottom of the design.

A symmetrically balanced design can appeal to our desire for equilibrium and communicate calm and stability. The Taj Mahal (3.25) was built by a seventeenth-century Indian emperor as a tomb for his beloved wife. The three white marble domes and the four flanking towers create architectural symmetry. In the reflecting pool, a mirror image appears, increasing visual symmetry. The building is both graceful and serene.

**Approximate symmetry** is created when similar imagery appears on either side of a central axis. For example, in Richard Estes' *Miami Rug Company* (3.26), actual and reflected light poles divide the space as decisively as a gate. Radiating from the center of the composition, a network of diagonal lines pulls us into the painting. At the same time, the large pane of glass on the left side pushes toward us, shimmering with darkened reflections of the buildings on the right side. The overall effect is unnerving. The seemingly symmetrical shapes are actually quite different, and the resulting image is disorienting rather than serene.

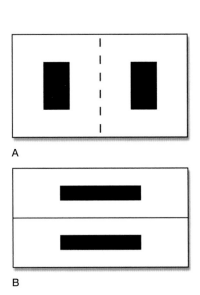

A

B

**3.24A–B** Examples of symmetrical balance.

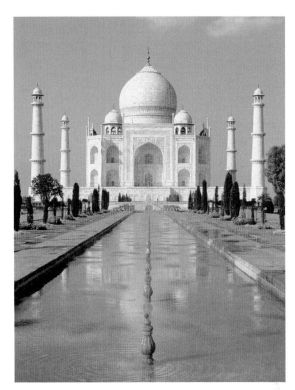

**3.25 Taj Mahal, Agra, India, 1630–1648.**

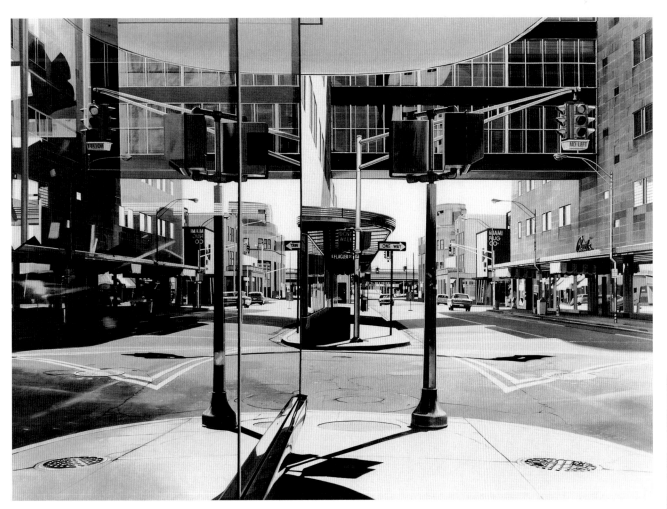

**3.26 Richard Estes,** *Miami Rug Company,* **1974.** Oil on canvas, 40 × 54 in. (101.6 × 137.16 cm).

# Radial Symmetry

With **radial symmetry,** lines and shapes are mirrored both vertically and horizontally, with the center of the composition acting as a focal point (3.27). An expanded approach to radial symmetry is shown in Judy Chicago's *Rejection Quintet: Female Rejection Drawing* (3.28). Because the format is now divided diagonally as well as vertically and horizontally, the entire design radiates from the center. Glowing and gradated colors accentuate the effect.

A variant on radial balance is the spiral. A spiral can increase energy in a circular format or add movement to a rectangular composition. In Rubens' *Tiger Hunt* (3.29A–B), the spiral pulls the tiger and the hunters together in the center of the painting. It then spins outward, breaking apart near the edges. The resulting composition harnesses the compressive power of centripetal force and the expansive power of centrifugal force.

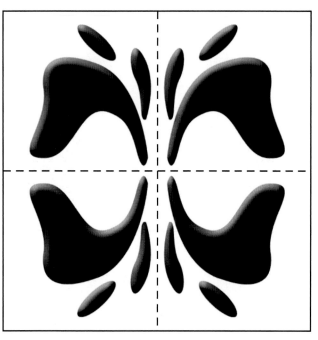

**3.27** Radial symmetry can be created when lines and shapes are mirrored both vertically and horizontally.

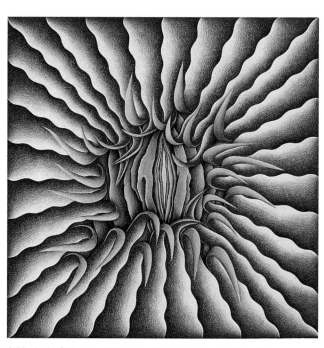

**3.28** Judy Chicago, *Rejection Quintet: Female Rejection Drawing*, **1974.** Prismacolor and graphite on rag board, 39⅝ × 29⅝ in. (101 × 75 cm).

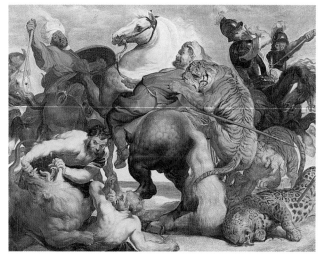

**3.29A Workshop of Peter Paul Rubens,** *Tiger Hunt,* **c. 1616.** Oil on canvas, 38⅞ × 49¼ in. (98.8 × 125 cm).

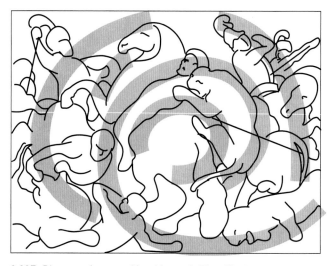

**3.29B** Diagram of compositional forces in *Tiger Hunt.*

## Asymmetrical Balance

**Asymmetrical balance** creates equilibrium among visual elements that do *not* mirror each other on either side of an axis. Depending on the degree of asymmetry, the resulting design may be quite stable, very dynamic, or nearly chaotic.

Many strategies can be used to create asymmetrical balance:

- A large shape is placed close to the fulcrum, while a small shape is placed farther away. Just as a child at the end of a seesaw can balance an adult near the center, so large and small shapes can be balanced in a design (3.30A).

- Multiple small squares, acting together, can balance a large square (3.30B).

- A small, solid square can balance a large, open circle. The solidity and stability of the square give it additional weight (3.30C).

- A textured shape placed near the fulcrum can be balanced by a distant open shape (3.30D).

Asymmetrical balance becomes even more interesting when a boundary is added. Because the negative space is just as important as each positive shape, more complex compositions can now be created:

- A small shape placed near the bottom of the format balances a large shape placed along the top. Especially within a tall rectangle, shapes placed near the top tend to rise, while shapes placed near the bottom tend to sink (3.31A).

- When the small square intersects the bottom edge and the large square moves away from the edge, the differences in weight become even more pronounced (3.31B).

- The top shape now gains energy through its diagonal orientation. Three bottom shapes are needed to create balance (3.31C).

- Finally, a small, aggressive triangle can balance a large, passive rectangle (3.31D).

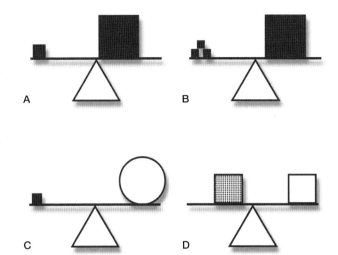

**3.30A–D** Creating asymmetrical balance.

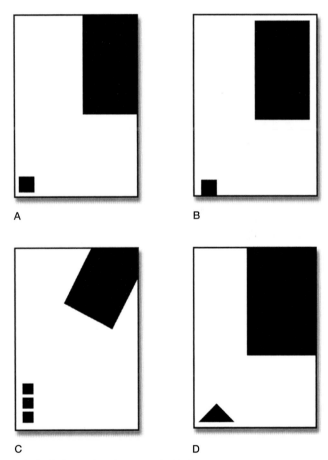

**3.31A–D** Examples of asymmetrical balance.

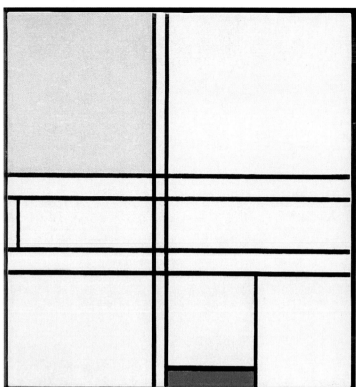

Balance in a composition shifts each time a visual element is added or subtracted. A complex network of negative and positive lines and shapes creates the balance in Mondrian's *Composition with Blue and Yellow* (3.32). The large yellow square positioned along the top edge is easily balanced by the small blue rectangle, which sinks to the bottom. As shown by the small vertical line positioned near the center left edge, even very minor changes can shift compositional balance.

The balance in Frank Miller's digital design (3.33) is even more complex. A horizontal line extends from the left to the right, in slightly descending steps. Four broken vertical lines divide the design into three major sections, each roughly one-third of the total length. Within these sections, the curving satellite dishes, clock, and letters add a series of repeated curves. Multiple lines, shapes, and clusters of information have been balanced in this image.

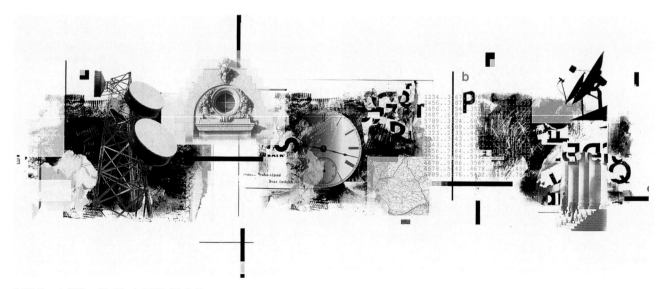

3.33 Frank Miller, *Untitled,* **1997.** Digital image.

# Expressive Uses of Balance

Each type of balance has its advantages. The approximate symmetry Frida Kahlo used for her double self-portrait (3.34) is symbolically appropriate and compositionally effective. Painted in response to her divorce from painter Diego Rivera, it presents the beloved Frida in a native costume on the right and the rejected Frida in European dress on the left. A linear vein connects the women's hearts. In figure 3.28, Judy Chicago used radial symmetry to pull the viewer into the composition. In figure 3.1 (see page 73), Mark Riedy used asymmetrical balance to animate his beach scene and accentuate the red umbrella.

There are even some cases in which a degree of **imbalance** is necessary. Eric Fischl used distortion to create imbalance in *Barbeque* (3.35). The table in the foreground is tilted and the bowl of fish is impossibly large. Pulled by the diagonal lines leading to the house, the pool also seems tilted, while the tiny women are more like dolls than people. Manning the grill, the father looks on approvingly as his son engages in a little recreational fire-breathing. Spatial distortion combined with a bizarre collec-

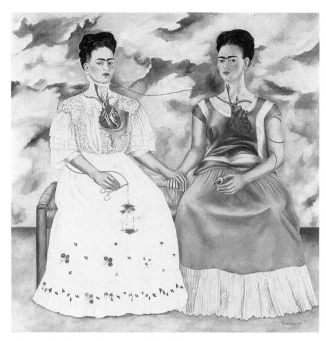

3.34 Frida Kahlo, *Las Dos Fridas*, 1939. Oil on canvas, 69⅛ × 69⅛ in. (176 × 176 cm).

tion of objects and events turns a family picnic into a suburban nightmare.

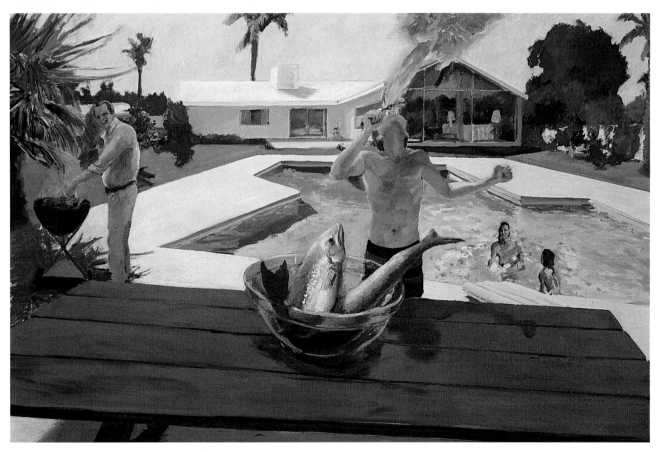

3.35 Eric Fischl, *Barbeque*, 1982. Oil on canvas. 5 ft. 5 in. × 8 ft. 4 in. (165 × 254 cm).

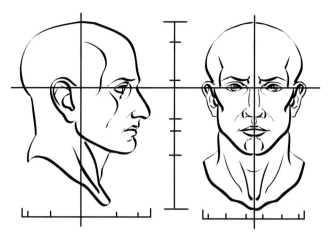

**3.36** Proportion is an essential part of figure drawing.

# SCALE AND PROPORTION

Scale and proportion create two types of size relationships. Both strongly affect compositional balance and emotional impact. **Proportion** refers to the relative size of visual elements *within* an image. When we compare the width of the head with its height or divide a composition into thirds, we are establishing a proportional relationship (3.36). **Scale** commonly refers to the size of a form when compared with our own human size. Thus, a 50-foot-long painting is a large-scale artwork, while a 10-square-inch square painting is an example of small scale.

Most designs distribute information fairly evenly within the format, with only modest size variation among the parts. Exaggerating these proportions can be eye-catching, because the image immediately stands out from the norm. In *Save Our City*, by Michael Bierut (3.37), the large black rectangle at the top presses down on the white shape below, covering the top part of the word *Save*. Meanwhile, the vertical white text suggests a city skyline and helps pull the white section of the poster upward. This tension between the upper and lower sections of the design perfectly matches the urgency of the message.

Likewise, various expressive possibilities occur when scale is exaggerated. *Intermission* (see page 107) presented many challenges to painter Ken Stout. The 50-foot-long format had to become an asset, rather than a liability. We visually enter the theater through the pink doorway at the far left. Cool blue light bathes the restless audience. Two men in the balcony add to the action, as one aims a peashooter and another launches a paper airplane. On

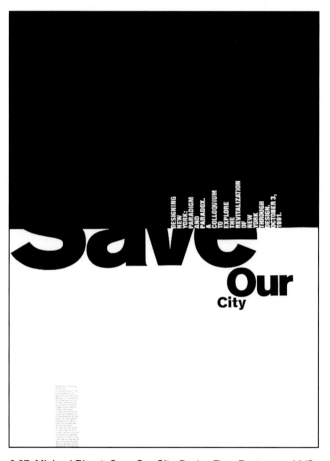

**3.37 Michael Bierut, *Save Our City.*** Design Firm: Pentagram, NYC.

the stage, a tiny actor creates a transition between the audience and the stage crew. The painting ends in a final burst of red, at the far right side. Taking advantage of each square inch, Stout created a swirling panorama of figures engaged in a wide variety of activities, onstage, backstage, and in the audience.

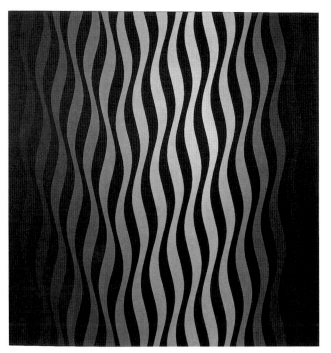

3.38 Bridget Riley, *Drift No. 2,* 1966. Acrylic on canvas, 7 ft 7½ in. × 7 ft 5½ in. (2.32 × 2.27 m).

3.39 A repeated word becomes a rhythmic design through color choices.

# RHYTHM

**Rhythm** is a sense of movement that is created by repetition of multiple units in a deliberate pattern. Visual rhythm is similar to musical rhythm. In music, rhythm is created through the organization of sound in time. Meter (the basic pattern of sound and silence), accents (which emphasize specific notes), and tempo (the speed with which the music is played) can be combined to create a dazzling array of compositional possibilities.

As with music, the rhythm in a visual composition can take many forms. In Bridget Riley's *Drift No. 2* (3.38), a simple line has been repeated to create an undulating rhythm similar to the waves on water. Vibrant words create a spatial rhythm in figure 3.39. Warm and cool colors in various values and intensities cause some words to advance while others recede.

Michael James combined undulating and spatial rhythms in his *Rhythm/Color: Improvisation* (3.40). A series of square blocks creates a unifying grid. Diagonal lines within each block and the curving shapes between blocks add another layer of movement. Fifteen blocks covered with diamond shapes provide accents, while a pattern of radiating diagonals energizes the border.

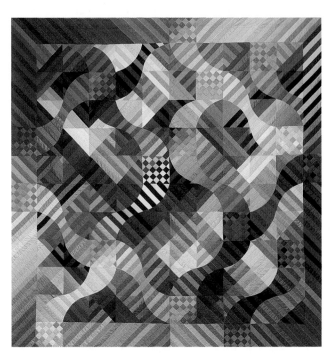

3.40 Michael James, *Rhythm/Color: Improvisation,* 1985. Machine-pieced and -quilted cotton and silk, 99½ × 99½ in. (253 × 253 cm).

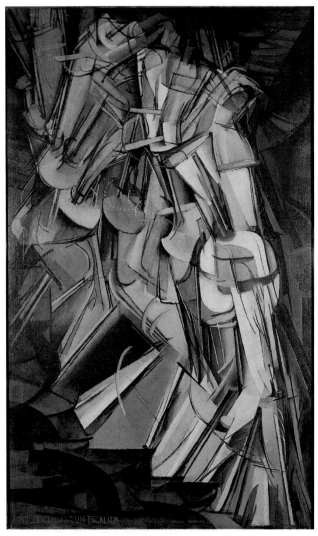

**3.41** Marcel Duchamp, *Nude Descending a Staircase, No. 2*, **1912.** Oil on canvas, 58 × 35 in. (147.3 × 88.9 cm).

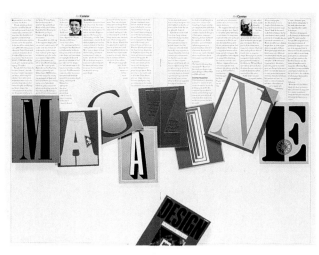

**3.42 Pentagram Design, Magazine.** Publisher: Art Center College of Design, Pasadena, CA.

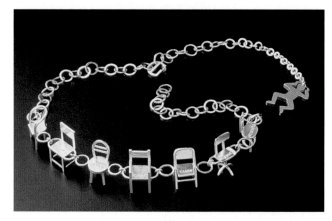

**3.43 Joana Kao, *I Never Liked Musical Chairs.*** Bracelet, sterling, 24K, 2¾ × 1¾ in. (7 × 4 cm). In this example of emphasis by isolation, the figure at the end of the chain represents a child ejected from a game.

Visual rhythm can be as regular as a waltz or as syncopated as jazz. Multiplication, fragmentation, and superimposition propel the nude descending Duchamp's staircase (3.41). The jerking rhythm demonstrates the alternating stability and instability of human locomotion, rather than physical grace.

# EMPHASIS

Each player in a basketball game has a particular role to play. The guards primarily focus on defense, the forwards on offense. The point guard plays a dominant role, calling plays and controlling the action. Likewise, the various visual elements in a composition must work together as a team. In most cases, a few carefully selected visual elements dominate, or stand out, while others are subordinate, or supportive.

**Emphasis** gives prominence to part of a design. A **focal point** is a compositional device used to create emphasis. Both emphasis and focal point are used to attract attention and increase visual and conceptual impact.

## Emphasis by Isolation

Any **anomaly,** or break from the norm, tends to stand out. Because we seek to connect the verbal and visual information we are given, a mismatched word or an isolated shape immediately attracts our attention. In figure 3.42, the word *design* is emphasized through its separation from the word *magazine*. Its placement right at the bottom edge makes this shape even more eye-catching.

Just as a pattern tends to increase connection among visual elements, so any break in the pattern emphasizes isolation. In figure 3.1 (page 67), 18 white umbrellas establish the pattern that is so beautifully broken by the single red umbrella. In *I Never Liked Musical Chairs* (3.43), metalsmith Joana Kao created a pattern using 7 tiny chairs connected by a silver chain. The figure at the end of the chain breaks the pattern. This break conveys the isolation felt by a child ejected from the game.

## Emphasis by Placement

Every square inch of a composition has a distinctive power. As a result, placement alone can increase the importance of a selected shape.

The compositional center is especially potent. In his *The Power of the Center*, psychologist Rudolph Arnheim discusses **centricity** (compressive compositional force), and **eccentricity** (expansive compositional force). Both centricity and eccentricity activate *Flash Point*, shown on page 14. The central white square pulls us into the middle of the painting, while the explosive red rectangle pushes toward the outer edge.

This effect is even more pronounced in figure 3.44. Any representation of another human attracts our attention, and faces are of particular interest. Four major lines and a series of concentric circles direct us inward, toward the man's left eye. Fragments of text extend outward, beyond the edge of the composition. Continually compressing and expanding, the seemingly simple image pulls the viewer inward while simultaneously appearing to extend outward, beyond the boundary.

## Emphasis Through Contrast

**Contrast** is created when two or more forces operate in opposition. By reviewing the elements and prin-

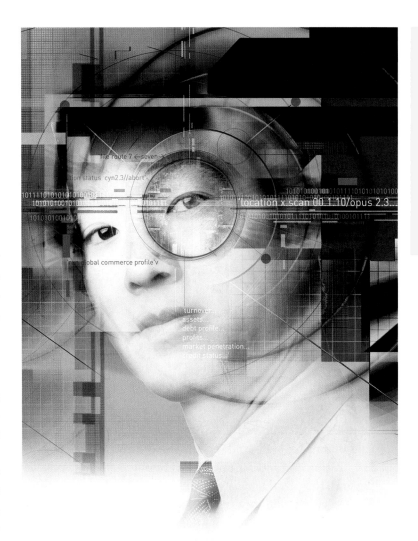

3.44 **Jacey,** *Untitled,* computer graphics. Example of centricity and eccentricity.

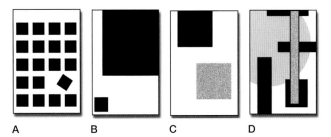

A   B   C   D

3.45A–D Examples of contrast: static/dynamic, small/large, solid/textured, curvilinear/rectilinear.

ciples of design discussed in this section, we can quickly create a long list of potential adversaries, including static/dynamic, small/large, solid/textured, and curvilinear/rectilinear (3.45A–D).

When the balance is just right, powerful compositions can be created from any of these combinations. Devoting about 80 percent of the compositional space to one force and about 20 percent to the other is especially effective. The larger force sets the standard, while the smaller force creates the exception. Just as a single basketball player wearing a blue uniform will stand out if the other four players wear yellow, so a smaller force can dominate a design. Consider these examples:

- *Contrast in scale.* In figure 3.46, the small airplane and the moon become charged with meaning when combined with the image of the sleeping child. Dreams take flight.

- *Contrast in shape.* Zurbarán's *Saint Serapion* (3.47) provides a brilliant example of contrast by shape as well as emphasis by separation. The small note pinned at the right edge of the canvas gains so much power that it easily balances the large figure filling the rest of the frame.

- *Contrast in color.* One of the most compelling uses of emphasis by color occurs in *Schindler's List,* by Steven Spielberg (3.48). Midway through the black-and-white film, a small girl in a red coat is shown walking toward her death. She breaks away from the line and runs back to hide under a bed in a nearby house. This is the only use of color in the main body of the film. When her red coat appears again, her body is being transported to a bonfire. This simple use of color creates one of the most emotional moments in a remarkable film.

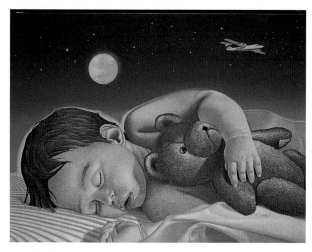

**3.46 Robert Crawford, *Jamie Sleeping*, 1988.** Acrylic on canvas, 20 × 14 in. (50.8 × 35.5 cm).

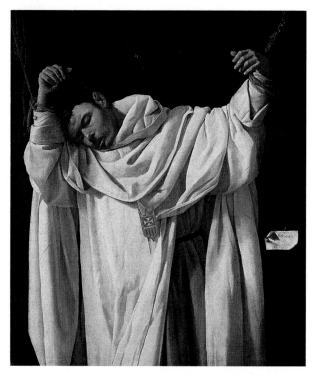

**3.47 Francisco de Zurbarán, *Saint Serapion*, 1628.** Oil on canvas, 47½ × 41 in. (120.7 × 103.5 cm).

## Key Questions

- What would happen to your composition if you dramatically changed its scale or shifted its proportions?
- Is there a dominant shape in your composition? If so, is it the shape you most *want* to emphasize?
- Is there a focal point in your composition? If not, should there be?

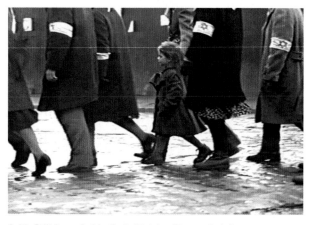

**3.48 Still from *Schindler's List*, by Steven Spielberg.**

# SUMMARY

- Using composition, we can organize multiple parts into a harmonious whole. In a well-composed design, visual elements work together as a team.

- Gestalt psychology describes six unifying strategies: grouping, containment, repetition, proximity, continuity, and closure.

- Effective design requires a dialogue between unity and variety. Too much unity can lead to boredom, while too much variety can lead to chaos.

- Any similarity between visual elements tends to increase unity; any difference between visual elements tends to increase variety.

- Symmetry, radial symmetry, and asymmetry are three common forms of balance. Visual balance creates equilibrium among compositional units, regardless of their size, weight, or shape.

- Scale and proportion are two types of size relationships. Proportion refers to the size relationships within an image, while scale involves a size comparison to our physical reality.

- Emphasis is most commonly created through isolation, placement, or contrast. A focal point can strengthen emphasis.

# KEYWORDS

| | | | |
|---|---|---|---|
| anomaly | continuity | grouping | rhythm |
| approximate symmetry | contrast | imbalance | scale |
| asymmetrical balance | eccentricity | movement | symmetrical balance |
| balance | emphasis | pattern | unity |
| centricity | focal point | proportion | variety |
| closure | fusion | proximity | visual weight |
| composition | Gestalt | radial symmetry | |
| containment | grid | repetition | |

# IN DETAIL

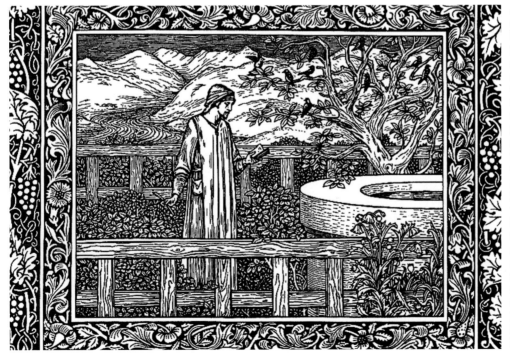

As a leader of the Arts and Crafts movement in England, socialist William Morris combined his love of medieval pattern with a commitment to the individual. He believed that mass production alienated workers from their labor. By contrast, handmade objects were more beautiful and provided the worker with a sense of personal accomplishment. Published in a limited edition by Morris' Kelmscott Press, *The Works of Geoffrey Chaucer Newly Augumented* was printed on hand-made linen paper using hand-set type designed by Morris himself. English painter Edward Burne-Jones completed 87 wood engravings for the book.

# Profile:
## Bob Dacey, Illustrator

*Tell Me a Story: Illustrating Miriam's Cup*

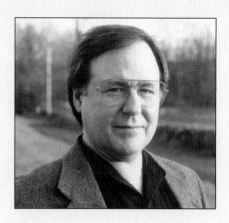

Bob Dacey is an internationally renowned artist whose drawings and paintings have been published as limited- and multiple-edition prints, as well as in a wide range of books and periodicals, including *McCall's,* Ballantine Books, Book-of-the-Month Club, *Playboy,* and Scholastic Publications. His commercial clients include The White House, ABC, CBS, NBC, PBS, Mobil Oil, Sony, the U.S. Post Office, Air Japan, and many others. Dacey received a Silver Medal from the Society of Illustrators in New York for 1 of the 16 paintings he produced for Scholastic Publications illustrating *Miriam's Cup,* which is themed on the Exodus of the Israelites from Egypt. Dacey collected an extensive library of books on Egypt and spent almost a year on research. From costumes to musical instruments, Dacey insisted on getting all the details just right.

**MS:** Give me a bit of background on *Miriam's Cup*. What was the significance of this project, and what aspects of the story did you want to emphasize in the illustrations?

**BD:** *Miriam's Cup* gave me a chance to expand on my single-image work. I've always approached each illustration as a moment in time, as if it had a "before" and an "after." This book gave me a chance to push that much further. I started every painting by focusing on the emotion in the moment being depicted. I always ask myself: "What is the essence of this moment?" The composition follows. Shapes and values serve the emotional content, while movement is used to unify the composition.

**MS:** You have said that 75 percent of your work on this project was devoted to research. Can you describe your research and tell me why it was so important?

**BD:** For *Miriam's Cup,* I had to understand the culture of Egypt and the Jewish culture of the time. Fortunately, I've always had an extensive interest in both. My personal library contains more books on Egypt than the local library system. Research helped open new ideas, leading in some unexpected directions. Those bullrushes are one example. I looked up the word in three dictionaries and two encyclopedias. One of these sources mentioned that the bullrushes of ancient Egypt are papyrus, those beautiful fan-shaped reeds that can be fashioned into a kind of paper. Without that knowledge, the image I arrived at would have been impossible.

**MS:** I understand that you have a seven-step process by which you refine and expand your ideas. Can you describe this process as it applies to the cover image for *Miriam's Cup?*

**BD:** I first consider the intent of each painting: what must this piece communicate? In this painting, I focused on Miriam's exuberance as she celebrates her escape from Egypt. Second, the composition must support my intent. The circular movement of the tambourine and flowers dominates this painting. The movement from the raised hand holding the tambourine, to Miriam's hair, to her face, and on to her cupped hand provides a secondary pattern. And that cupped hand repeats the curve of the flowers. Third, the shapes depend on both the intent and the composition. If I am painting a very stoic character, I use a lot of verticals. Diagonals are used when the character or event is very dynamic. Value is fourth on my checklist. I assign value according to the mood of the painting. Lighter values are used for celebratory images, like this one; darker values dominate when the mood is somber. A mix of light and dark value is best. I base my compositions on the Golden Section [a classic use of proportion], and I often use a 60/40 proportion between light and dark values. Texture, step five, often results from the placement of shape and value—but it really deserves a place of its own, due to its importance as a constructive or destructive factor. When everything else works but the image still suffers, textural discord is usually the culprit! Color comes next. I really have to have the other questions resolved first. Color without composition, value, or intent just doesn't cut it. This painting is dominated by rich pastel colors, which help convey the exuberant emotion.

All of this contributes to the overall image, the final step. If all of the preceding factors serve my intent, the image can emerge naturally and effectively.

**MS:** In addition to the extensive research you did for *Miriam's Cup*, it seems that you have a very wide range of interests in general.

**BD:** Well, everything feeds into my work—and I've always been interested in everything! My undergraduate majors included theater and anthropology before I settled on ad design as the field in which I finally got my degree. Now, my readings range from archaeology to philosophy to psychology to paleontology, and more. I'm also developing my interest in writing and plan to pursue a master's in writing in order to increase my understanding of narrative.

**MS:** One of the questions my students often have is this: how do I get from where I am as a student to where you are as a professional?

**BD:** Focus on your goals and research the field. Talk to professionals you admire. Set high standards for yourself and be realistic about the level of professionalism and quality required.

**MS:** Any final bits of advice?

**BD:** Don't limit yourself. We all have great potential that serves the higher purpose of society. Pursue your goals with the knowledge that you can succeed. And remain flexible and open-minded, so that you can redirect your efforts as opportunities present themselves. Read everything! Draw everything!

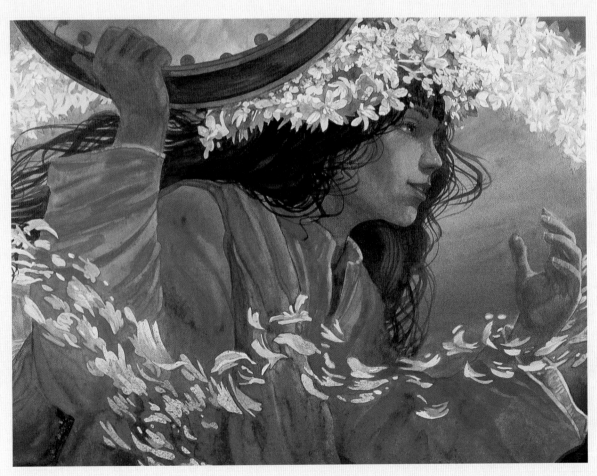

Bob Dacey, Cover of *Miriam's Cup*, by Fran Manushkin, 1988. Scholastic Press.

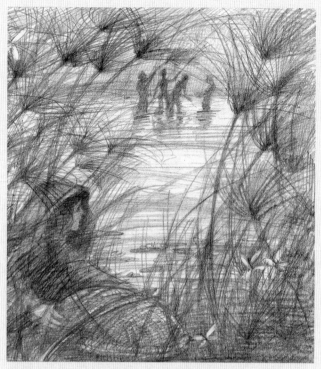

Bob Dacey, *In the Bulrushes* compositional study.

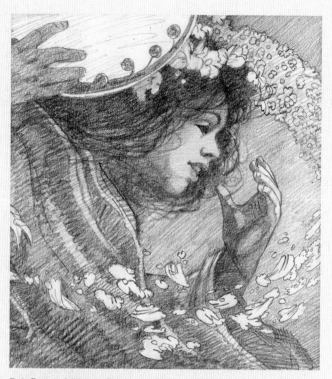

Bob Dacey, *Miriam's Celebration* compositional study.

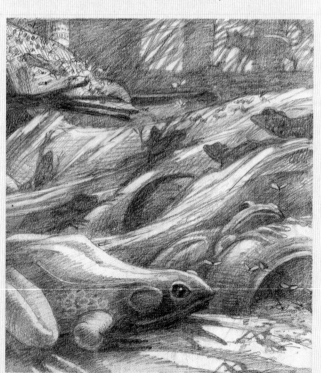

Bob Dacey, *Plague of Frogs* compositional study.

Preliminary drawings Bob Dacey developed for *Miriam's Cup*.

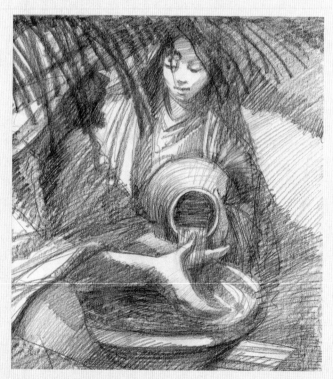

Bob Dacey, *Washing Hands* compositional study.

# Illusion of Space,
# Illusion of Motion

Let's return to an imaginary basketball game for a moment. First, place your-self in the bleachers, high above the court. As a spectator, you can easily observe the overall distribution of players and follow the flow of the game. Now, mentally place yourself in the middle of the game, passing the ball and making shots. As a player, you are physically engaged in a complex and ever changing event. The game swirls with activity as players advance and recede in space.

Just as symmetrical balance is appropriate for some images while asym-metrical balance is appropriate for others, so each type of space offers distinct advantages. The opening page of the medieval *Book of Kells* (4.1) is spatially shallow. Assorted human figures huddle to the right of the dominant vertical shape, while intricate border patterns flatten the space. At the other extreme, the spatial depth in Altdorfer's *Battle of Alexander* (4.2) is so convincing that we almost feel we can enter this battle between Alexander the Great and King Darius of Persia. The flat wooden panel has been transformed through the illusion of space.

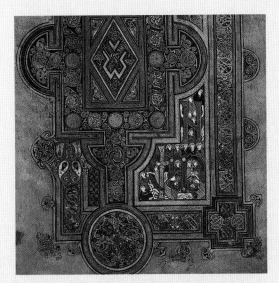

4.1 *Book of Kells:* **Detail from Opening page, St. Luke's Gospel.** Trinity College, Dublin, 9½ × 13 in. (24 × 33 cm).

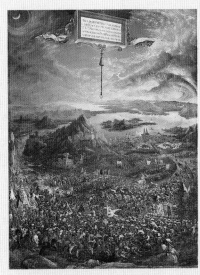

4.2 Albrecht Altdorfer, *Battle of Alexander,* 1529. Limewood, 47¼ × 62¼ in. (120 × 158 cm).

# chapter four

# CREATING THE ILLUSION OF SPACE

## Linear Perspective

**Linear perspective** is a mathematical system for projecting the apparent dimensions of a three-dimensional object onto a flat surface. This surface, called the **picture plane,** is comparable to a window overlooking a city street. By tracing the outlines of the buildings on the pane of glass, you can make a simple perspective drawing.

Developed during the Renaissance, perspective offered a methodical approach to depicting the rational reality perceived by artists in the fifteenth century. It soon gained wide acceptance as a means of systematically diminishing the size of objects as they recede in space. Raphael's *School of Athens* (figure 4.3) is one example. A broad arch in the foreground frames the compositional stage. Three additional arches diminish in size, pulling us into the painting. The diagonal lines in the buildings and floor converge at a point in the center. The viewer is invited to enter into an illusory world.

Even though many recent philosophical and aesthetic theories challenge this conception of reality, perspective remains the most pervasive Western system for suggesting three-dimensionality on the two-dimensional surface. Linear perspective is based on five basic concepts, shown in figures 4.4 and 4.5:

1. Objects appear to diminish in size as they recede into the distance. Perspective is possible because the rate at which objects appear to diminish is regular and consistent.

2. The point at which objects disappear entirely is called a **vanishing point.** Sets of parallel lines (such as train tracks) converge at a vanishing point as they go into the distance, creating deep space.

3. In basic one- and two-point perspective, all vanishing points are positioned on the **eye level,** or **horizon line,** which is level with the artist's eyes.

4. Because all proportional relationships shift with each change in position, a fixed viewing position is an essential characteristic of linear perspective.

5. Only a limited area is clearly visible from a fixed position. To accommodate a larger viewing area, you must move farther away from the object to be drawn. This expands the **cone of vision** and increases the area being viewed.

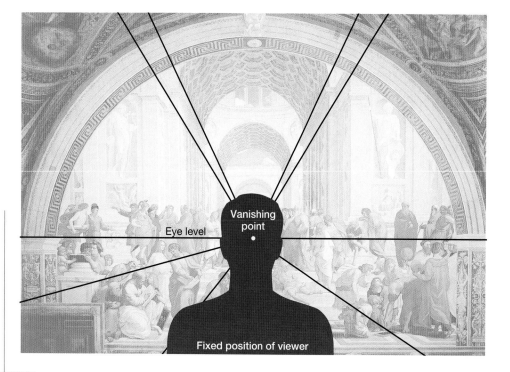

**4.3** Perspective used in Raphael's *School of Athens*.

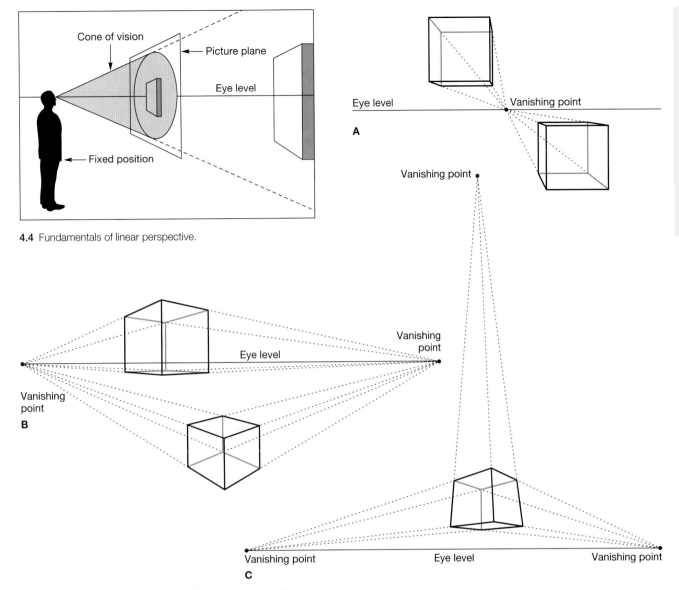

**4.4** Fundamentals of linear perspective.

**4.5A–C** Examples of one-, two-, and three-point perspective.

**One-point perspective** occurs when the lines receding into space appear to converge at a single point on the eye level. This occurs when the viewer is confronted with the flat front of the cube, and results in a drawing in which vertical lines and horizontal lines run parallel to the edges of your sheet of paper (4.5A). One-point perspective is relatively simple and can be very dramatic. However, as we move to the far right or left of the cube being drawn, many of the horizontal lines appear to shift, becoming more diagonal. They are no longer parallel to the top and bottom edges of your rectangular sheet. At this point, a second vanishing point is needed.

**Two-point perspective** is used when the lines receding into space appear to converge at two vanishing points on the eye level. This occurs when the viewer is confronted with the vertical edge of the cube, rather than the flat front (4.5B). Now, only the vertical lines remain parallel to each other and the edge of the paper. All other lines recede back to the two vanishing points on the eye level.

**Three-point perspective** is used when the lines receding into space appear to converge at two vanishing points on the eye level, plus a third point placed above or below the eye level. This occurs when the artist is positioned far above or below the cube, creating a "bird's eye" or "worm's eye" view (4.5C). Now, all the lines converge at the various vanishing points: none of the sets of lines parallel the edge of the paper.

## Using Perspective

There are distinct advantages to each of these basic types of perspective. One-point perspective is simple and straightforward. As demonstrated by figure 4.6, this type of perspective pulls the viewer into the image using a single, dramatic focal point. Two-point perspective is often used for diagrams and architectural drawings, such as Frank Lloyd Wright's *Fallingwater* (4.7). Three-point perspective creates an exaggerated sense of space and a unique viewpoint. We feel that we are being actively pulled upward or downward by the illusion of space it creates. As shown by Charles Sheeler's *Delmonico Building* (4.8), this type of perspective is often used when an artist or designer wants to communicate the power and energy of the technological or architectural setting.

## Other Ways to Create the Illusion of Space

- *Overlap.* Overlap is the simplest way to suggest space, and it can be especially effective when combined with size variation. In *Deposition* (4.9), Rogier van der Weyden used overlap combined with value to create a convincing drama within a crowded compositional space.

- *Size variation.* Because the diminishing size of distant objects is a basic characteristic of human vision, any systematic variation in size can enhance the illusion of space. This effect is demonstrated most clearly when the distance is great. In Ansel Adams' *Monolith, The Face of Half Dome* (see page 17), the imposing cliff in the foreground rapidly diminishes in size as it moves back in space.

- *Definition.* Sharply focused shapes also tend to advance, while blurred shapes tend to recede. When we look at a landscape, dust and water droplets in the air blur outlines and add a blue-gray color to distant shapes. This effect is known as **atmospheric perspective.** In *The Rocky Mountains, Lander's Peak* (4.10), Albert Bierstadt combined dramatic lighting with atmospheric perspective to increase the illusion of space.

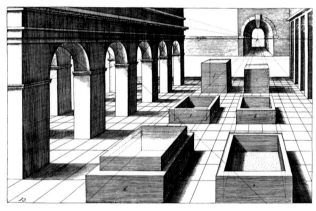

4.6 Jan Vredeman de Vries, *Perspective Study,* from *Perspective,* Leiden, 1604.

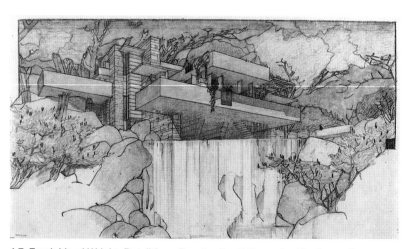

4.7 Frank Lloyd Wright, Detail from Drawing for *Fallingwater,* Kaufmann House, Bear Run, Pennsylvania, 1936. 15⅜ × 27¼ in. (39 × 69 cm).

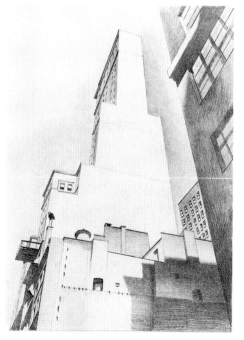

4.8 Charles Sheeler, *Delmonico Building,* 1926. Lithograph, 9¾ × 6⅞ in. (24.7 × 17.4 cm).

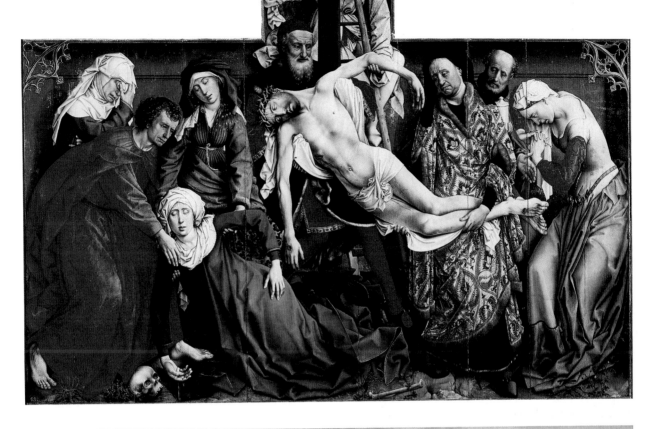

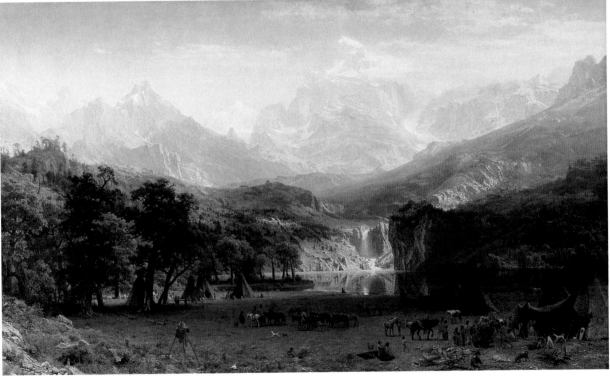

4.10 Albert Bierstadt, *The Rocky Mountains, Lander's Peak,* 1863. Oil on canvas, 6 ft 1¼ in. × 10 ft ¾ in. (186.7 × 306.7 cm).

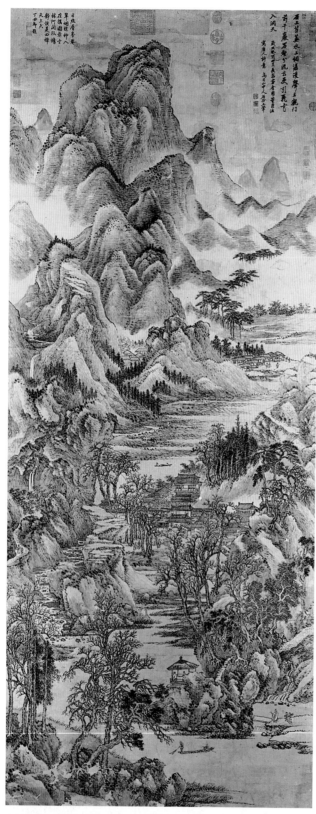

**4.11 Wang Hui, *A Thousand Peaks and Myriad Ravines*, Qing dynasty, 1693.** Hanging scroll, ink on paper, 8 ft 2½ in. × 3 ft 4½ in. (2.54 × 1.03 m).

- *Location.* Visual elements placed near the top of the page tend to recede, while shapes placed at the bottom tend to advance. In *A Thousand Peaks and Myriad Ravines* (4.11), the mountains at the top of the scroll appear more distant, despite their large size.

- *Color.* Under most circumstances, high-intensity colors tend to advance. Contrast in hue, value, or temperature can enhance the illusion of space.

## Using the Illusion of Space

Through the illusion of space, artists invite viewers to enter an imaginary world. Expression can be heightened when the world so created is particularly intriguing or when the spatial illusion is especially dramatic.

**Amplified perspective** can be defined as the exaggerated use of linear perspective to achieve a dramatic and engaging presentation of the subject. Amplified perspective is often created using an unusual viewing position, such as a bird's eye view, accelerated convergence, or through distortion.

In Dalí's *Christ of St. John of the Cross* (4.12), amplified perspective changes our interpretation of the crucifixion of Jesus. Dramatic three-point perspective emphasizes the importance of the note pinned at the top of the cross. As we look down, the vulnerability of Jesus emphasizes his humanity, while the hovering position of the figure suggests his divinity.

**Fractured space** can be created when multiple viewpoints are combined in a single image. In his portrait of sculptor Henry Moore (4.13), David Hockney used multiple photographs to manipulate space and suggest the passage of time. The repeated hands gesture to us as we visually converse with the old master.

**Layered space** can be created when the foreground, middle ground, and background are clearly defined. Layered space is used extensively in the film *Citizen Kane*. In figure 4.14, young Charlie Kane plays in the background, while his mother in the foreground signs over his care to a lawyer. His father, who is opposed to this action, occupies

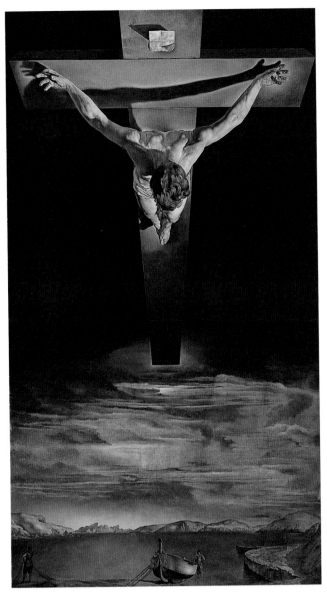

**4.12 Salvador Dalí, *Christ of St. John of the Cross*, 1951.** Oil on canvas, 80⅜ × 45⅞ in. (204.8 × 115.9 cm).

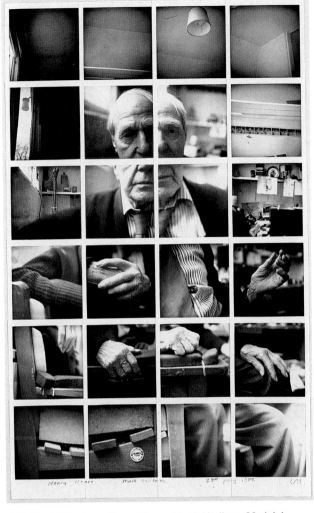

**4.13 David Hockney, *Henry Moore Much Hadham 23rd July 1982*, 1982.** Composite Polaroid, 21 × 14 in. (53 × 36 cm).

the middle ground, caught between the mother and the child. The tensions in the family, the determination of the mother, and the innocence of the child are heightened when Charlie shouts, "The Union forever!" as part of his game. When the lawyer takes charge of Charlie, the family will be split apart forever. These three compositional layers communicate complex emotions while telling a story.

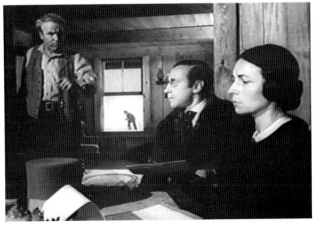

**4.14 Scene from *Citizen Kane.*** Three layers of space divide this shot from *Citizen Kane:* the mother in the foreground, the father in the middleground, and the child in the background.

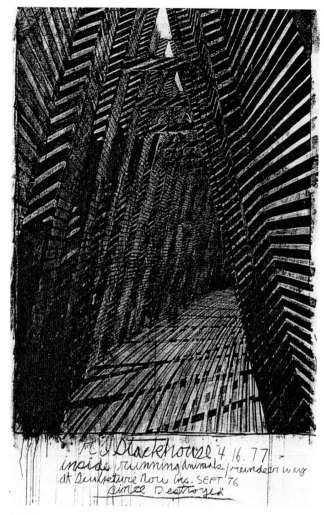

4.15 Robert Stackhouse, *Inside Running Animals/Reindeer Way,*
**1977.** Mixed mediums, 64 × 43¾ × 2 in.

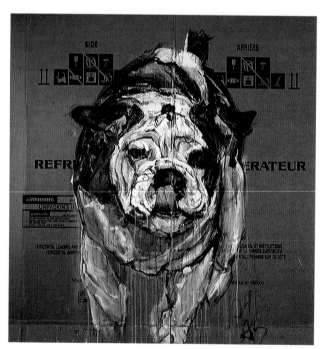

4.16 Ann Strassman, *Humphrey I,* **2004.** Acrylic on cardboard,
70 × 65 in. (177.8 × 165.1 cm).

Three examples of **dynamic space** are shown on this page. In *Inside Running Animals/Reindeer Way,* Robert Stackhouse combined diagonal lines with definition and size variation to pull us into a mysterious tunnel (4.15). Ann Strassman's *Humphrey I* (4.16) comes charging out of the picture plane, ready to lick us or attack us. Cropping (the cutting away of part of the image) combined with vigorous brushstrokes helps push the dog forward. In Mark Messersmith's *Edge of Town* (4.17), a logging truck rushing into the background pulls the viewer into the painting while the dead animals atop the hunter's car are thrust forward. However, the tree in the foreground traps this apocalyptic action, forcing the space to swirl around a central compositional pole. As we look down into the flaming car and upward toward the white birds, we become even more disoriented. The space seems to bulge, twist, and rotate in the madness and mystery of the night. For a full-page example of figure 4.17, go to page 172.

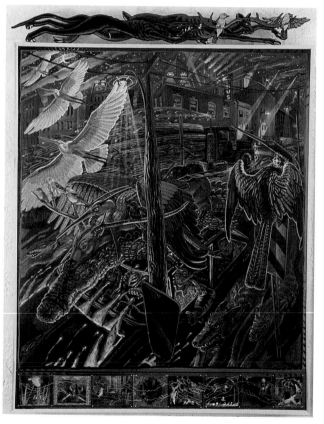

4.17 Mark Messersmith, *Edge of Town,* **2005.** Oil on canvas and mixed media.

# ANIMATED SPACE: CONSTRUCTING *MULAN*

Animators use the illusion of space with great inventiveness. Freed from the restrictions of reality, they can invent and explore space with abandon. Indeed, every type of space discussed in this chapter was used beautifully in Walt Disney's *Mulan*. From the opening shots to the grand finale, the illusion of space is of critical importance to the visual and conceptual power of the film.

- *Overlap.* After a brief battle with Shan-Yu and his men, a Chinese soldier lights a signal fire to warn of the invasion. With Shan-Yu filling the foreground, we see six towers, with signal fires gradually blazing forth from each (4.18A). Here, overlap and size variation enhance the illusion of space.

- *Linear perspective.* Linear perspective is used in the next sequence, when General Li enters the imperial palace to inform the emperor of the invasion. One-point perspective is used to create the large, majestic hall (4.18B). Because our eye-level is that of a child, the hall seems even more intimidating and imposing.

- As the general approaches the throne, the angle of vision shifts to an aerial view. Three-point perspective is now used to emphasize the insignificance of the figures within this great hall (4.18C). We look down on the standing emperor and the prostrate soldiers.

- *Atmospheric perspective.* Atmospheric perspective is often used as the troops travel through the mountains. After learning of the death of his father in battle, Captain Shang walks to the edge of a cliff. Like the massive mountains in the background, his seemingly invincible father has dissolved in the mist. A small figure within a large landscape, Captain Shang remains sharply focused, dignified, and powerful, even as he grieves (4.18D).

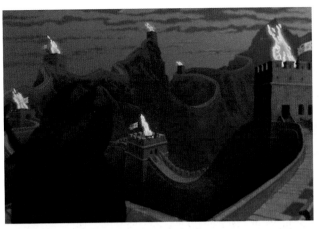

4.18A

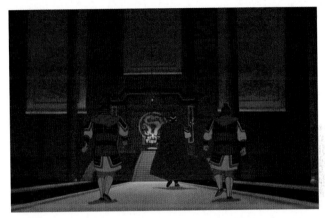

4.18B

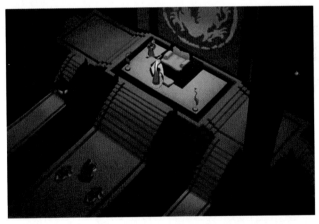

4.18C

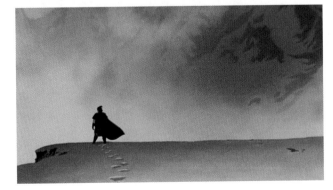

4.18D

**Camera angles** help orient the viewer and can determine the amount and type of space in each shot. An aerial view can provide the sweeping panorama needed to convey the enormity of a battle, while a low camera angle can provide an expansive view of the sky. The major battle scene in *Mulan* beautifully demonstrates the critical role camera angle can play in a film. The enormity of the enemy army is shown in figure 4.18E. A low camera angle positions the Mongols along a ridge, above the small company of Chinese soldiers.

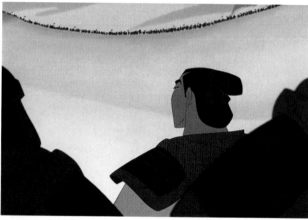

4.18E

As the Mongols pour over the ridge and gallop toward Mulan, the camera angle shifts to a slanted, oblique view (4.18F).

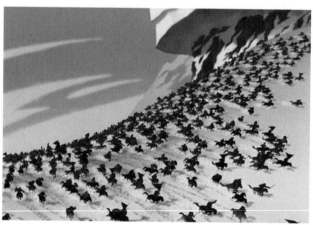

4.18F

A complete aerial view is used in the next shot (4.18G). The riders now pour across the screen.

The shifting perspectives give us a more comprehensive view of the extent of the battle and emphasize the hopelessness of the emperor's warriors, who are confronted with an apparently invincible enemy. When Mulan grabs the one remaining cannon and races forward to create an avalanche, an aerial view is again used to show her vulnerability against the advancing enemy. Throughout the battle, shifts in camera angle provide the emotional and compositional power needed to create a dramatic battle sequence using the fewest number of shots.

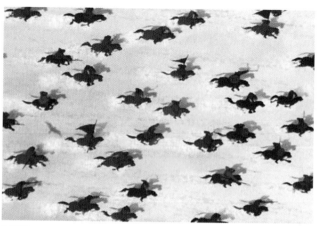

4.18G

## Key Questions

- How can spatial depth be increased or decreased in your composition?
- How can spatial depth increase meaning in your work?
- What happens when flat and spatially deep areas are combined?

# THE ILLUSION OF MOVEMENT

*Mulan* is constructed from thousands of tiny frames. When run through a film projector, they create the fluid movement that is a hallmark of Disney animation. Animation is possible because we have the perceptual ability to integrate the sequential images into a continuous flow.

Substantial audience involvement is also required to create the illusion of movement within a drawing or sculpture. When presented with multiple images on a single surface, we must feel the movement, complete the action, or anticipate the next event. Based on our day-to-day experience in an ever changing world, we use our imagination to connect static images to create the illusion of movement.

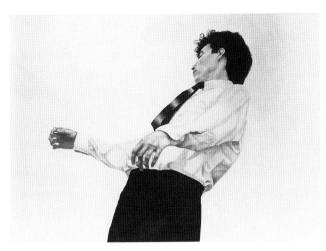

4.19 Robert Longo, *Untitled*, 1980. From the *Men in Cities* series. Crayon and graphite on paper, 40½ × 28 in. (102.9 × 71.1 cm).

## The Kinesthetic Response

**Kinesthetics** is the science of movement. Through the very process of walking, we consistently engage in a complex balancing act as we fall forward, then catch ourselves with the next step. When confronted by a life-sized figure, such as the man from Robert Longo's *Men in Cities* series (4.19), the lunging movement of the model resonates on a physical level. Based on our personal experience, we feel as well as see the gesture. Capturing the gesture at the right moment is critical. In Myron's *Discus Thrower* (4.20), the athlete is caught at the moment *before* the whirling vortex of energy explodes, releasing the disc. By capturing this moment rather than the moment of release, the sculptor has trapped within the marble the implied energy of the throw.

## The Decisive Moment

Photographer Henri Cartier-Bresson used his understanding of impending change to formulate a theory of photography he called "the decisive moment." A pioneer in the use of the 35-mm camera, he specialized in capturing the most telling moment in time. The space, emotions, and events he recorded in *Valencia* (4.21) are both fascinating and disturbing. Sharply focused and framed by the window, the policeman's fierce face dominates the foreground. Squeezed between the target shapes and the wall on the left, a boy turns toward us apprehensively. A dissected target shape is

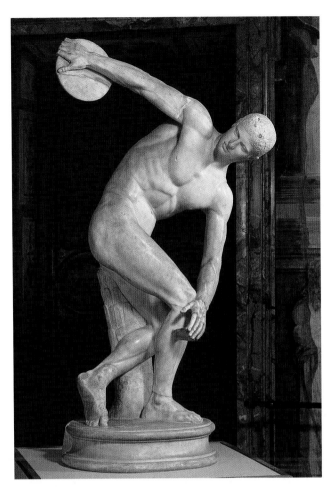

4.20 Myron, *Discus Thrower (Diskobolos)*. Roman copy after the original bronze of c. 450 B.C. Marble, height 5 ft 1 in. (1.54 m).

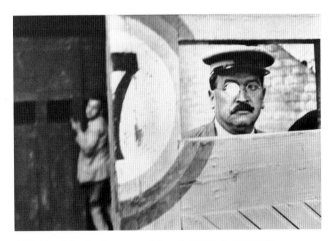

4.21 Henri Cartier-Bresson, *Valencia*, 1933. Photograph, 7¹¹⁄₁₆ × 11½ in. (19.6 × 29.2 cm).

balanced by the man's monocle on the right and the boy's face on the left. Horizontal rectangles compress three of the four corners of the composition. The resulting interplay of shapes creates a complex dialogue between childhood fears and adult authority.

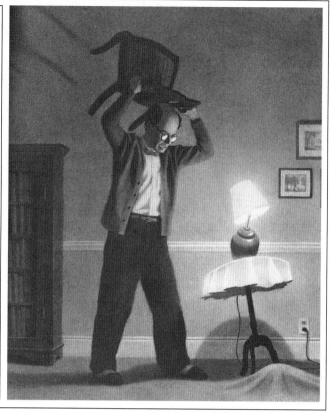

UNDER THE RUG

*Two weeks passed and it happened again.*

4.22 Chris Van Allsburg, "Under the Rug" from *The Mysteries of Harris Burdick*, Houghton-Mifflin, 1984.

## Before and After

The kinesthetic response and the perception of a decisive moment are both based on our past experience and our ability to relate this experience to the images we see. Based on our physical experience, we can feel the awkward and unbalanced position of the Longo figure. Likewise, through our emotional experience, when we look at the Cartier-Bresson photograph, we realize that we are seeing a single moment in a more extensive story.

To create a story through a single image, many illustrators deliberately plan the moment that takes place *before* and the moment that takes place *after* an actual event. An example of this is illustrated in Chris Van Allsburg's book entitled *The Mysteries of Harris Burdick* (4.22). Each drawing in the book is accompanied by a title and a short piece of text. Based on the clues in the title, text, and image, we can invent all sorts of stories.

## Fragmentation

As an object moves, it sequentially occupies various positions in space. Visual fragmentation can be used

to simulate this effect in art. For example, the superimposed figures in Thomas Eakins' *Double Jump* (4.23) record the multiple positions the man occupies during an athletic event. Even when figures are simply repeated, as in Edgar Degas' *Frieze of Dancers* (4.24), movement is strongly suggested.

What attracted these two painters to explore the illusion of motion? Thomas Eakins was one of the first artists in America to use photography as a tool in the art-making process. His *Double Jump* was taken in the early days of photography when artists became fascinated by the study of movement and the new notion that they could capture an action through photography. Eakins was especially interested in human anatomy and used photography to explore kinesthetics. Even though it is a still image, the viewer clearly understands that figure 4.23 shows one body captured at different stages in an action.

Although Edgar Degas was primarily a painter, he also became a talented photographer later in his career. He had always been fascinated by both human and animal locomotion, and photography expanded his ability to observe and record the

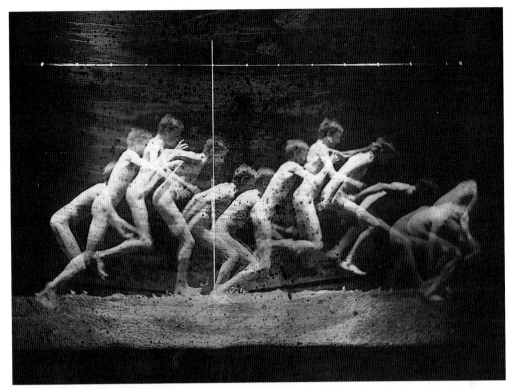

4.23 Thomas Eakins, *Double Jump*, 1885. Modern print from a dry-plate negative, 10.2 × 12.7 cm.

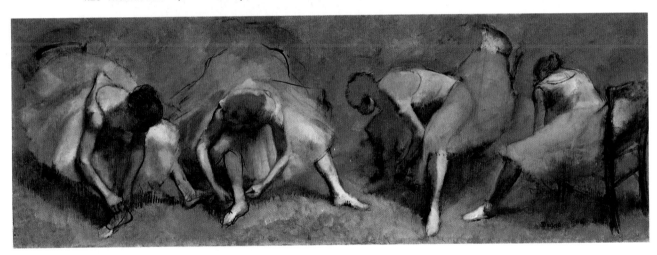

4.24 Edgar Degas, *Frieze of Dancers*, c. 1895. Oil on canvas, 70 × 200.5 cm.

nuances of movement. Many of his paintings reflect his interest in ballet dancers as well as his interest in the nature of movement. *Frieze of Dancers* is a painting of four different dancers, yet it can also be perceived as a study of a single dancer in multiple poses.

For Eakins, Degas, Longo, and Van Allsburg, the illusion of motion expanded both the conceptual and emotional possibilities in an image. Always searching for more effective means of visual exression, any artist or designer can gain from appropriate use of this powerful tool.

## Key Questions

- Will the illusion of motion enhance the idea you want to express? If so, how can you create this illusion?
- To what extent is the illusion of motion affected by the illusion of space?
- What happens when static (unmoving) and dynamic (moving) shapes are used together in a design?

# Multiplication

Multiplication can also play a role in visual storytelling. In this page from *Inhumans* (4.25), by Paul Jenkins and Jae Lee, a dialogue between an alien child and a human politician unfolds over five panels. Notice how "time" moves faster in the smaller four panels, and how a close-up is used when the child delivers his ultimatum. Multiplication creates a very different effect in George Tooker's *Government Bureau* (4.26). Repeated images of the central male figure combined with endless bureaucratic faces creates a scene from a nightmare. No matter where the man goes in this hall of mirrors, he always returns to the beginning.

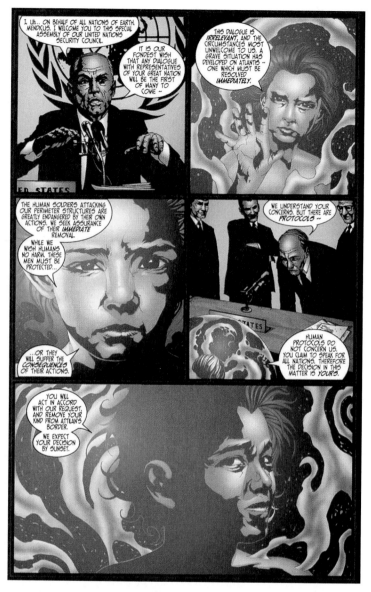

4.25 Paul Jenkins and Jae Lee, from *Inhumans:* "First Contact." Volume 2, Issue 5, March 1999. Comic book.

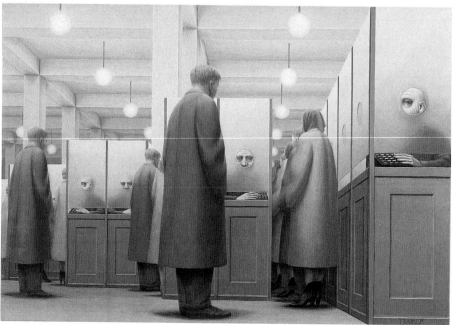

4.26 George Tooker, *Government Bureau,* 1956. Egg tempera on gesso panel, 19⅝ × 29⅝ in. (50 x 75 cm).

# SUMMARY

- The illusion of space can be created through linear perspective, overlap, size variation, location, definition, atmospheric perspective, and use of color.

- Linear perspective is based on five fundamental concepts, listed on page 96.

- Three common types of linear perspective are one-point, two-point, and three-point.

- Overlap, size variation, definition, location and color can also create the illusion of space.

- The illusion of motion is often created by selecting the most decisive moment in an event, through fragmentation, or through various types of multiplication.

# KEYWORDS

| | | | |
|---|---|---|---|
| amplified perspective | dynamic space | layered space | picture plane |
| atmospheric perspective | eye level (horizon line) | linear perspective | three-point perspective |
| camera angle | fractured space | movement | two-point perspective |
| cone of vision | kinesthetics | one-point perspective | vanishing point |

# IN DETAIL

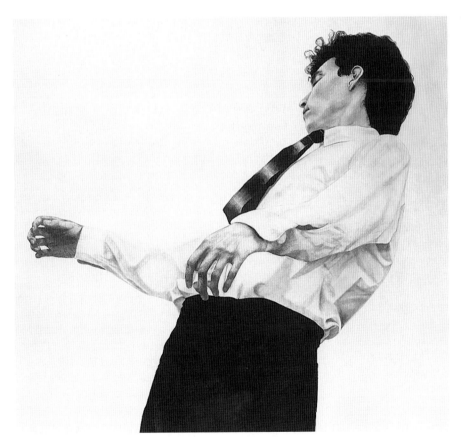

To create his "Men in Cities" series, Robert Longo positioned his models on the roof of his studio building, then threw small objects at them. As they flinched, he snapped a photograph. Dressed in formal attire (such as expensive dresses and tuxedos), this reflexive action created a disturbing contrast. We don't expect to see well-dressed people recoiling or stumbling. Longo then drew the life-sized images in rich, soft graphite, adding further energy to the images.

# Profile:
## Ken Stout, Painter
Immediacy and Energy in Large Scale

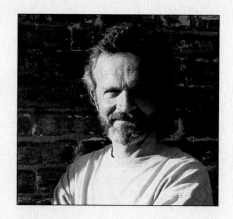

Ken Stout is an internationally renowned figurative painter. He has shown his work widely, including group shows at the Nelson-Atkins Museum of Art in Kansas City and the Butler Museum of American Art, as well as solo shows at the Goldstrom Gallery in New York City and the Cité Internationale des Arts in Paris. *Intermission* was commissioned by the Walton Arts Center in Fayetteville, Arkansas, funded by Saatchi and Saatchi in 1992 and permanently installed in 1994.

**MS:** How did *Intermission* begin?

**KS:** I began work on the mural in 1989. During visits to Paris and Madrid, I was bowled over by a Toulouse-Latrec mural I saw at the Orsay Museum and by a mural by Delacroix at St. Sulpice. Both were vibrant with energy, and the strident reds and greens in the Delacroix sent the viewer's eyes hurtling around and through the composition. I was interested in the mural project because it gave me an opportunity to combine the immediacy of drawing with the richness of painting.

**MS:** Why show the intermission, not the play?

**KS:** It is a moment in time that is highly charged. The mural depicts a cross section of the theater, from backstage to stage and from audience to lobby. The performer on stage is like a toggle switch, connecting the audience to the action backstage. As he bows through the closing curtain, the audience begins to break apart, dissolving into its own private plays. Applause fills the theater, children begin to awaken, and neighbors discuss the performance. I wanted to pull the viewer into a scene bursting with energy, as if all things were in orbit, pushing and pulling, as in dance. The whole painting is a gesture, an embodiment of bodies in motion, with both the volumes and voids ignited with energy.

**MS:** I know that you love art history and that your preliminary research on this project was extensive. What did you learn from the masters?

**KS:** Mostly, I learned ways to increase compositional complexity without sacrificing gestural energy.

These compositional lessons helped me sustain a vigorous visual pace for all 50 feet of the painting.

Technically, though, my work method was more exploratory and direct than is the usual practice.

First, the 300 preliminary drawings and paintings I did stand as autonomous images in themselves. I learned from all of them—but didn't copy any of them when I painted the mural. I confronted the painting directly, rather than replicating ideas I had worked out beforehand.

Second, I didn't graph out, slide project, or otherwise draw the outlines on the canvas. I just drew blue lines to divide the canvas into halves, quarters, and eighths, then drew freehand, using a brush attached to a 3-foot-long bamboo pole, starting with light washes in earth colors.

Finally, every figure was painted from life, using over 50 community members as models. They were amazingly generous and patient, considering it wasn't putting a penny in their pockets. This process increased the connection between the audience and the artwork, and we had a great party for everyone when the painting was installed. I continue to meet these townspeople on the street, and, as participants in the project, they have a continuing relationship with the painting.

**MS:** So it sounds like you didn't really know what would happen when you began to paint each day.

**KS:** Each model, each pose, and each prop provided variations and surprises. I actually used at least two models for each figure in the painting, which basically means that there is another 50-foot-long painting underneath the one that you see!

**MS:** What advice do you have for my students?

**KS:** Take risks. Without daring—indeed, without great daring—there is no beauty. We must go beyond ourselves if we are ever to fulfill our real potential.

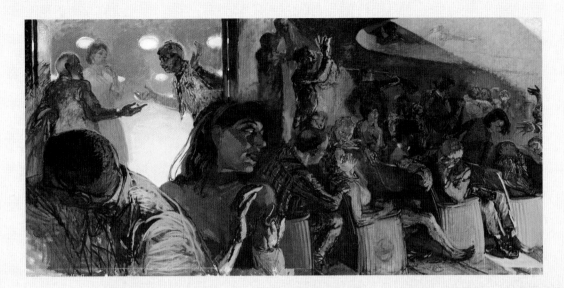

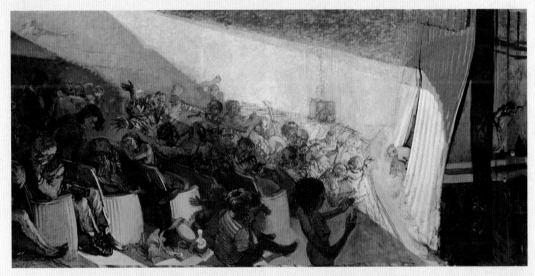

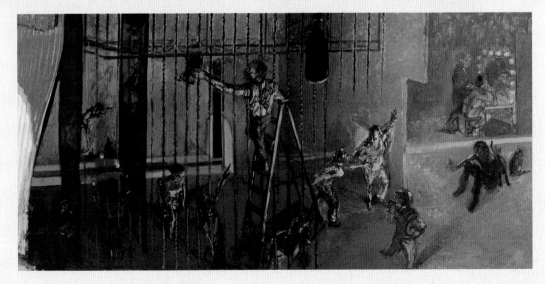

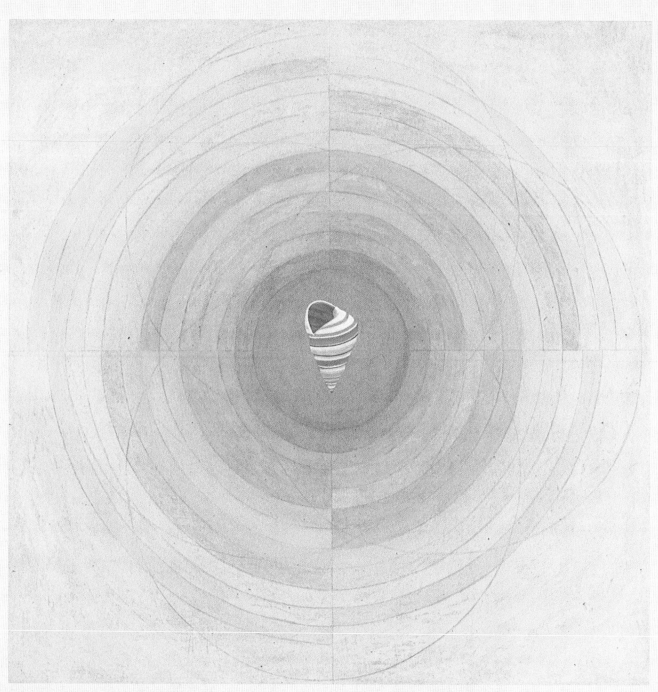

**Georgiana Nehl,** *Sun/Star* **(Detail), 1996.** Oil paint on gessoed wood, 25¾ × 13¼ × 1 in. (65 × 34 × 3 cm).

# Concepts and Critical Thinking

In *A Kick in the Seat of the Pants,* Roger Von Oech identifies four distinct roles in the creative process.

First, the *explorer* learns as much as possible about the problem. Research is crucial. Ignorance may result in a superficial concept or in a compositional cliché.

Second, the *artist* experiments with a wide variety of solutions, using all sorts of combinations, proportions, and materials. By creating 10 answers to each question, the artist can select the best solution rather than accepting the only solution.

Third, the *judge* assesses the work in progress and determines what revisions are required. Innovative ideas are never fully developed when first presented; most need extensive revision and expansion. Rather than discard an underdeveloped idea, the judge identifies its potential and determines ways to increase its strength.

Finally, the *warrior* implements the idea. When the project is large and complex, implementation can be a challenge. When obstacles appear, the warrior assesses the situation, determines the best course of action, and then completes the project.

We will explore each of these roles in the next four chapters. Strategies for cultivating creativity and improving time management are discussed in Chapter Five. Chapter Six deals with concept development and visual problem solving. Chapter Seven is devoted to critical thinking and provides specific ways to improve any design. In Chapter Eight, we expand our discussion of visual communication and consider ways to make more meaningful designs.

A
IS FOR APOLLO, WHOSE ARROWS NEVER MISS

U
IS FOR URANIA THE MUSE OF CELESTIAL FORCES IS SHE

# Cultivating Creativity

# chapter five

"The heart of all new ideas lies in the borrowing, adding, combining or modifying of old ones. Do it by accident and people call you lucky. Do it by design and they'll call you creative."

Michael LeBoeuf, in *Imagineering*

Once viewed as peripheral, creativity and innovation have become highly valued in contemporary life. In the Information Age, intellectual property can be the most important asset in a business. New technologies have expanded the range of approaches available, and ideas drawn from literature, philosophy, science, and history inspire contemporary artists and designers. The sky is the limit. An effective artist or designer cannot simply follow instructions. Cultivating creative thinking is as fundamental as mastering any technical skill.

## SEVEN CHARACTERISTICS OF CREATIVE THINKING

"Conditions for creativity are to be puzzled, to concentrate, to accept conflict and tension, to be born every day, to feel a sense of self."

Erich Fromm, in *Creativity and Its Cultivation*

Creativity is inherently unpredictable. Through creative thinking, old habits are broken and familiar patterns of thought are transformed. Anything can happen. Predicting the future based on past experience becomes inadequate when a creative breakthrough occurs. Like a shimmering drop of mercury, creativity eludes capture.

We can actively encourage creative thinking, however. Rather than waiting for inspiration, we can set up the conditions favorable to creativity. Based on observation and on interviews, various researchers have noted the following characteristics in many creative people.

### Receptivity

Creative people are open to new ideas and welcome new experiences. Never complacent, they question the status quo and embrace alternative solutions to existing problems. Listening more and talking less is helpful. As journalist Larry King says, "I never learn anything new when I'm the one talking!"

## Curiosity

A good designer brings an insatiable curiosity to each project. Researching unfamiliar topics and analyzing unusual systems is a source of delight for most creative people. "How does it work?" and "How can it work better?" are frequently asked questions.

## Wide Range of Interests

With a broad knowledge base, a creative person can make a wider range of connections. Consider the number of words you can create from the letters in the word *image:*

**age, game, gem, am, aim, a, I, me**

Try the same game with the word *imagination:*

**gin, nation, gnat, ton, tan, not, man, again, gain, oat, got, tag, am, aim, ant, no, on, tin, gamin, inn, ingot, main, a, I**

With more components, the number of combinations increases. Likewise, an artist who has a background in literature, geology, archery, music, and history can make more connections than a narrow-minded specialist.

## Attentiveness

Realizing that every experience is valuable, creative people pay attention to seemingly minor details. Scientists often develop major theories by observing small events, which they then organize into complex patterns. Artists can often see past superficial visual chaos to discern an underlying order. Playwrights develop dramatic works by looking past the surface of human behavior to explore the substance of the human condition. By looking carefully, creative people see possibilities that others miss.

## Connection Seeking

Seeing the similarity among seemingly disparate parts has often sparked a creative breakthrough. For example, Egyptian hieroglyphs became readable when a young French scholar realized that they carried the same message as an adjacent Greek inscription on a slab of stone. By comparing the two and cracking the Rosetta Stone code, Jean-François Champollion opened the door for all subsequent students of ancient Egyptian culture.

## Conviction

Creative people value existing knowledge. Since new ideas are often derived from old ideas, it is foolish to ignore or dismiss the past. However, creative people also love change. Never satisfied with routine answers to familiar questions, they constantly consider new possibilities and often challenge the status quo.

## Complexity

In lecture classes, we must take notes, memorize facts, and collect and analyze data. We are encouraged to think rationally, write clearly, and present our ideas in a linear progression. In studio classes, exploration, experimentation, and intuition are encouraged, especially during brainstorming sessions. Synthesis, intuition, visualization, spatial perception, and nonlinear thinking are highly valued.

To be fully effective, a creative person needs to combine the rational with the intuitive. While intuition may be used to generate a new idea, logic and analysis are often needed for its realization. As a result, the actions of creative people are often complex or even contradictory. As noted by psychologist Mihaly Csikszentmihalyi,[1] creative people often combine

- Physical energy with a respect for rest. They work long hours with great concentration, then rest and relax, fully recharging their batteries. They view balance between work and play as essential.

- Savvy with innocence. Creative people tend to view the world and themselves with a sense of wonder, rather than cling to preconceptions or stereotypes. They use common sense as well as intellect in completing their work.

- Responsibility with playfulness. When the situation requires serious attention, creative people are remarkably diligent and determined. They realize that there is no substitute for hard work and drive themselves relentlessly when nearing completion of a major project. On the other hand, when the situation permits, a playful, devil-may-care attitude may prevail, providing a release from the previous period of work.

- Risk-taking with safe-keeping. Creativity expert George Prince has noted two behavioral extremes in people.[2] Safe-keepers look before they leap, avoid surprises, punish mistakes, follow the rules, and watch the clock. A safe-keeper is most comfortable when there is only one right answer to memorize or one solution to produce. Risk-takers are just the opposite. They break the rules, leap before they look, like surprises, are impetuous, and may lose track of time. A risk-taker enjoys inventing multiple answers to every question.

  An imbalance in either direction limits creativity. Fear inhibits the safe-keeper, while irresponsibility inhibits the extreme risk-taker. Creative thinking requires a mix of risk-taking and safe-keeping. When brainstorming new ideas, open-ended exploration is used. But, when implementing new ideas, deadlines, budgets, and feasibility become major concerns. The risk-taker gets the job started; the safe-keeper gets the job done.

- Extroversion with introversion. When starting a new project, creative people are often talkative and gregarious, eager to share insights and explore ideas. When a clear sense of direction develops, however, they often withdraw, seeking solitude and quiet work time. This capacity for solitude is crucial. Several studies have shown that talented teenagers who cannot stand solitude rarely develop their creative skills.

- Passion with objectivity. Mature artists tend to plunge into new projects, convinced of the significance of the work and confident of their skills. Any attempt to distract or dissuade them at this point is futile. However, when the model or rough study is done, many will pause to assess their progress. This period of analysis and judgment may occur in a group setting or may be done by the artist alone. In either case, the emotional attachment required while creating is now replaced by a dispassionate objectivity. Work that does not pass this review is redone or discarded, regardless of the hours spent in its development. In major projects, this alternating process of creation and analysis may be repeated many times.

- Disregard for time with attention to deadlines. Time often dissolves when studio work begins.

An artist or a designer can become engrossed in a project: when the work is going well, 6 hours can feel like 20 minutes. On the other hand, an acute attention to deadlines is necessary when preparing an exhibition or working for a client.

- Modesty with pride. As they mature, creative people often become increasingly aware of the contributions to their success made by teachers, family, and colleagues. Rather than brag about past accomplishments, they tend to focus on current projects. On the other hand, as creative people become aware of their significance within a field, they gain a powerful sense of purpose. Distractions are deleted from the schedule, and increasingly ambitious goals are set. When the balance is right, all of these complex characteristics fuel even greater achievement.

# GOAL SETTING

As humans, our behavior is strongly goal-directed. Every action occurs for a reason. When we focus our attention on a specific task, we can channel our energy and better manage our time. When we reach our goals, our self-esteem increases, which then helps us overcome obstacles. And, with each goal met, our knowledge increases. Michael LeBoeuf has diagrammed this effect clearly (5.1).

## A Goal-Setting Strategy

Self-knowledge is essential. To be effective, goals must be authentic. No matter how hard we try, we can never really fulfill our potential when pursuing goals set by others. Identifying our true interests, strengths, and objectives can be liberating. The following exercise can help clarify personal interests.

1.  Get a package of small Post-it notes. Working spontaneously, write one of your characteristics on each note, such as "I am creative," "I love music," "I write well." Identify as many attributes as possible.

2.  When you finish, lay out the notes on a table and look at them for a while. Consider the type of person they describe. What are this person's

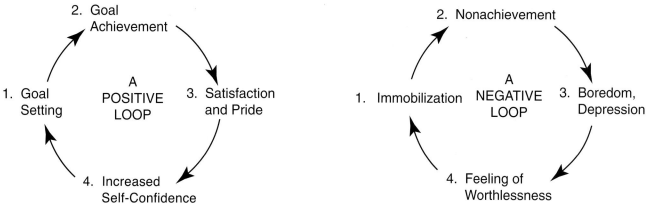

**5.1 Michael LeBoeuf,** *Imagineering,* **1980.** Achievement feeds self-confidence while nonachievement induces inertia.

strengths? What additional interests might this person need to develop?

3. On a fresh stack of notes, write a new set of responses, this time dealing with the question "Why not?" as an expansion of these interests. Why not travel to Tibet? Why not learn Spanish? Why not master canoeing? Add these to the grid.

4. Then, leave the room. Go for a walk, have dinner, or head to class. Let your subconscious mind play with the possibilities suggested by your notes.

5. Next, organize the notes into four general categories: intellectual goals, personal-relationship goals, spiritual or emotional goals, physical fitness goals. If you are an extreme safe-keeper, add a category called "Adventure." If you are an extreme risk-taker, add a category called "Organization." Since a mix of activities helps feed the psyche, working with each of these categories is important.

6. Choose one goal from each category and develop an implementation strategy. Be specific! "I want to become a better artist" is too vague. Consider specific actions you can take to improve your artwork. "I need to improve my drawing" is better. "I want to learn anatomy" is better still. To learn anatomy, you can take a class, study an anatomy book, or draw from a skeleton. These are tangible actions: you now know what to do.

7. Prioritize your goals and develop a rough timetable, listing weekly goals, semester goals, and one-year goals. It is not necessary to list career goals just yet. Most of us explore many ideas during our first year of college, and formalizing career goals prematurely

is counterproductive. After you are clearly committed to a major field of study, you can add a page of long-term goals, projecting your priorities for the next three to five years.

8. At least once a month, review your chart and add or delete information as necessary. If you realize that you are overextended this term, shift one of your minor goals to next semester. This system is intended to provide clear targets, not to create a straitjacket. Make adjustments as necessary, making sure that your primary goals are met.

9. If you achieve all your goals, congratulate yourself — then set more ambitious goals next term. If you achieve half of your goals, congratulate yourself — then prioritize more carefully next term. You may have taken on too many tasks and thus dissipated your energy. Because there is always a gap between intention and outcome, a 70 to 80 percent completion rate is fine.

## Characteristics of Good Goals

### Challenging but Attainable

Too modest a goal will provide no sense of accomplishment. Too ambitious a goal will reduce, rather than increase, motivation. No one wants to fight a losing battle! Knowing your strengths and weaknesses will help you set realistic goals.

### Compatible

Training for the Boston Marathon while simultaneously trying to gain 20 pounds is unwise, since you will burn off every calorie you consume. Trying to save a thousand dollars while touring Europe is unrealistic, since travel always costs more than you expect. On the other hand, by taking a dance class or joining a hiking club, you may be able to combine a fitness goal with a social goal.

### Self-Directed

Avoid goals that are primarily dependent on someone else's actions or opinions. "I want to earn an A in drawing" is a common example. Since the grade is determined by a teacher, your control in this area is limited. Instead, focus on improving your drawing as much as possible. This will increase your receptivity to learning and will focus your attention on actions you can control. When you do your best work, good grades generally follow.

### Clearly Defined

We all have "too much to do." No matter how carefully we organize our time, there are only 24 hours in a day. Identifying daily and weekly priorities can help focus attention, increase productivity, and reduce stress.

1. Identify your target. It may be a specific action (such as doing your laundry) or a broader intention (such as improving your knowledge of anatomy). Specificity is important. It is nearly impossible to hit a target you cannot see.

2. Focus. Reduce distractions as much as possible. If visiting friends have taken over your living space, plan another time for socializing, then chase them out. If you need music to improve your concentration, plug in your favorite tunes. If you can't seem to focus due to an assortment of worries, try writing them down; then refocus on the task at hand. Getting worries off your mind often helps.

3. Then, hit your target with the necessary force and energy.

### Temporary

Set clear target dates, get the job done, and move on to the next project. Each completed task increases your self-confidence and adds momentum. By contrast, unfinished work can drain energy and decrease momentum. If you are overloaded, delete secondary goals, so that you can complete primary goals.

# TIME MANAGEMENT

Time management can help you achieve your goals. Working smarter is usually more effective than simply working harder. In a world bursting with opportunity, using your work time well can increase the time available for travel, volunteer work, or socializing. The following time-management strategies have been used by many artists and designers.

## Set the Stage

Choosing when and where to work can significantly increase your output. If you are a lark, bursting with energy and enthusiasm early in the morning, tackle major projects before noon. If you are an owl, equipped with night vision and able to hunt after dark, work on major projects after dinner. If you are distracted by clutter, clean your desk before beginning your workday, and tidy up your desk before you leave. These seemingly minor actions can substantially increase your productivity.

## Prioritize

Use your goal list to help determine your priorities. Note which tasks are most *urgent* and which tasks are most *important*. Timing can be crucial. When you pay your phone bill on time, you easily complete an urgent but unimportant task. When your phone bill is overdue and the service is cut off, this unimportant task becomes a major headache. Dispense with urgent tasks quickly so that you can focus on more important issues.

## See the Big Picture

Use monthly calendar pages to record your major projects and obligations. A calendar that is organized by months can help you see which weeks will be packed with deadlines and which weeks will be relatively quiet. To avoid all-nighters, distribute large, important tasks over several weeks. To avoid missing a pivotal lecture or critique, schedule out-of-town trips during "slow" weeks.

## Work Sequentially

Many activities are best done in a specific sequence. If you are writing a 20-page paper, it is best to start with research, make an outline, complete a rough draft, make corrections, then write the final draft. If you are designing a poster, it is best to start with research, make thumbnail sketches, assess the results, make a full-size rough layout, consult the client, and *then* complete the poster. Trying to cut out the intermediate steps and move directly to the final draft is rarely effective. With most large projects, you learn more, save time, and do better work by following the right sequence of events.

## Use Parts to Create the Whole

Seen as a whole, a major project can become overwhelming. In an extreme case, creative paralysis sets in, resulting in a condition similar to writer's block. Breaking down big jobs into smaller parts helps enormously. In *Bird by Bird,* Anne Lamott gives a wonderful description of this process:

> Thirty years ago my other brother, who was ten years old at the time, was trying to get a report on birds written that he'd had three months to write. [It] was due the next day. . . . He was at the kitchen table close to tears, surrounded by binder paper and pencils and unopened books on birds, immobilized by the hugeness of the task ahead. Then my father sat down beside him, put his arm around my brother's shoulder, and said, "Bird by bird, buddy. Just take it bird by bird."[3]

By doing the job incrementally, you are likely to learn more and procrastinate less.

## Make the Most of Class Time

Psychologists tell us that beginnings and endings of events are especially memorable. An experienced teacher knows that the first 10 minutes of class sets the tone for the rest of the session and that a summary at the end can help students remember the lesson. Similarly, the wise student arrives 5 minutes early for class and maintains attention to the end of class.

Be an active learner. You can use that 5 minutes before class to review your notes from the previous session and organize your supplies. This helps create a bridge between what you know and the new information to be presented. Try to end the class on a high note, either by completing a project or by clearly determining the strengths and weaknesses of

the work in progress. By analyzing your progress, you can organize your thinking and provide a solid beginning point for the next work session.

## Start Early

Momentum is extremely powerful. It is much easier to climb a hill when you are already moving forward, rather than reclining. When you receive a long-term assignment, such as a 20-page paper, start it right away. Even one hour of research will help focus your attention on the problem and get you going. A slow start is better than no start!

## When in Doubt, Crank It Out

Fear is one of the greatest obstacles to creative thinking. When we are afraid, we tend to avoid action and consequently miss opportunities.

Both habit and perfectionism feed fear. If you consistently repeat the same activities and limit yourself to familiar friendships, you will become more and more fearful of new experiences. Perfectionism is especially destructive during brainstorming, which requires a loose, open approach.

Creativity takes courage. As IBM founder Thomas Watson noted, "If you are not satisfied with your rate of success, try failing more." Baseball player Reggie Jackson is renowned for his 563 home runs—but he also struck out 2,597 times. Thomas Edison's research team tried over 6,000 materials before finding the carbon-fiber filament used in lightbulbs.

"When in doubt, don't!" is the safe-keeper's motto. "When in doubt, do!" is the risk-taker's motto. By starting each project with a sense of adventure, you increase your level of both learning and creativity.

## Work Together

Many areas of art and design, including filmmaking, industrial design, and advertising design, are often done collaboratively. Working together, artists and designers can complete projects that are too complex or time-consuming to be done alone. Collaborative thinking helps us break familiar patterns and teaches us to listen to alternative or opposing ideas.

Here is one example. Gather 20 people. Start with a copied fragment from an existing image, such as *Metamophosis II,* an 8 × 160 in. banner by

M. C. Escher (5.2). In this case, design students were provided with a 1-inch strip of the banner to create a beginning point and another 1-inch strip of the banner to create the ending point (5.3A). Each person invented an 8½ × 11 in. connection between the two strips. Buildings, plants, chess pieces, and other images were used to bridge the gap between the strips at the beginning and the end. The images were then connected end to end, like cars in a train. When combined, they created a collaborative banner, 20 feet long. One piece of the banner is shown in figure 5.3B. Students had to negotiate with the person ahead of them in the line and with the person behind them, in order to make a continuous image with graceful transitions. In effect, all 20 participants become members of a creative team. Finally, each 8½ × 11 in. section was photocopied and traded, providing each person with the completed artwork. In a collaboration of this kind, everyone gains, both in the learning process and in the sharing of the product.

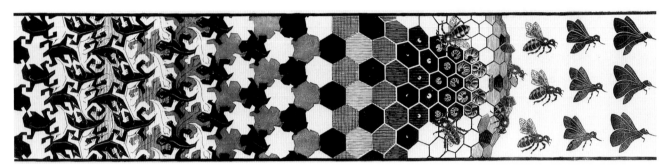

5.2 M. C. Escher, Part of *Metamorphosis II,* 1939–40. Woodcut in black, green, and brown, printed from 20 blocks on three combined sheets, 7½ × 153⅜ in. (19 × 390 cm). © 2002 Cordon Art B. V. Baarn, Holland. All rights reserved.

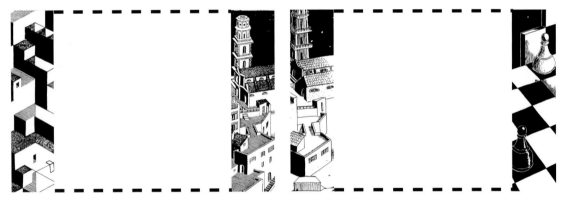

5.3A Examples of Escher Starter Images.

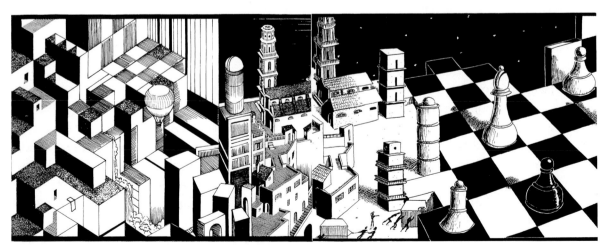

5.3B Mary Stewart and Jesse Wummer, Expanded Escher Collaboration. Student work.

## Habits of Work

Constructing a sculpture, designing a poster, or writing a story are labor-intensive: there are no real shortcuts. To provide beginning designers with a realistic list of targets, Professor Rusty Smith and his colleagues in the School of Architecture at Auburn University have developed a list of "habits of work" for architects. It emphasizes:

### Self-Reliance

Essentially, self-reliance creates an active approach to work. Rather than waiting for directions or blaming others for delays, each architecture student actively generates possibilities, weighs benefits, and makes choices. To a substantial degree, self-reliant students drive their own learning process.

### Organized Persistence

Beating your head against a brick wall is an example of mindless persistence. It is impressive, but ineffective. Chiseling away at the mortar between the bricks until the wall falls apart is an example of organized persistence. It may take weeks, but eventually organized persistence results in a solution. It gives us the ability to prevail, even when faced with the most daunting task.

### Daily Practice

Momentum is extremely powerful when you are working on a difficult problem. Daily practice helps maintain momentum. For example, when learning a new computer program, practicing for a couple of hours each night is better than working one full day a month.

### Appropriate Speed

Some tasks are best completed quickly, with brisk decision making and decisive action. Slowing down to re-frame a question and weigh alternative solutions is necessary in other cases. Knowing when to speed up and when to slow down is one mark of a "master learner."

### Incremental Excellence

Most art and design problems are best developed in a series of stages. Ideas evolve, skills improve, compositions are distilled. Rather than trying for the "perfect solution" on the first day or work, it is better to start with a "funky junky" draft.

### Valuing Alternative Viewpoints

Listening to others, understanding diverse points of view, and considering alternatives expands our capacity to solve a wide variety of problems. Even when the advice is off base, we can often use the idea as a springboard into a fresh approach.

### Direct Engagement

Talk is cheap. Work is hard. The only way to solve most art and design problems is to get involved. You will never win a race when you are standing at the sidelines!

# SUMMARY

- Creativity and design both require new combinations of old ideas.

- Creative people are receptive to new ideas, are curious, have a wide range of interests, are attentive, seek connections, and work with great conviction.

- A combination of rational and intuitive thinking feeds creativity. While intuition may be used to generate a new idea, logic and analysis are often needed for its completion. As a result, the actions of creative people are often complex or even contradictory.

- Goals you set are goals you get. Establishing priorities and setting appropriate goals will help you achieve your potential. Good goals are challenging but attainable, compatible, self-directed, clearly defined, and temporary. Deadlines encourage completion of complex projects.

- Completing tasks in an appropriate sequence, making the most of each work period, maintaining momentum, and reducing stress are major aspects of time management.

- Collaborative work can help us expand our ideas, explore new fields, and pursue projects that are too complex or time-consuming to do alone.

- Self-reliance, organized persistence, daily practice, appropriate speed, direct engagement, valuing alternative viewpoints, and incremental excellence are effective habits of work.

# Profile:
## Nancy Callahan, Artist, and Diane Gallo, Writer

Storefront Stories: Creating a
Collaborative Community

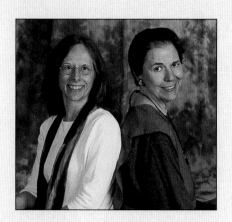

Nancy Callahan (left in photo) is a leader in the field of artists' books and is known for her creative work in screen printing. She has exhibited her work widely, and, in 1994, she was one of four artists chosen to represent the United States at the International Book and Paper Exhibition in Belgium. In 1999, she participated in the International Artists' Book Workshop and Symposium in Mor, Hungary. In addition to her full-time teaching at the State University of New York at Oneonta, Callahan has taught workshops at major book centers around the country, including the Center for Book Arts in New York City and The Women's Studio Workshop.

Diane Gallo (right in photo) is an award-winning writer and performance poet, as well as a master teacher. Her filmwork has received awards from American Women in Radio & Television and nominations from the American Film Institute. Gallo teaches creative writing and life-story workshops at universities and cultural institutes throughout the country and is a visiting poet with the Dodge Foundation Poetry Program, a humanist scholar with the National Endowment for the Humanities Poets in Person program, and co-founder of the newly formed Association of Teaching Artists.

Callahan and Gallo began working together in 1984 as a photographer/writer team for the Binghamton Press. As a result of many years of collaborative teaching, they became the first teaching artist team working with the Empire State Partnership project, jointly sponsored by the New York State Education Department and the New York State Council of the Arts. In 1996, they received fellowships to the Virginia Center for the Creative Arts, where they began working on a major project, which led to their selection by the Mid-Atlantic Foundation for their millennium project. Funded by the National Endowment for the Arts, the project—Artists & Communities: America Creates for the Millennium—named Callahan and Gallo as two of America's 250 most creative community artists.

**MS:** You've gained a lot of recognition for your recent text-based installations. Please describe *Storefront Stories*.

**NC:** Over the past two years we've had an extraordinary collaborative experience. As an extension of our writing, we developed a new type of textbased installation. One day as we worked on a story about ironing, we playfully hung a single wrinkled white shirt in the front window of our studio in Gilbertsville, New York. Below the shirt, we placed a small sign that said "No one irons anymore." As the lone shirt turned, it attracted attention, causing people on the sidewalk to stop, read the window, and react. *Storefront Stories* was born.

**DG:** Objects became words; words transformed objects. Week by week, using storefront windows as a public stage, we wrote and presented installments of autobiographical stories. In one town, a single window was changed every 10 days, creating an ongoing narrative. In another, we used five windows in a row, like pages in a book. Bits of text and symbolic objects were used to tell stories about personal change. Stories and objects—combined with the unexpected street location—sparked curiosity and started a community dialogue.

MS: How did members of the community become participants?

NC: They just began telling us their stories. An elderly woman on her way to the post office stopped to tell us the story of how she had learned to type on an old Smith typewriter, just like the one in the window. Eleven-year-old boys on bicycles stopped by. A mother brought her children to the windows each week to read the story aloud. Couples strolling by in the evening asked, "What's coming next?"

DG: People talked to us easily, asking questions and encouraging us. Many times, we'd return to find handwritten stories, comments, and suggestions. We watched passersby examine the windows and heard them laughing and talking to each other as they pieced together the story. When a viewer made a good suggestion, we incorporated the idea into the next window. When community members saw their ideas so quickly incorporated, they realized they were more than passive viewers. They were now active participants, with a vital involvement in the artistic process. The collaboration which began between two artists quickly expanded, engaging the entire town.

MS: In your household installations you create complete environments to frame your stories. To create these environments, you spend many hours scouting thrift shops and garage sales, searching for just the right objects to evoke an exact time and place. Why are these objects so important?

NC: Household objects are the vocabulary of the everyday world. Everyone feels comfortable with them. The objects are a bridge—they allow the viewer to cross easily from everyday life into the world of our installations.

DG: After the object is safely in the viewer's mind, it becomes a psychic spark which triggers associations and amplifies memories. For example, while we were doing the ironing installation, a delivery man who stopped for a moment to watch us work said, "I don't know anything about art," and began talking deeply and at length about how, when he was a boy, his mother took in ironing to make extra money so that he could have a bicycle.

NC: His narrative then created another layer of collaboration.

MS: When you began creating the installations, did you expect this kind of public reaction?

NC: No. It was a shock. From the moment we hung that first wrinkled shirt in the studio window,

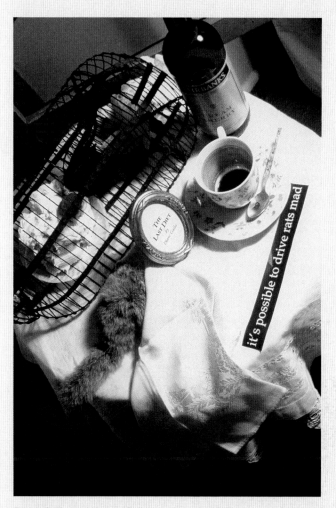

Diane Gallo and Nancy Callahan, *Storefront Stories*, 1999. Mixed medium installation, 6 × 6 × 6 ft (1.83 × 1.83 × 1.83 m).

people on the street were responsive. The immediate feedback was exhilarating.

MS: What are the characteristics of a good collaboration?

DG: Quiet attention is crucial. We both have to really listen, not only to words but also to the implications.

NC: Always tell the truth. There can be no censoring. If something's bothering you, it's important to talk about it right away. Honesty and careful listening build trust. When you trust your partner, you can reveal more.

MS: When people first see your installations, many are almost overwhelmed. Why?

DG: We're balancing on a fine line between life and art, between the personal and the universal, the public and the private, the conscious and the unconscious. We're working on the edge of consciousness, looking for things you might only be half aware of under ordinary circumstances. It's like watching a horizon line in your mind, waiting for a thought or an answer to rise.

# Problem Seeking and Problem Solving

# chapter six

Artworks are generally experienced visually. By learning the basic elements of design and exploring many approaches to composition, you can increase the visual power of your work. Composition, however, is only part of the puzzle. With the increasing emphasis on visual communication, the ideas being expressed by artists and designers have become more varied and complex. Conceptual invention is just as important as compositional strength. New ideas invite development of new types of artwork. When the concept is fresh and the composition is compelling, expression and communication expand.

## PROBLEM SEEKING

### The Design Process

In its most basic form, the design process can be distilled down to four basic steps. When beginning a project, the designer asks

1.   What is needed?
2.   What existing designs are similar to the design we need?
3.   What is the difference between the existing designs and the new design?
4.   How can we transform, combine, or expand these existing designs?

By studying the classic Eames chair, we can see this process clearly. Charles and Ray Eames were two of the most innovative and influential designers of the postwar era. Trained as an architect, Charles was a master of engineering and had a gift for design integration. Trained as a painter, Ray contributed a love of visual structure, a sense of adventure, and an understanding of marketing. Combining their strengths, this husband-and-wife team designed furniture, toys, exhibitions, and architecture and directed over 80 experimental films.

Their first breakthrough in furniture design came in 1940, when they entered a chair competition sponsored by the Museum of Modern Art. Many architects had designed furniture, and the Eameses were eager to explore this field.

Many similar products existed. The most common was the overstuffed chair, which continues to dominate American living rooms. Extensive padding on a boxy framework supported the sitter. Another popular design was the Adirondack chair, made from a series of flat wooden planes. Of greatest interest,

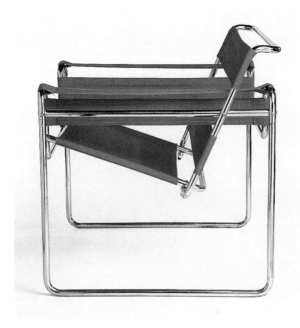

**6.1 Marcel Breuer, *Armchair*, 1925.** Tubular steel, canvas, 28¹⅟₁₆ × 30⁵⁄₁₆ × 26¾ in. d. (72.8 × 77 × 68 cm).

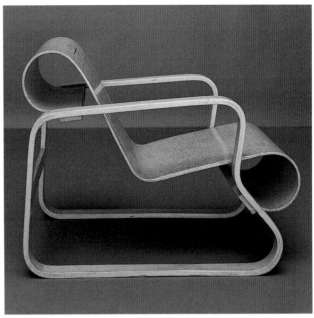

**6.2 Alvar Aalto, *Paimio Lounge Chair*, 1931–33.** Laminated birch, molded plywood, lacquered, 26 × 23¾ × 34⅞ in. (66 × 60.5 × 88.5 cm).

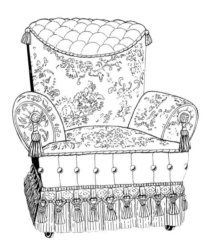

**6.3** Overstuffed chair.

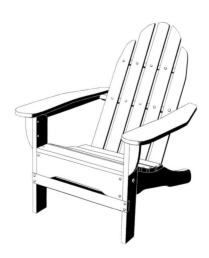

**6.4** Adirondack chair.

however, were designs by architects such as Marcel Breuer (6.1) and Alvar Aalto (6.2). These designs used modern materials and clearly displayed their structure.

By comparing existing chairs with the chair they wanted, Charles and Ray could identify qualities they needed to retain and qualities that needed to be changed. The familiar overstuffed chair (6.3) was bulky and awkward, but it was comfortable. The Adirondack chair (6.4) was easy to mass-produce, but too large for interior use. The modern chairs were elegant and inventive but were expensive to produce and often uncomfortable. The Eameses wanted to create a modern chair that was comfortable, elegant, and inexpensive.

During World War II, the Eames team had designed and manufactured molded plywood splints, which were used by doctors in the U.S. Navy. After extensive research and experimentation, they had mastered the process of steaming and reshaping the sheets of plywood into complex curves. In developing their competition entry, they combined their knowledge of splints, love of modern chairs, understanding of painting, and mastery of architecture. Their plywood chair, designed in collaboration with architect Eero Saarinen, was awarded the first prize.

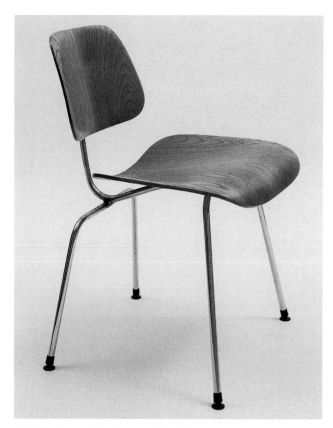

**6.5 Charles and Ray Eames,** *Side Chair, Model DCM,* **1946.**
Molded ash plywood, steel rod, and rubber shockmounts,
28¾ × 19½ × 20 in. (73 × 49.5 × 50.8 cm).

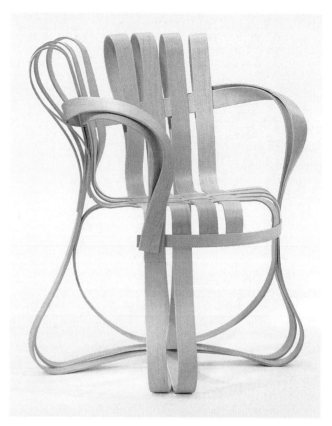

**6.6 Frank Gehry,** *Cross Check Armchair,* **1992.** Maple,
33⅝ in. h. × 28½ in. d. × 28½ in. w. (85.3 × 72.4 × 72.4 cm).

A series of Eames designs followed, including a metal and plywood version in 1946 (6.5) and numerous cast plastic versions. To create the plastic chairs, the Eames team invented a new manufacturing process. This led to a breakthrough in the field of furniture design.

By addressing a need, researching existing designs, making comparisons, and combining the best characteristics of existing chairs, the Eames team produced a new kind of chair and thus firmly established themselves as leaders in the design field.

## The Fine Art Process

For a designer, the problem-solving process begins when a client requests help or the designer identifies a specific need. With the Eames chair, the museum competition provided the impetus for an experiment that reshaped an industry.

Contemporary sculptors, filmmakers, painters, and other fine artists generally invent their own aesthetic problems. Ideas often arise from personal experience and from the cultural context. Combining

self-awareness with empathy for others, many artists have transformed a specific event into a universal statement. For example, Picasso's *Guernica* (see figure 8.21, page 167) painted in response to the 1937 bombing of a specific Spanish village, is now seen as a universal statement about the horrors of war. Working more independently and with fewer deadlines, artists can explore ideas and issues of personal interest. Adam Kallish's interview at the end of this chapter emphasizes the design process while Rodger Mack's interview emphasizes the fine art process.

## Sources of Ideas

Regardless of the initial motivation for their work, both artists and designers constantly scan their surroundings in an omnivorous search for images and ideas. As demonstrated by the profiles that appear throughout this book, the most improbable object or idea may provide inspiration. Memories of growing up in small-town America provide the stimulus for *Storefront Stories,* by Nancy Callahan and Diane Gallo. Biological systems inspire sculptor Heidi Lasher-Oakes. Ordinary vegetables and African vessels influence ceramicist David MacDonald. If you are at a loss for an idea, take a fresh look at your surroundings. Here are three strategies.

## Transform a Common Object

Architect Frank Gehry based the exuberant armchair in figure 6.6 on the wood-strip bushel basket used by farmers (6.7). If you consider all the ideas that can be generated by a set of car keys, a pair of scissors, or a compass, you will have more than enough to get a project started.

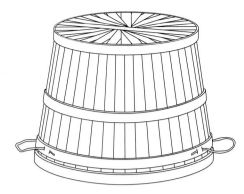

**6.7** Wood-strip bushel basket.

## Study Nature

Ceramicist Ray Rogers is inspired by many natural forms, including mushrooms, stones, and aquatic life. His spherical pots (6.8) often suggest the colors, textures, and economy of nature. In figure 6.9, Vera Lisková used the fluidity and transparency of glass to create a humorous version of a prosaic porcupine. Through an inventive use of materials, both artists have reinterpreted nature.

## Visit a Museum

Artists and designers frequently visit all kinds of museums. Carefully observed, the history and physical objects produced by any culture can be both instructive and inspirational. Looking at non-Western artwork is especially valuable. Unfamiliar concepts and compositions can suggest new ideas and fresh approaches.

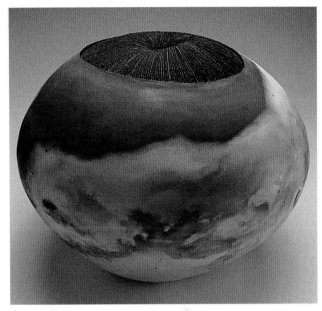

**6.8 Ray Rogers,** *Vessel,* **New Zealand, 1984.** Large, pit-fired (porous and nonfunctional) with "fungoid" decorative treatment in relief. Diameter approximately 21⅝ in. (55 cm).

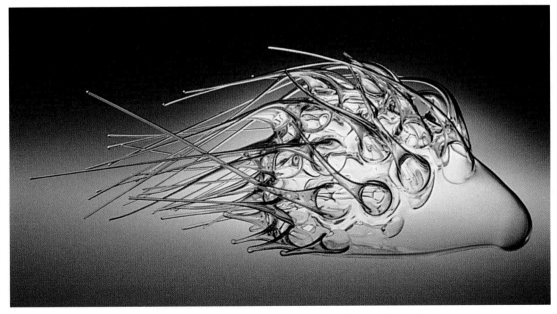

**6.9 Vera Lisková,** *Porcupine,* **1972–80.** Flame-worked glass, 4¼ × 11 in. (10.8 × 28.2 cm).

Beau Dick's *Mugamtl Mask* (6.10) is one example. First developed by a man who had revived from a deadly illness, it depicts the supernatural abilities (including flight) that he gained during his experience. His descendants now have the right to construct and wear this special mask. By understanding the story and studying this mask, you can more readily design a mask based on your own experiences.

## Characteristics of a Good Problem

Regardless of its source, the problem at hand must fully engage either the artist or the designer. Whether it is assigned or invented, a good problem generally includes the following characteristics.

### Significant

When substantial amounts of time, effort, and money are being spent, it is wise to prioritize problems and focus on those of greatest consequence. Identifying and prioritizing your major goals can help you determine the significance of a job.

### Socially Responsible

With the human population above 6 billion, it is unwise to pursue a project that squanders natural resources. What resources will be required for a major project, and how will you dispose of resulting waste? Increasingly, designers consider the environmental as well as the economic implications of each project.

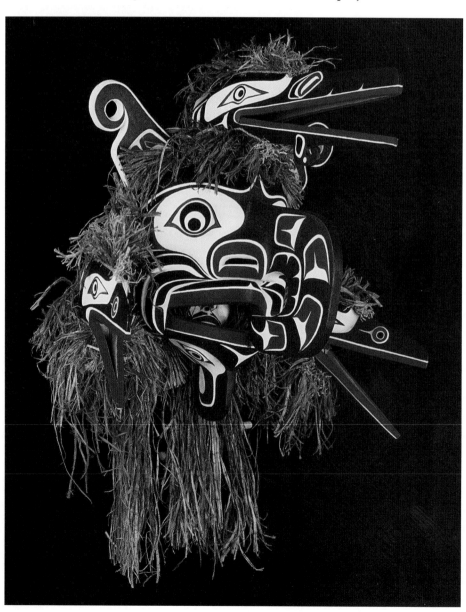

6.10 Beau Dick, *Mugamtl Mask (Crooked Beak)*, 1993. Red cedar, cedar bark, paint, 24 × 26 × 16 in. (61 × 66 × 40.6 cm).

### Comprehensible

It is impossible to solve a problem you don't fully understand. When working on a class assignment, ask questions if the assignment specifications and objectives are unclear to you.

### Open to Experimentation

It is important to distinguish between clear definition and restrictive limitations. Consider the following two assignment descriptions:

1. Organize at least 20 photocopies in such a way that they convey an idea or emotion.

2. Organize 20 photographs by American Civil War photographer Mathew Brady in order to tell a story about the life of Abraham Lincoln.

In the first case, the requirements of the project are clearly stated, but the solution remains open. In the second case, the *solution* as well as the *problem* is described. For the professional artist or designer, there are no "bad" problems, only bad solutions. However, when limited to a narrow range of possible solutions, even the most inventive person will become frustrated. If you find yourself in a straitjacket, rethink the problem and try a new approach.

### Ambitious yet Achievable

When the problem is too easy or the solution is too familiar, little is learned and nothing is gained. When the problem is too difficult or the solution is too time-consuming, completion is delayed and costs increase. Continued indefinitely, even the most exciting project can become a trap!

### Authentic

Regardless of the source, every person approaches each problem on his or her own terms. Each of us has a unique perspective, and the connections we make will vary. As a student, you will learn more when you really embrace each assignment and make it your own. Ask questions, so that you can understand the conceptual substance as well as the surface of each assignment. When you re-frame the assignment in your own terms and plunge into the work wholeheartedly, the creative possibilities will expand and your imagination will soar.

# CONVERGENT AND DIVERGENT THINKING

To see how it all works, let's work our way through an actual assignment, using two different problem-solving strategies.

*Problem*: Organize up to 20 photocopies from the library so that they tell a story. Use any size and type of format as appropriate. Any image can be enlarged, reduced, cropped, or repeated.

## Using Convergent Thinking

**Convergent thinking** involves the pursuit of a predetermined goal, usually in a linear progression and using a highly focused problem-solving technique. The word *prose* can help you remember the basic steps:

1. Define the *problem.*

2. Do *research.*

3. Determine your *objective.*

4. Devise a *strategy.*

5. *Execute* the strategy.

6. *Evaluate* the results.

In convergent thinking, the end determines the means. You know what you are seeking before you begin. For this reason, clear definition of the problem is essential: the most brilliant idea is useless if it doesn't solve the problem.

Convergent thinking is familiar to most of us through the scientific method, which follows the same basic procedure. It is orderly, logical, and empirical; there are clear boundaries and specific guidelines. Clearly focused on the final result, convergent thinking is a good way to achieve a goal and meet a deadline. Let's analyze each step.

### Define the Problem

Determine all of the physical and technical requirements of the assignment and ask whether there are any stylistic limitations. Be sure that you understand the preliminary steps as well as the final due date.

Next, assess your strengths and weaknesses relative to the problem assigned, and determine your best work strategy. Let's consider the approaches taken by two hypothetical students, Jeremy (as a convergent thinker) and Angela (as a divergent thinker).

Jeremy begins by defining *story, images,* and *library.* From the dictionary, he finds that a *story* is shorter than a novel, that it may be true or fictitious, that a series of connected events is needed, and that it may take many forms, including a memoir, a play, or a newspaper article.

Next, he finds that an *image* is a representation of a person or thing, a visual impression produced by reflection in a mirror, or a mental picture of something: an idea or impression. This means that photographs from books or magazines and reproductions of paintings are fair game. Jeremy realizes that he can even include a mirror in the project, to reflect the viewer's own image.

Finally, by exploring the computer system in the *library,* he finds that Internet resources as well as books are available. He spends the first hour of class on brainstorming, then decides to develop a story about Irish immigration to America at the turn of the century.

## Do Research

Creativity is highly dependent on seeking connections and making new combinations. The more information you have, the more connections you can make. Through research, you can collect and assess technical, visual, and conceptual information. For this assignment, Jeremy develops a plausible story based on immigrant diaries. He begins to collect images of ships, cities, and people.

## Determine Your Objective

Jeremy now has the raw material needed to solve the problem. However, many questions remain unanswered, including

- What happens in this story? Is it fiction or nonfiction?

- Who is the storyteller? A 12-year-old boy will tell a very different story than a 20-year-old woman.
- What is the best format to use? A dozen letters sent between fictitious brothers in Dublin and Boston? A Website describing actual families? A photo album?

At this point, Jeremy pauses to re-think his strategy. What does he really want to communicate? He considers:

- *Does it solve the problem?* He reviews the assignment parameters.
- *Is the solution conceptually inventive?* Is it really intriguing, or is it something we've all seen before, a cliché?
- *Is the planned solution visually compelling?*
- *Can this solution be completed by the due date?* To meet the due date, it may be necessary to distill a complex problem down to an essential statement. In this case, Jeremy decides to simplify his project by focusing on one main character.

## Devise a Strategy

While some assignments can be done in an afternoon, three-dimensional projects and multiple-image works tend to take longer. Jeremy determines the supplies he needs and considers the best time and place to work on the project.

## Execute the Strategy

Now, Jeremy just digs in and works. He has found it best to work with great concentration and determination at this point, rather than second-guessing himself.

## Evaluate the Results

At the end of each work session, Jeremy considers the strengths and weaknesses of the work in progress. What areas in each composition seem cluttered or confusing? How can those areas be strengthened? He finally presents the project for a class critique.

### Convergent Thinking Applications

Convergent thinking is most effective when

- The problem can be defined clearly.
- The problem can be solved rationally.
- The problem must be solved sequentially.
- Firm deadlines must be met.

Because many problems in science and industry fit these criteria, convergent thinking is widely used by scientists, businesspeople, and graphic designers.

## Using Divergent Thinking

The advantages of convergent thinking are clarity, control, focus, and a strong sense of direction. For many tasks, convergent thinking is ideal. In some cases, however, convergent thinking can offer *too* much clarity and not enough chaos. Inspiration is elusive. Over-the-edge creativity is often messy and rarely occurs in an orderly progression. If you want to find something completely new, you will have to leave the beaten path.

In **divergent thinking,** the means determines the end. The process is more open-ended; specific results are hard to predict. Divergent thinking is a great way to generate completely new ideas.

There are two major differences between convergent and divergent thinking. First, in divergent thinking, the problem is defined much more broadly, with less attention to "what the client wants." Research is more expansive and less tightly focused. Experimentation is open-ended: anything can happen. Second, because the convergent thinker discards weak ideas in the thumbnail stage, the final image is preplanned and predictable. The divergent thinker, on the other hand, generates many variables, is less methodical, and may have to produce multiple drafts of a composition in order to get the desired result.

While convergent thinking is usually more efficient, divergent thinking is often more inventive. It opens up unfamiliar lines of inquiry and can lead to a creative breakthrough. Divergent thinking is a high-risk/high-gain approach. By breaking traditional rules, the artist can explore unexpected connections and create new possibilities.

Let's try the same assignment again, now using Angela's divergent thinking.

*Problem:* Organize up to 20 photocopies from the library so that they tell a story. Use any size and type of format as appropriate. Any image can be enlarged, reduced, cropped, or repeated.

Realizing that the strength of the source images is critical, Angela immediately heads for the section of the library devoted to photography. By leafing though a dozen books, she finds 30 great photographs, ranging from images of train stations to trapeze artists. She photocopies the photographs, enlarging and reducing pictures to provide more options. Laying them out on a table, she begins to move the images around, considering the stories that might be generated. Twenty of the images are soon discarded; they are unrelated to the circus story she begins to develop. She then finds 5 more images to flesh out her idea.

At this point, her process becomes similar to the final steps described in the preceding section. Like Jeremy, she must clarify her objective, develop characters, decide on a format, and construct the final piece. However, because she started with such a disparate collection of images, her final story is more likely to be nonlinear. Like a dream, her images may evoke feelings rather than describe specific events.

### Divergent Thinking Applications

Divergent thinking is most effective when

- The problem definition is elusive or evolving.
- A rational solution is not required.
- A methodical approach is unnecessary.
- Deadlines are flexible.

Many creative people have used divergent thinking to explore the subconscious and reveal unexpected new patterns of thought. Surrealism, an art movement that flourished in Europe between the world wars, provides many notable examples of divergent thinking in art and literature. More interested in the essential substance of ideas and objects than in surface appearances, painter

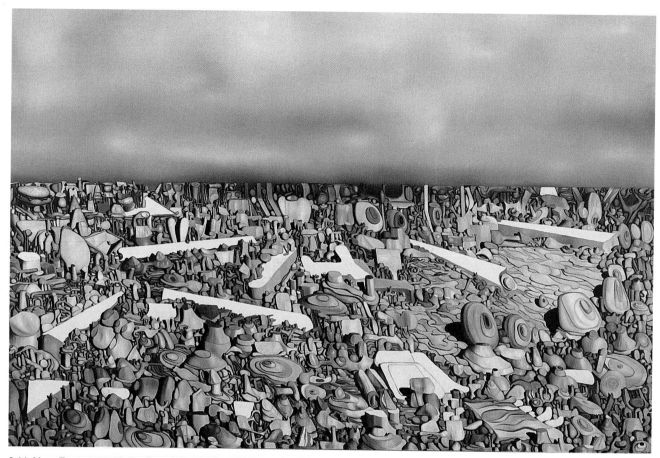

**6.11** Yves Tanguy, *Multiplication of the Arcs,* **1954.** Oil on canvas, 40 × 60 in. (101.6 × 152.4 cm).

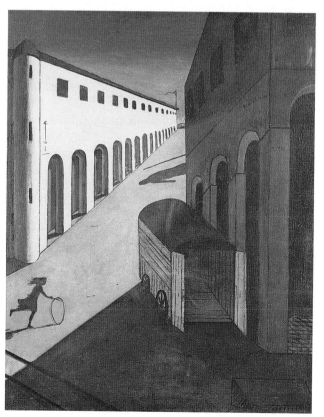

**6.12** Giorgio de Chirico, *The Mystery and Melancholy of a Street,*
**1914.** Oil on canvas, 24¼ × 28½ in. (62 × 72 cm).

Yves Tanguy constructed *Multiplication of the Arcs* (6.11) from evocative abstract shapes. In *The Mystery and Melancholy of a Street* (6.12), Giorgio de Chirico used distorted perspective and threatening cast shadows to create a feeling of anxiety. More interested in stimulating the viewer's own response than in imposing a specific vision, the surrealists rejected rational thought.

Which is better—convergent or divergent thinking? A good problem-solving strategy is one that works. If five people are working on a Website design, a clear sense of direction, agreement on style, an understanding of individual responsibilities, and adherence to deadlines are essential. Such a design team may primarily use convergent thinking. On the other hand, when an artist is working independently, the open-ended divergent approach can lead to a major breakthrough. As noted in the Kallish interview at the end of this chapter, combining convergent and divergent thinking is ideal. When you need to expand an idea, use divergent thinking. When focus is needed, shift to convergent thinking.

# BRAINSTORMING

**Brainstorming** plays an important role in both convergent and divergent thinking. It is a great way to expand ideas, see connections, and explore implications. The following are four common strategies.

## Make a List

Let's say that the assignment involves visualizing an emotion. Start by listing every emotion you can, regardless of your interest in any specific area. Getting into the practice of opening up and actively exploring possibilities is crucial: just pour out ideas!

> **joy    sorrow    anger    passion    jealousy**
> **sympathy    horror    exaltation**

From the list of emotions, circle one that looks promising. To move from the intangible name of the emotion to a visual solution, develop a list of the *kinds*, *causes*, and *effects* of the emotion. Following is one example, using *anger* as a starting point.

| KINDS | CAUSES | EFFECTS |
|---|---|---|
| annoyance | wrong number phone call at 5 A.M. | slammed down phone |
| smoldering rage | friend gets award you want | argument with friend |
| desperate anger | fired from job | shouted at your child |
| anger at self | poor performance on test | major studying |

By investigating specific kinds of anger and determining the causes and the effects, you now have some specific images to develop, rather than struggling with a vague, intangible emotion.

## Use a Thesaurus

Another way to explore the potential of an idea is to use a thesaurus. Be sure to get a thesaurus that lists words conceptually rather than alphabetically. Use the index in the back to look up the specific word you need. For example, *The Concise Roget's International Thesaurus* has a section titled "Feelings," including everything from *acrimony* to *zeal*. Here is a listing of synonyms from the section on resentment and anger: *anger, wrath, ire, indignation, heat, more heat than light, dudgeon, fit of anger, tantrum, outburst, explosion, storm, scene, passion, fury, burn, vehemence, violence, vent one's anger, seethe, simmer,* and *sizzle!* Thinking about a wide range of implications and connections to other emotions can give you a new approach to a familiar word.

## Explore Connections

By drawing a conceptual diagram, you can create your own thesaurus. Start with a central word. Then, branch out in all directions, pursuing connections and word associations as widely as possible. In a sense, this approach lets you visualize your thinking, as the branches show the patterns and connections that occurred as you explored the idea (6.13).

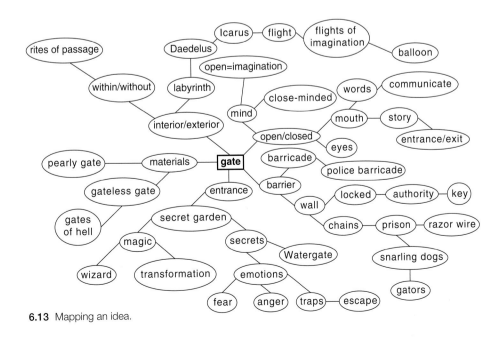

**6.13** Mapping an idea.

If I am going to make drawings or photographs which include a bicycle, I might go for a bike ride, but more importantly I would fantasize about a bike. I would picture a bike in my mind. The most obvious depiction is the side view because this is the significant profile. I would then imagine a standing bicycle with no rider, looking from above, directly down on the bike, or from behind or in front of the standing bike with my eye-level midway between the ground and the handlebars. In these three positions the bicycle is seen from the least significant profile. It is a thin vertical line with horizontal protrusions of the pedals, seat and handlebars. The area viewed is so minimal that the bicycle almost disappears.

Before long in examining a bike I would become involved with circles. Looking at the tires, I think about the suspension of the rim and the tire, indeed, the entire vehicle and rider, by the thin spokes. It amazes me that everything is floating in space, connected only by thin lines. I imagine riding the bike through puddles and the trace of the linear journey from the congruent and diverging water marks left by the tread on the pavement. I might think about two friends together and separated. Symbolism.

I think about cycles of being with friends and apart. And again I would think literally of cycles, circles and tires.

I would think of the full moon as a circle and how in its cycle it turns into a line. I would see the tires from the significant profile and in my mind I would turn it in space and it would become an ellipse.

If I turned it further, until it was on an axis 90 degrees from the significant profile, it would no longer be a circle or an ellipse, but it would be a line. So again, line comes into my thoughts.

A circle is a line.

A circle is a straight line.[1]

**6.14** Keith Smith, Brainstorming.

In *Structure of the Visual Book,* Keith Smith demonstrates the value of verbal connections. Smith seeks immersion in his subject. He wants to know it so well that, when he begins to work, he can pursue his images intuitively, with all the power and grace of a skillful cyclist. Try to follow the steps in figure 6.14, as he explores the word *bicycle*. Using a single object, he explores movement, friendship, and geometry.

## Keep a Journal

Keeping a journal or sketchbook is an ideal way to record your ideas and create connections. In it, you can

- Classify, arrange, and record information.
- Develop new ideas.
- Examine your current beliefs and analyze the beliefs of others.
- Record your responses to critiques.

- Make connections among your various classes.

Recording your ideas at the end of each class and reviewing them at the beginning of the next can help you construct your own learning process. Anything that expands your thinking is fair game, including

- Plans for projects, such as thumbnail sketches and rough drafts
- Comments on how your work can be improved
- Notes from textbook readings and clippings from magazines
- Notes on visiting artists or gallery visits
- Technical notes or information on materials used in class
- Questions you want to pose in the next class meeting

Your record keeping can take many forms, including

- Drawings and diagrams
- Written ideas, descriptions, and lists
- Poetry and song lyrics

Ask yourself the following questions:

- What was the most compelling image I saw today? What made it compelling?
- What similarities and differences were there among my studio classes this week?
- What connections were there between my lecture classes and studios?
- What do I need to know in order to push my ideas further?

Viewing the journal as a record of your creative process is liberating. Just let your ideas flow. A random idea today can help you solve a visual problem tomorrow. Indeed, it is wise to review the journal as you move into upper-level classes. Many ideas that were too ambitious for a first-year class are perfectly suited to further development later on.

## Collaborative Creativity

Designers generally use group brainstorming. This helps them explore a wider range of possibilities and better meet client needs. In *The Art of Innovation*, IDEO general manager Tom Kelley lists seven characteristics of effective group brainstorming. The following list is based on a chapter titled "The Perfect Brainstorm."

1. Sharpen your focus. A good brainstormer will generate a lot of ideas. When these ideas all address the same problem, many viable solutions result. On the other hand, when participants don't understand the problem, chaos can result.

2. Use playful rules, such as "write it down," and "think bigger." A visual and verbal record of your ideas is helpful. Premature criticism is not.

3. Number your ideas. Numbers ("let's aim for 50 ideas in the next hour") can create quantitative targets and provide a record of the order in which ideas occurred.

4. Build and jump. As the momentum builds, more and more ideas burst forth. A thoughtful question can then help the group leap to the next level, rather than getting stuck on a plateau.

5. The space remembers. Fill your brainstorming space with 22 × 30 in. Post-it notes covered with ideas the group has developed. By seeing the information, you can more easily spot bridges and build connections.

6. Warm up. If you are working with a completely new group, it may be necessary to provide an ice-breaker to build trust. This is especially true if the participants are unfamiliar with brainstorming. I often ask each participant to present one succinct question or to draw a quick cartoon of the problem as they see it. It may be an enraged elephant, a tangle of thorns, or a whirling chainsaw. Both the questions and the cartoons can reveal participant insights without demanding too much too soon.

7. Get physical. A wide range of simple materials opens up possibilities, especially if you are brainstorming a three-dimensional design problem. Cardboard, plasticine, and canvas all behave very differently. Playing with various materials can lead to a wider range of possibilities.

# VISUAL RESEARCH

## Thumbnail Sketches

Now, let's practice turning ideas into images.

Return to your original list of emotions you developed in the brainstorming exercise. Circle the most promising words or phrases you have generated and look for connections between them. Start working on thumbnail sketches, about 1.5 × 2 in. in size (6.15). Be sure to draw a clear boundary for the sketches. The edge of the frame is like an electric fence; by using the edge wisely, you can generate a lot of power!

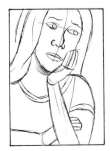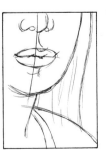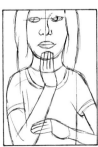

**6.15** Examples of thumbnail sketches.

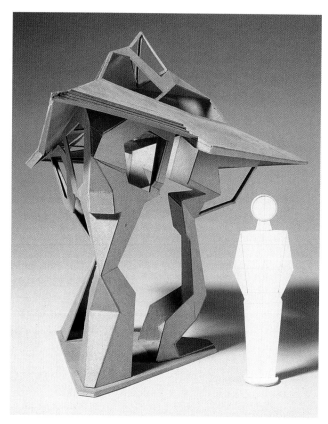

6.16A  Peter Forbes, Models for *Shelter/Surveillance Sculpture*, **1994.** Mixed media, 10½ × 9½ × 9 in. (27 × 24 × 23 cm).

developed a construction strategy. As a result, when he constructed the final, 11-foot-tall sculpture, Forbes was able to proceed with confidence. A **model** is a technical experiment. A **prototype** can be quite refined, as with the fully functional test cars developed by automobile companies. In addition to the aesthetic benefit of these preliminary studies, it is often necessary to solve technical problems at this stage. Is the cardboard you are using heavy enough to stand vertically, or does it bow? Is your adhesive strong enough? If there are moving parts, is the action fluid and easy, or does the mechanism consistently get stuck?

By completing these preliminary studies, you can refine the idea, strengthen the composition, and improve the craft of the final piece. As with a well-rehearsed performance, the work you bring to the critique is now really ready for discussion.

As with the verbal brainstorming, move fast and stay loose at this point. It is better to generate 10 to 20 possibilities than to refine any single idea. You may find yourself producing very different solutions, or you may make a series of multiple solutions to the same idea: either approach is fine. Just keep moving!

## Model Making

When working two-dimensionally, it is often necessary to make one or more full-sized rough drafts to see how the design looks when enlarged. Refinements made at this stage can make the difference between an adequate solution and an inspired solution.

Prototypes, models, and maquettes serve a similar purpose when you are working three-dimensionally. A **maquette** is a well-developed three-dimensional sketch. Figure 6.16A shows Peter Forbes' maquette for *Shelter/Surveillance Sculpture*. In this chipboard "sketch," Forbes determined the size of the sculpture relative to the viewer and

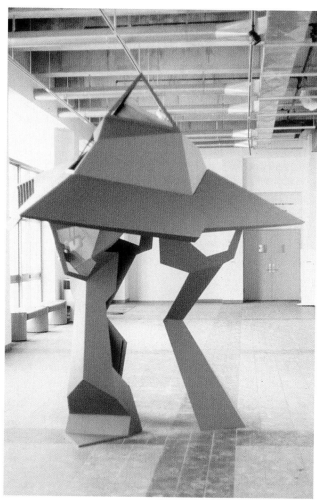

6.16B  Peter Forbes, *Shelter/Surveillance Sculpture*, **1994.** Mixed media, 11 ft 2 in. × 10 ft 4 in. × 10 ft (3.4 × 3.2 × 3 m).

# VARIATIONS ON A THEME

When we work creatively, the idea develops right along with the image. As the project evolves, we see other implications that go beyond our initial intention. By courageously pursuing these implications, we can exceed our original expectations. Just as the landscape appears to expand when we climb a mountain, so an image can expand when our conceptual understanding increases.

One way to get a lot of mileage out of an idea is through variations on a theme. Professional artists rarely do just one painting or sculpture of a given idea—most do many variations before moving to a new subject. *Thirty-Six Views of Mount Fuji* is one example. Printmaker Katsushika Hokusai was 70 years old when he began this series. The revered and beautiful Mount Fuji appeared in each of the designs in some way. Variations in the time of year and size of the mountain helped Hokusai produce very different images while retaining the same basic theme (6.17A–C).

A very different series of variations is presented in figures 6.18 and 6.19. Here, the two artists offer very individual interpretations of the basic bracelet. Leslie Leupp's three bracelets present a playful dialogue between form and space. Lines, planes, and simple volumes dance around the wearer's wrist. In contrast, Lisa Gralnick's three bracelets are dark, massive, and threatening. The crisp angles, simple forms, and black acrylic are more suggestive of armor than of jewelry.

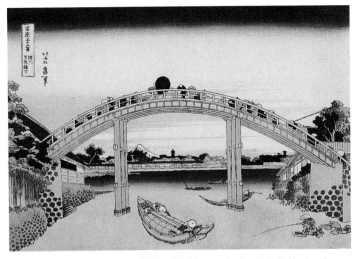

**6.17A** Katsushika Hokusai, *Thirty-Six Views of Mount Fuji: Under the Mannen Bridge at Fukagawa,* Edo Period, c. 1830. Color woodblock print, 10¹⁄₁₆ × 14¹¹⁄₁₆ in. (25.7 × 37.5 cm).

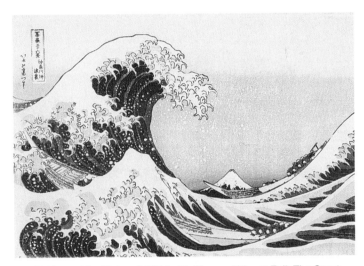

**6.17B** Katsushika Hokusai, *Thirty-Six Views of Mount Fuji: The Great Wave off Kanagawa,* Edo Period, c. 1830. Color woodblock print, 10³⁄₁₆ × 14¹⁵⁄₁₆ in. (25.9 × 37.5 cm).

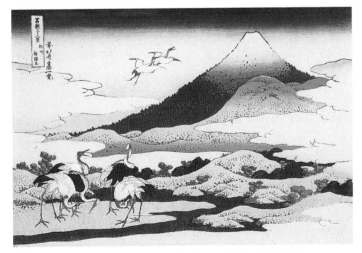

**6.17C** Katsushika Hokusai, *Thirty-Six Views of Mount Fuji: Near Umezawa in Sagami Province,* Edo Period, c. 1830. Color woodblock print, 10¹⁄₁₆ × 14⅞ in. (25.6 × 37.8 cm).

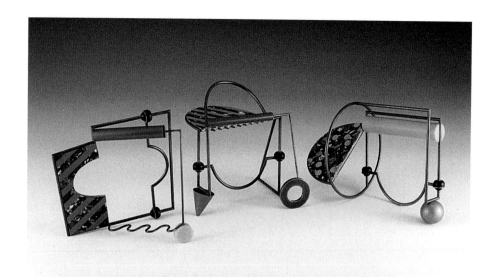

**6.18** Leslie Leupp, *Three Bracelets: Solidified Reality, Frivolous Vitality, Compound Simplicity,* **1984.** Steel, plastic, linoleum, laminate, aluminum. Each 3 × 4 × 3 in. (8 × 10 × 8 cm).

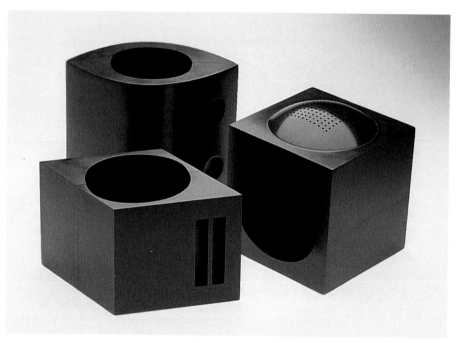

**6.19** Lisa Gralnick, *Three Bracelets,* **1988.** Black acrylic, gold, hollow construction, left to right: 3 × 3½ × 3½ in.; 4½ × 3½ × 3 in.; 3½ × 3½ × 3½ in. (7.6 × 8.9 × 8.9 cm; 11.4 × 8.9 × 7.6 cm; 8.9 × 8.9 × 8.9 cm).

# AN OPEN MIND

As noted in Chapter Five, most creative people have a wide range of interests. The very best artists and designers are often accomplished in more than one field. For example, Michelangelo was acclaimed as a painter, sculptor, and poet, while da Vinci was a master of art, biology, and engineering. The study of philosophy has had a major impact on videographer Bill Viola and on installation artist Robert Irwin. Performer Laurie Anderson is equally an artist and a musician and derives many of her ideas from literature. Whenever the base of knowledge expands, the range of potential connections increases. When the islands of knowledge are widely scattered, as with interdisciplinary work, the imaginative leap is especially great.

The message is clear: the more you know, the more you can say. Read a book. Attend a lecture. Take a course in astronomy, archaeology, psychology, or poetry. Use ideas from academic courses to expand your studio work. Art and design require conceptual development as well as perceptual and technical skill. By engaging your heart, your eye, your hand, and your mind, you can fully use your emotional, perceptual, technical, and conceptual resources to create your very best work.

## SUMMARY

- Concept and composition are equally important aspects of art and design.

- Designers usually solve problems presented by clients. Artists usually invent aesthetic problems for themselves.

- Ideas come from many sources, including common objects, nature, mythology, and history.

- Good problems are significant, socially responsible, comprehensible, achievable, and authentic. They provide basic parameters without inhibiting exploration.

- Convergent thinking is highly linear. The word *prose* can help you remember the steps.

- Divergent thinking is nonlinear and more open-ended than convergent thinking. It is less predictable and may lead to a creative breakthrough.

- Any idea can be expanded or enriched using brainstorming. Making lists, using a thesaurus, making a conceptual diagram, and creating connections are all common strategies.

- Visual and verbal research can provide the background information needed to create a truly inventive solution.

- Pursuing an idea through variations on a theme can help you realize its full potential.

## KEYWORDS

brainstorming
convergent thinking

divergent thinking
maquette

model

prototype

## IN DETAIL

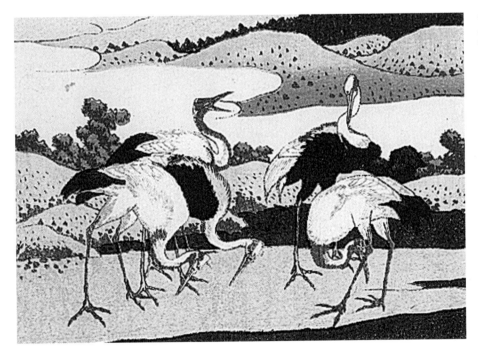

Carved from fine-grained cherry, Japanese woodblock prints from the Edo period combine power and grace to create a remarkable illusion of space. Multiple steps are needed for both the cutting and the printing of the blocks. First, a raised linear design is carved into the key block. The key block surface is then coated with black ink, and the design is transferred to multiple color blocks. In this case, there are two color blocks, one for blue and one for green. In flat color areas, ink is again applied evenly. In the distinctive gradated areas, waterbased ink is brushed onto the block, creating a gradual transition. When printed, every block must be carefully aligned, so that each part of the puzzle fits together perfectly.

# Profile:
## Adam Kallish, Designer/Consultant
### Creativity by Design

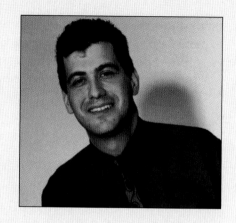

Adam Kallish has dedicated his career to brand design with underpinnings in business consulting and collaborative deployment of innovation teams for large corporations. His interests range from traditional graphic design and brand strategy to organizational design. These areas are integrated through multidisciplinary teams and program management, linking vision (desire) to requirements (specifications) to results (benefits).

**MS:** You are an advocate of "Design Methods," which is a particular approach to solving problems. Why?

**AK:** Designers are often invited into a project after many crucial decisions have been made. They are then urged to "be creative." While developing a great composition is important, the outcome may miss the mark because the designer is entering too late in the game. Design Methods presents a disciplined approach to creativity from the very start.

**MS:** Please give me some historical background.

**AK:** Design Methods was developed by John Chris Jones and others in reaction to the scientific reductivism of the post–World War II world. It recognized a new way to solve the world's problems by striking a balance between intuition (imagination, experience, and beliefs) and logic (objectivity, phenomenology, and repeatability).

The convergent and divergent strategies described in Chapter Six are a part of Design Methods. In fact, they are interdependent. Rather than simply solve a problem as presented, through Design Methods, we redefine the problem itself, which often leads to a creative breakthrough. From the outset Design Methods combines rationality, proof, and definitions with experience, feelings, and precedent.

**MS:** Why seek a balance between intuition and logic?

**AK:** Intuition is based on established patterns derived from our personal experiences. We use it every day, especially when making quick decisions. Yet, a purely intuitive response can only illuminate what has been experienced, not what *can* be experienced.

Thus, intuition provides a narrow doorway into the future. Rationality is based upon logical patterns that many people can understand. But a purely rational approach tends to oversimplify problems and the results are often mediocre.

Innovation acts as a bridge between the two by exploring three key areas: what is desirable, what is possible, and what is viable. Innovation is difficult to achieve because it requires us to move from desirability to viability.

**MS:** It sounds pretty daunting!

**AK:** In the beginning, it can feel counterintuitive. But with practice, Design Methods leads to a deeper understanding of both problem seeking and problem solving.

**MS:** You are really talking about ways to invent the future. What are the essential questions that apply to *all* change processes?

**AK:** The act of designing is difficult because we tend to seek future solutions using past and current information. For example, the solutions to global warming we develop today will work only if our predictions of the future are correct.

For simple problems involving incremental change, the future is pretty easy to understand. The redesign of an existing object like a poster or a coffee cup has many constraints that are fairly obvious, and a single designer can solve these problems. However, for highly complex problems involving many designers, many interdependencies, and many unknowns, the act of designing can easily fall apart. These four key questions can guide us when discussing the future. What should we stop doing; what should we start doing; what should we continue doing; and how can we become more effective in what we do?

MS: What is the typical Design Methods sequence?

AK: Step one is Divergence (sometimes called Analysis or Discovery). This stage is about generating doubts, posing insightful questions, exploring what is critical to the stakeholders, including the client and the users.

Step two is Transformation (sometimes called Genesis or Development). This stage is about creating appropriate boundaries and prioritizing information. The criteria and specifications that begin to emerge help the design team agree on a specific course of action.

Step three is Convergence. This stage is about focusing on an emerging solution and narrowing as many variables as possible in implementing a designed result.

With complex problems (such as systems or technological change), this sequence may need to be repeated several times before reaching a final result.

MS: It seems that Design Methods is best used in collaborative situations.

AK: It actually *requires* collaboration among various stakeholders, including clients, marketing personnel, manufacturing, users, and the designers themselves. While individualism seems easier, each of us has too many blind spots and prejudices to create a balanced future. Collaboration provides us with multiple lenses. Through these lenses, we can see our problem more fully. Even though they are harder to manage, teams bring the critical mass of skills and ideas we need when creating the best future for the greatest number of people.

MS: Let's see Design Methods in action.

AK: We can use a project from one of my classes as an example. The Nehring Center, a nonprofit art center in DeKalb, Illinois, needed to expand membership and increase attendance. Working with center director Jessica Witte, we began with an overview of the organization, discussing its goals and objectives, and noting areas for possible improvement. We interviewed a wide range of stakeholders, reviewed activities offered at the Center, analyzed its program content, and considered its affiliations to other institutions. Students began to delve deeply into its operational, marketing, and philanthropic activities and created a prioritized list of challenges.

Students then divided into two teams: one of which focused on issues of identity and the other on fundraising, which were seen as interdependent. Using convergent thinking, the teams redefined their topics, and recommended specific actions. Finally, the students presented their findings to Ms. Witte, a board member, and to School of Art faculty members. After the final presentation, she wrote:

"Design Methods sketches out a plan for the gallery's future and its current needs. I am really thankful that the presentation did not just put a Band-aid of a logo together for me. Addressing the issue of the gallery in a greater scope . . . is really valuable."

MS: Essentially, it sounds like you took the long way around, and arrived at a more interesting endpoint.

AK: Yes. Despite its initial difficulty, the full process provoked the students to intensify their investigation. Their conceptual toolkit then allowed them to dig deeper and wrestle with much more expansive problem space.

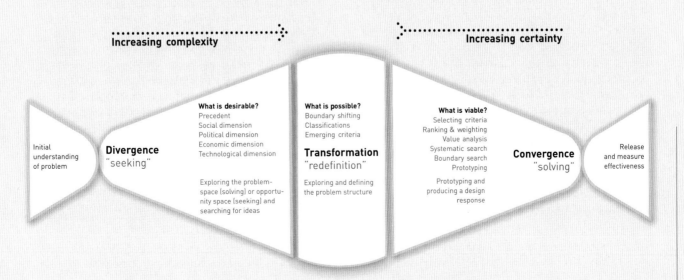

# Profile:
## Rodger Mack, Sculptor
*The Oracle's Tears:* Conception, Composition, and Construction

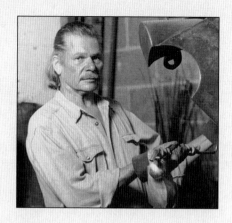

Rodger Mack is an internationally renowned sculptor best known for his work in bronze and steel. His work is included in the collections of the Museum of Modern Art in Barcelona, Spain; the Grand Hotel in Guayaquil, Ecuador; the Arkansas Arts Center Museum, Little Rock; the Albrecht-Kemper Museum of Art in St. Joseph, Missouri; the Munson-Williams-Proctor Institute in Utica, New York; and the Everson Museum in Syracuse, New York. Mack, who always used travel as a major inspiration for his imagery, was the recipient of a Fulbright grant for study in Italy, grants from the National Endowment for the Arts and the New York State Council on the Arts, and workshop grants for projects in England, Barcelona, and South Africa.

My meeting with Mack in 2000 was delayed for almost a year, due to his many commissions and elaborate projects. We got together over lunch just before he left for Italy. I had always admired Mack's abstract sculptures that so elegantly combine power and grace. Indeed, I expected our conversation to focus on the elements and principles of design. As you will see, the conversation that actually developed was equally devoted to concepts and composition.

**MS:** One of the biggest questions my students have is this: how do I get from where I am, as a beginner to where you are, as a professional? Can you describe that path briefly?

**RM:** I always knew that I wanted to study art, and I began my undergraduate work at the Cleveland Institute of Art, planning to become an automotive designer. In the fourth year of the five-year BFA program, I had the good fortune of being picked by General Motors to participate in an experimental summer internship. It was an exciting time: I was well paid and directly involved in my intended career.

I realized, though, that automotive design limited my possibilities as an artist, and I turned instead to a major in sculpture, with a minor in ceramics. At Cleveland, ceramicist Toshiko Takaezu was a great influence. She taught me a level of professionalism and an understanding of a new level of quality, both in concept and in craft. I was further influenced by Toshiko's teacher, Maija Grotell, who had developed the ceramics program at Cranbrook, where I did my graduate work. At the age of 70, she was continuing to do pioneering work with ceramic glazes.

Finally, as an apprentice to William McBey, I learned about working on commissions and the realities of day-to-day work in the studio. With sculpture, clean-ing up is important: if you don't control your work space, it will control you!

**MS:** How do you get started on a sculpture?

**RM:** I don't have to get started, because I never stop! I'm always watching, listening, and thinking. When I do stop the merry-go-round long enough, I record my ideas in a notebook. I always carry this notebook on the plane: while others read, I draw. I always have many more ideas than I can handle: I wish I could build them as fast as I can think them up.

Whenever I stop generating new material, I just visualize the inventory of sculptural parts I already have in the studio. Putting them together in new ways provides even more possibilities: an idea gets me working with the metal, which then generates more ideas. I always try to have something ready for casting each month, if only to add to this inventory of parts.

I only make maquettes when they are required for a commission. The small scale of a maquette is so different from the actual scale of the piece, especially for a major project. I remember one maquette I made for a commission in North Little Rock, Arkansas. It was made of bronze, and I charged them $200 for the maquette. Before the meeting to review the project, one of the city councilors put a box of multi-colored sticks of plasticine in front of me and said, "Next time, make it out of this." He was annoyed that I had made the maquette in bronze. In fact, the city council was against the project—they just didn't want to spend the money—but a grassroots civic group saw the importance of the work, and the commission was approved.

MS: How do you choose which of the drawings to make into sculptures?
RM: I might choose a drawing because I can't see the other side. I get curious. There is something in the drawn side that compels me to spend the time and money on the sculpture, so that I can see the other side. Drawings that I really finish are the sculptures that I never make.

MS: It seems that you actually "draw" with the metal; that is, you approach it with the same openness with which I approach a sheet of paper. How malleable is it?
RM: Just malleable enough! I like it because it is NOT easy. It is hard, and you have to really commit

yourself to the piece. I am most intuitive when I am working with existing fragments from my inventory, essentially collaging parts together. Starting with a collection of parts, I create connections, often heating a bar of bronze to just the right temperature and bending it to form a bridge or activate a space. I see the space around each volume as much as I see the volume itself.

MS: Please describe your latest piece, *The Oracle's Tears*.
RM: I've always been drawn to ancient cities and architectural forms and have been working with mythological themes for the past six years, with a series of maidens, a minotaur, a Trojan horse, and several oracles completed so far. When I visit these ancient civilizations, it saddens me that they are gone, destroyed to make way for new civilizations.

This sculpture is made from six major parts. The column is the dominant feature, structurally and conceptually. Just above it, I have placed a form which has reappeared in my work for 30 years, the Oracle. It is like an image on a tarot card, the hanging man, perhaps. A smaller piece, based on a shape I found in a market in Athens, connects the oracle and the column. On the top, the "capitol" repeats the triangular spaces seen throughout the sculpture. The tears are created by the three descending lines. The base is the final element. It provides a stable support and adds a sense of completion.

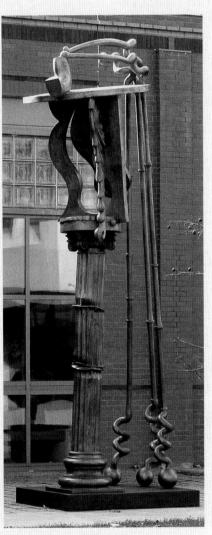

MS: How was the sculpture made?
RM: I used a combination of fabrication and casting. The oracle form was made by cutting out shapes from a sheet of ⅛-inch bronze and welding them together. The tears and the column were cast in sections, then welded. A potassium dichloride patina, applied using a blowtorch, gives the piece its golden color.

MS: This is an especially important piece for you, I think.
RM: You always hope your latest piece is the best! But yes, it combines ideas I've been working on for three years, with an overall theme, which first appeared in my work when I was in undergraduate school.

MS: What advice do you have for a beginning student?
RM: There's the old cliché: learn the rules before you break them. Always worked for me.

Rodger Mack, *The Oracle's Tears*, 1999. Cast and welded bronze, 17 × 6 × 4 ft (5.18 × 1.83 × 1.2 2 m).

# Developing Critical Thinking

# chapter seven

Critical thinking combines

- Evaluation of all available information
- Analysis of visual relationships
- Exploration of alternative solutions

Never complacent, the best artists and designers continually seek to improve each image and expand each idea. Critical thinking is used to determine compositional strengths, develop concepts, and improve visual communication. Knowing what to keep and what to change is crucial. By enhancing the best aspects of a design and deleting the weak areas, we can dramatically strengthen both communication and expression.

## ESTABLISHING CRITERIA

Establishing the criteria on which judgments will be made is the first step. For example, if technical skills are being emphasized in an assignment, craftsmanship will be highly valued. Likewise, if the assignment must be done in analogous colors, a black-and-white painting will not meet the criteria, no matter how well it is composed. By determining the major questions being raised in each problem, we can understand the basis on which judgments will be reached. Consider the following questions:

- What is the purpose of the assignment? Does your teacher want you to learn any specific skills? What compositional and conceptual variables will you need to explore?
- What are the assignment parameters? Are there limitations in the size, style, or materials?
- When is the assignment due and in what form must it be presented?

It is important to distinguish between understanding assignment criteria and seeking the "right answer." In the first case, by determining the boundaries, you can fully focus your energy when you begin to work. Just as a magnifying glass can be used to focus sunlight into a powerful beam, so assignment parameters can help you focus creative energy. On the other hand, students who try to determine the right answer to a problem often simply want to know the teacher's solution. Such knowledge is rarely helpful. The problem simply sets a learning process in motion: you learn through your work.

# FORM, SUBJECT, CONTENT

**Form** may be defined as the physical manifestation of an idea or emotion. Two-dimensional forms are created using line, shape, texture, value, and color. The building blocks of three-dimensional forms are line, plane, volume, mass, space, texture, and color. Duration, tempo, intensity, scope, setting, and chronology are combined to create time-based art forms. For example, film is the form in which *Star Wars* was first presented.

The **subject,** or topic, of an artwork is most apparent when a person, an object, an event, or a setting is clearly represented. For example, the conflict between the rebels and the Empire provides the subject for *Star Wars.*

The emotional or intellectual message of an artwork provides its **content,** or underlying theme. The theme of *Star Wars* is the journey into the self. Luke Skywalker's gradual understanding of himself and acceptance of Darth Vader as his father provides an essential emotional undercurrent to the entire series.

# STOP, LOOK, LISTEN, LEARN

Any of these three aspects of design can be discussed critically. A **critique** is the most common structure used. During the critique, the entire class analyzes the work completed at the end of an assignment. Many solutions are presented, demonstrating a wide range of possibilities. The strengths and weaknesses in each design are determined, and areas needing revision are revealed. These insights can be used to improve the current design or to generate possibilities for the next assignment.

Critiques can be extremely helpful, extremely destructive, or just plain boring, largely depending on the amount and type of student involvement. The main purpose of the critique is to determine which designs are most effective and why. Specific recommendations are most helpful: be sure to substantiate each judgment, so that your rationale is clear. Whether you are giving or receiving advice, come with your mind open, rather than your fists closed. A critique is not a combat zone! Listen carefully to any explanations offered and generously offer your insights to others. Likewise, receive their suggestions gracefully rather than defensively. You will make the final decision on any further actions needed to strengthen your design; if someone gives you bad advice, quietly discard it. An open, substantial, and supportive critique is the best way to determine the effect your design has on an audience, so speak thoughtfully and weigh seriously every suggestion you receive.

When beginning a critique, it is useful to distinguish between objective and subjective criticism.

**Objective criticism** is used to assess how well a work of art or design utilizes the elements and principles of design. Discussion generally focuses on basic compositional concerns, such as

- The type of balance used in the composition and how it was created

- The spatial depth of a design and its compositional effect

- The degree of unity in a design and how it was achieved

Objective criticism is based on direct observation and a shared understanding of assignment parameters. Discussion is usually clear and straightforward. Alternative compositional solutions may be discussed in depth.

**Subjective criticism** is used to describe the personal impact of an image, the narrative implications of an idea, or the cultural ramifications of an action. Discussion generally focuses on the subject and content of the design, including

- The meaning of the artwork

- The feelings it evokes

- Its relationships to other cultural events

- The artist's intent

Because subjective criticism is not based on simple observation, it is more difficult for most groups to remain focused on the artwork itself or to reach any clear conclusions regarding possible improvements. The discussion may become more general and wide-ranging, as political or social questions raised by the works of art and design are analyzed. Because of the potential lack of clarity, subjective criticism may be used sparingly during the foundation year.

# TYPES OF CRITIQUES

## Description

The first step is to look carefully and report clearly. Without evaluating, telling stories, drawing conclusions, or making recommendations, simply describe the visual organization of the work presented. A **descriptive critique** can help you see details and heighten your understanding of the design. The student whose work you describe learns which aspects of the design are most eye-catching and readable and which areas are muddled and need work.

This is a particularly useful exercise when analyzing a complex piece, such as figure 7.1A. In an art history class you might write:

> *Place de l'Europe on a Rainy Day* is a rectangular painting depicting a street in Paris. A vertical lamppost and its shadow extend from the top edge to the bottom edge, neatly dividing the painting in half. A horizon line, extending from the left side and three-quarters of the way to the right, further divides the painting, creating four major quadrants. Because this horizon line is positioned just above center, the bottom half of the composition is slightly larger than the top half.
>
> A dozen pedestrians with umbrellas occupy the bottom half of the painting. At the right edge, a man strides into the painting, while next to him a couple moves out of the painting, toward the viewer. To the left of the lamppost, most of the movement is horizontal, as people cross the cobblestone streets.

When using description in a spoken critique, it is useful to consider the following compositional characteristics:

- What is the shape of the overall composition? A circle or sphere presents a very different compositional playing field than a square or a cube.

- What range of colors has been used? A black-and-white design is very different from a design in full color.

- What is the size of the project? Extremes are especially notable. A sculpture that is 10 feet

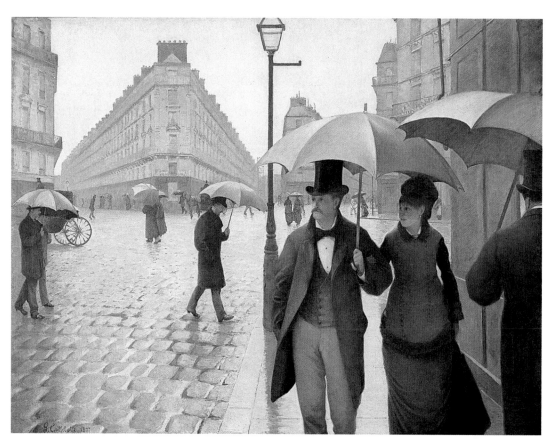

**7.1A** Gustave Caillebotte, *Place de l'Europe on a Rainy Day,* 1877. Oil on canvas, 83½ × 108¾ in. (212.2 × 276.2 cm).

tall or a painting that is 1-inch square will immediately attract attention.

- Is the visual information tightly packed, creating a very dense design, or is the design more spacious, with a lot of space between shapes or volumes?

## Cause and Effect

A descriptive critique helps us analyze the compositional choices made by the artist. A **cause-and-effect critique** builds on this description. In a simple description, you might say that the design is primarily composed of diagonals. Using cause and effect, you might conclude that, *because* of the many diagonals, the design is very dynamic. In a cause-and-effect critique, you discuss consequences as well as choices. Analyzing the same painting, you might write:

*Place de l'Europe on a Rainy Day* depicts a city street in Paris near the end of the nineteenth century. A lamppost, positioned near the center, vertically dissects the painting in half. The horizon line creates a second major division, with 45 percent of the space above and 55 percent below this line.

A dozen pedestrians in dark clothing cross the cobblestone streets from left to right, creating a flowing movement. To the right of the post, the pedestrians move in and out of the painting, from background to foreground. Both types of movement add compositional energy. Two men and one woman are the most prominent figures. The man at the far right edge pulls us into the painting, while the couple to his immediate left moves toward us, pushing out of their world and into our world. The movement that dominates each side of the painting is arrested by the lamppost. It is almost as if we are getting two paintings on one canvas.

As shown in figure 7.1B, a visual diagram can be used to support your written comments.

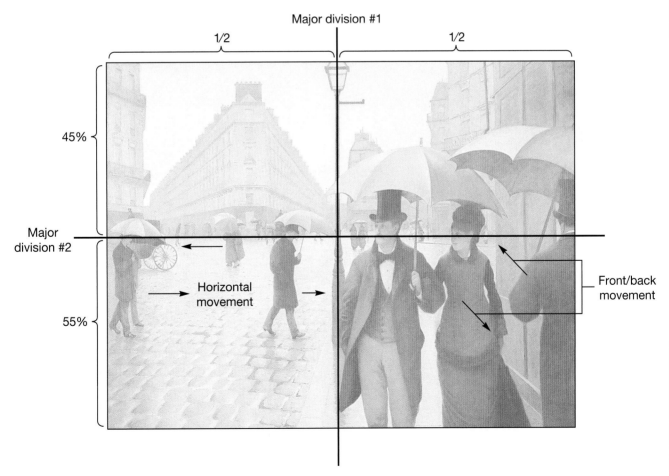

**7.1B Gustave Caillebotte, *Place de l'Europe on a Rainy Day*, 1877.** Compositional diagram.

## Compare and Contrast

In a **compare/contrast critique,** similarities and differences between two images are noted. We will use the Caillebotte painting one more time, now comparing the perspective used with the perspective in Raphael's *The School of Athens* (7.2).

The city streets depicted in *The School of Athens* and *Place de l'Europe* demonstrate many differences between Renaissance and Impressionist perspective.

The one-point perspective used in Raphael's painting leads our eyes to Plato and Aristotle, positioned just below the center of the composition. The other figures in the painting are massed in a horizontal band from the far right to the far left side and in two lower groups, to the right and left of the central figures. Our eyes are led back to the philosophers by a man sprawled on the steps to the right and by the scribes' tables on the left. Like a proscenium arch in a theater, a broad arch in the foreground frames the scene. Overlapping arches add to the depth of the painting. This composition combines the stability of one-point perspective with a powerful illusion of space.

In the Caillebotte painting, a lamppost occupies center stage, rather than a philosopher. The perspective in the cobblestone street and in the buildings on the right is complicated by the perspective used for a large background building on the left. This unusual illusion of space, combined with the movement of the pedestrians, creates a feeling of instability.

Compare and contrast essays are often used in art history classes. This form of analysis helps demonstrate differences in historical periods or artistic styles. The same approach, however, may be used in the studio, for either spoken or written critiques. The following is an example, written by two students in a basic design class. The assignment was to complete an 18 × 24 in. design, transforming the music building (Crouse College) into a labyrinth.

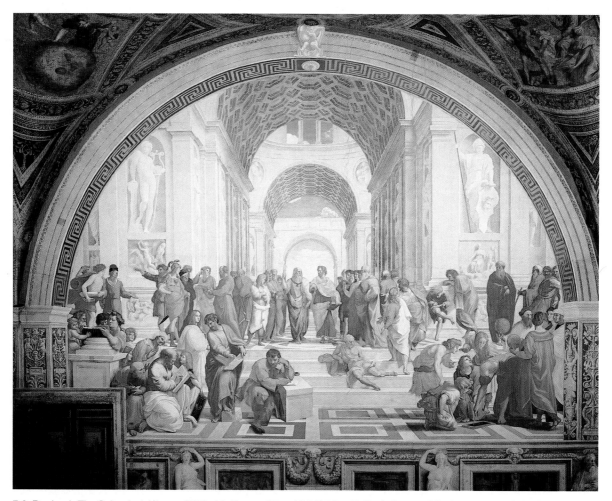

**7.2 Raphael, *The School of Athens*, 1509–11.** Fresco, 26 × 18 ft (7.92 × 5.49 m). Stanza della Segnatura, Vatican, Rome.

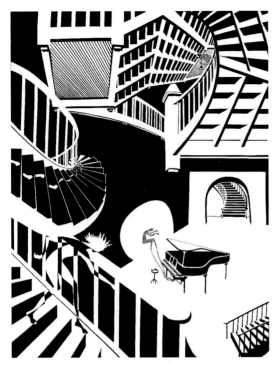

**7.3 Cally Iden,** *Transforming Crouse College into a Labyrinth.* Student work, 18 × 24 in. (45.7 × 61 cm).

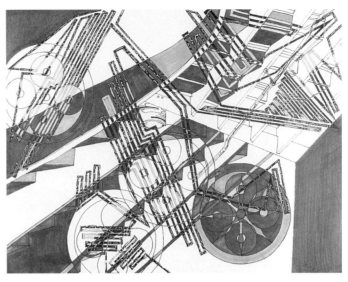

**7.4 Tricia Tripp,** *Transforming Crouse College into a Labyrinth.* Student work, 24 × 18 in. (61 × 45.7 cm).

Looking at Cally's design (7.3), Trish wrote:

Cally's piece uses strong black-and-white contrast, with both negative and positive space clearly defined. In contrast, my design is brightly colored, representing a kaleidoscope based on the stained glass windows in the building.

We both use the staircase as a major element. Cally's stair leads you in and around the building, creating a way to explore the space. My stair becomes part of the overall pattern.

I thought of the labyrinth as an abstract puzzle, a design you could draw your pencil through to find the ending. I wanted my design to be playful. Cally's design focuses on the psychological, creating an entry into the human mind. Cally's design is mysterious. Her staircases lead nowhere.

We both use lines very deliberately. Where one line ends, another begins. Without lines in a labyrinth, it wouldn't be as puzzling or mysterious. It would just be another design, rather than a puzzle to solve or a fun house to explore.

Looking at Trish's design (7.4), Cally wrote:

My labyrinth uses black and white to form a high-contrast composition, whereas Trish uses color to transform the building into a complex pattern. My vertical format helps suggest the height of the building, which is dominated by two amazing staircases. Trish's horizontal format contains a design that is as abstract as a computer circuit board.

Next, I notice conceptual differences between our solutions. My drawing is representational, depicting a psychological labyrinth, whereas Trish's turns the labyrinth into a puzzle. The space is essentially flat in her design: color is used to create a balanced composition rather than being used to create any illusion of space. On the other hand, because my design is representational, I used the illusion of space to create a convincing interior space.

One similarity between our drawings is in the inclusion of the staircase. Trish used the stairs as a background shape that adds dynamism to the composition. I used the stair as a primary motif, a means by which people using the building can explore their own minds.

For me, Trish's design creates a sense of alienation. There is no evidence of human experience here—it is a purely visual world, made up of complex shapes. It produces no strong emotion for me, no sense of mystery. It is purely visual.

On the other hand, there are hints of "the human" in my composition, but it is lost within the maze of repetitive stairs: only traces remain. I want to convey the feeling of being caught in a labyrinth, solving mysteries, and finding one's self.

Both critiques are honest without being abusive and offer a discussion of both concept and composition. While they are very different, each of the students clearly respects the approach taken by the other.

## Greatest Strength/ Unrealized Potential

Many projects have one notable strength and one glaring weakness. To create a positive atmosphere, start by pointing out the strength in the work. Begin by looking for

- The level of unity in the design and how was it achieved

- The amount of variety in the design and how much energy it generates

- The visual rhythms used and their emotional effect

- The attention to detail. This could include craftsmanship, conceptual nuance, or compositional economy.

- A conceptual spark. We all love to see an unexpected solution that redefines the imaginative potential of a project.

Using figure 7.5A as an example, you could say,

> The primary strength of this project is unity. The use of black marker throughout gives the design a simple, clean, and consistent look. The repetition of the arches helps tie it all together. Vertical and horizontal lines dominate, creating a type of grid.

Next, consider ways to improve the project. Mentally arm yourself with a magic wand. If you could instantly transform the design, what single aspect would you change? How can the potential of the project be more fully realized? Some basic questions follow.

- Is it big enough? Is it small enough?

- Is it bold enough? Is it subtle enough?

- How rich is the concept? Can it be expanded?

- How can the concept be communicated more clearly? How can the concept be communicated more fully?

The assignment was to create a labyrinth. Figure 7.5A is spatially shallow. To strengthen the composition, you might suggest:

> When I think about a labyrinth, I think of it as a mysterious place that I can enter and explore. As it

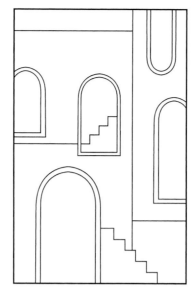 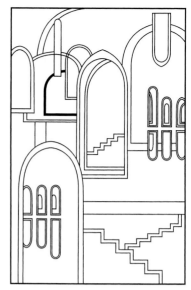

**7.5A** Initial design.       **7.5B** Design variation.

now stands, this design is spatially flat: it gives me no place to go. You might try increasing the illusion of space. Greater size variation in the arches, with larger ones in the front and smaller ones in the back, could help. Overlapping some of the arches could increase the space and add rhythm to the work. And have you considered using gray marker for the background shapes? This would reduce the contrast and push those shapes back in space.

The resulting design (7.5B) is more spatially complex.

# DEVELOPING A LONG-TERM PROJECT

Critical thinking is useful at many points in a project, not just at the end. When working on a project for 10 hours or more, it is useful to assess progress at the beginning or the end of each work period. This may be done in a large-group critique, in small teams, in discussion with your teacher, or on your own. Several effective strategies follow.

## Week One Assessment

### Determine Essential Concept

As a project begins to evolve from brainstorming, to thumbnails, to rough drafts, the concept may also evolve. Your initial idea may expand or shift during the translation from the mind to the hand to the page. Stopping to reconsider your central concept and refine your image can bring great clarity and purpose to the work. What is the design *really* about? You can speak more forcefully when you know what you want to say.

### Explore Polarities

Sometimes, the best way to strengthen an idea is to present the exact opposite. For example, if you want to show the *joy* a political prisoner feels on being released from jail, you may need to show the *despair* she felt before her release. To increase the *dynamism* in a design, add some emphatically *static* elements. The contrast created by polarities can heighten communication.

### Move from General to Specific

"Be specific!" demands your writing teacher. Just as vague generalities weaken your writing, so vague generalities can weaken your designs. Details are important. "A bird watched people walk down the street" is far less compelling than "Two vultures hovered over University Avenue, hungrily watching the two hapless students stagger from bar to bar." Specifying the kind of bird, type of people, and exact location makes the image come alive.

### Move from Personal to Universal

Autobiography is a particularly rich source for images and ideas. The authenticity of personal experience is extremely powerful. However, if you focus too tightly on your own family, friends, and experiences, the viewer must know you personally in order to appreciate your design. Try expanding your field of vision. Use a story about your high school graduation to say something about *all* rites of passage from childhood to adulthood.

## Week Two Assessment

A well-developed rough or a full-scale model may be presented at this stage. The purpose of this critique is to help the artist or designer determine ways to increase the visual and conceptual impact of an existing idea. Following are three major strategies.

### Develop Alternatives

By helping someone else solve a problem, we can often solve our own problem. Organize a team of four or five classmates. Working individually, design 5 to 10 possible solutions to a visual problem using 2 × 3 in. thumbnail sketches. Then, have one person present his or her ideas verbally and visually. Each team member must then propose an alternative way to solve the problem. This can be done verbally; however, once you get going, it is more effective and stimulating if everyone (including the artist) draws alternative solutions. This process helps the artist see the unrealized potential in his or her idea. And, because of the number of alternatives presented, the artist rarely adopts any single suggestion. Instead, the exercise simply becomes a means of demonstrating ways to clarify, expand, and strengthen intentions already formed.

### Edit Out Nonessentials

Have you ever found it difficult to determine the real point of a lengthy lecture and thus lost interest? In our zeal to communicate, teachers sometimes provide so many examples and side issues that students get lost. Likewise, if your design is overloaded with peripheral detail or if a secondary visual element is given the starring role, the result will be cluttered and impact will be lost. Look carefully at your design, focusing on visual relationships. Are there any extra shapes or volumes that can be deleted?

### Amplify Essentials

Just as it is necessary to delete extraneous information, it is equally important to strengthen the essential information. Review the section on emphasis in Chapter Three and consider ways to increase your compositional power. Try "going too far," wildly exaggerating the size, color, or texture of an important visual element. The only way to get an extraordinary image is to make extraordinary compositional choices.

## Developing a Self-Assignment

In the following two pages, Jason Chin describes the development of a month-long self-assignment he completed near the end of his freshman year. The original project proposal is given at the top of the first page. The rest of the text is devoted to Jason's analysis of his actual work process. This type of personal assessment can bring an extended project to a memorable conclusion.

# Self-Assignment:
## Jason Chin
The Mythological Alphabet

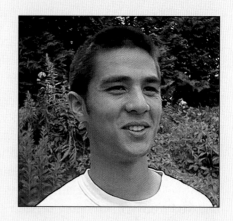

## Original Proposal

**Description:** I plan to make an illustrated alphabet book with 32 pages and a cover. The theme of the book will be myths and heroes. I am interested in illustrating the essence of each hero's story. Specifically, how can I visually communicate the story of a tragic hero versus a triumphant one? Further concerns with the book will be making it work as a whole. That means keeping it balanced and making it flow: I don't want the images to become disjointed.

## Primary Concerns

1.  How do I communicate the individual nature of the characters?

2.  How do I connect each hero to all the others?

3.  How will the book affect the reader? I want to get the reader fully involved in the book.

4.  How can I best use the unique characteristics of the book format?

## Time Management

Week 1: Research myths and heroes. Identify possible characters for the book.

Week 2: Bring at least 20 thumbnail sketches to the first team meeting.

Week 3: Bring finalized design/layout for book. Each page must have a final design in the form of thumbnails.

Week 4: Complete half of the pages.

Week 5: Finish remaining pages and present at the critique.

## Commentary

The independent project was both a blessing and a curse. Given the freedom to do what I chose was liberating, but the burden of what to do with that freedom was great. Ultimately, it became one of the best learning experiences of my freshman year.

I had decided to pursue illustration as my major, because of my interest in storytelling. This interest in stories led me to choose to make a book for my project. The next step was to find a story to tell. To limit my workload, I looked for a story that had already been told, one that I could reinterpret, as opposed to writing my own story. At this point, I came across two books, one of Greek myths, and an alphabet book illustrated by Norman Rockwell, and my initial concept was born.

Once the idea was initiated, I set to work researching Greek myths. The idea was to find one character for each letter of the alphabet. It proved more difficult than I had first thought. I found about 20 names with no problem, but I soon realized that several letters in our alphabet did not exist in the Greek alphabet. To overcome this hurdle, I took some liberties on the original problem and did not limit myself strictly to characters from myths (for example, I included the White Island for the letter W). Once the subject of each illustration was chosen, I set about the task of doing the images and designing the format of the book.

Doing the illustrations and designing the format of the book all came together at about the same time.

As I was working out the drawings I made several key decisions that heavily influenced the outcome of the project. First, I decided that each picture would have to be black and white if I was going to pull this whole thing off. Second, I knew that they would have to be relatively small. Through my art history class, I gained a strong interest in Japanese woodblock prints and was especially attracted to their strong compositional sensibility. This became the focus of my attention while working out the illustrations. Finally, the decision to make the illustrations small helped determine the way I used text in the book, because it all but eliminated the possibility of overlaying text on image.

I designed each image in my sketchbook, doing thumbnails and comp sketches of all sizes and shapes, until I found the image that I felt best represented the character. For example, Zeus has the biggest and busiest frame in the book because he is the king of the gods, while the image of the White Island is quite serene because it is a burial ground.

When I had each individual image worked out, I redrew them in order in the pages of my sketch book as if they were in the real book. I could now see how each image would work as a double-page spread, as well as how well the book could flow visually. With this mockup of the book in front of me it was very easy to see obvious mistakes and correct them before going to final art.

I did the final illustrations in pen and ink, on illustration board, and when they were finished, it was time to drop in the text. My first concept for the text was to be very minimal; each page would read, "A is for," "B is for," and so on. However,

I soon realized that making each page rhyme would drastically increase the reader's interest in the book. So I wrote a more extensive text and put the rhyming parts on opposite pages in order to give the reader one more incentive to turn the page.

The final touch for the book was putting the colored paper down. The decision to do this came when I went to place the type. The only means I had to get good type was to print it out on the computer, but I had no way to print it on the illustration board. So I had to put it on printer paper and cut and paste it. No matter how carefully I cut the paper and pasted it on, it just didn't look right. I came up with two solutions: one, print the words on colored paper and paste it on, or two, cut frames of colored paper to cover over the entire page except for the image and the text. I chose the latter and was pleased to discover that the local art store had a vast selection of handmade and colored papers.

Today I look back on this project as a pivotal experience in my art education, because I had free range to pursue storytelling, something that has since become an essential aspect of my art. In the professional world, bookmaking is rarely an individual process. It is a collaborative process, involving editors, artists, and writers, so for me to be able to pursue it on my own was in fact a blessing. I got to make a book the way that I thought it should be done, and pursue my own personal vision of what a Mythological Alphabet should be. By making this book, I discovered something that I love to do, and want to make a career of doing, and to me the vision that I have gained from this experience is invaluable.

Jason Chin, *A Is for Apollo* (left) and *U Is for Urania* (right). Student work.

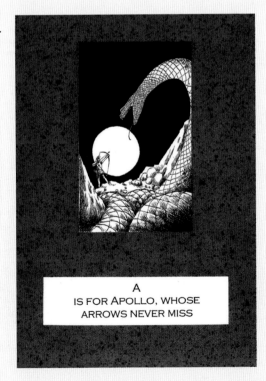

A
IS FOR APOLLO, WHOSE
ARROWS NEVER MISS

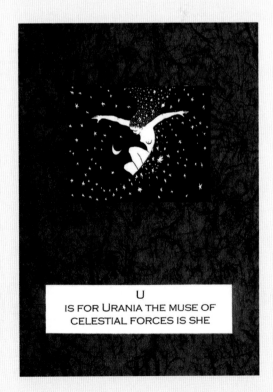

U
IS FOR URANIA THE MUSE OF
CELESTIAL FORCES IS SHE

# TURN UP THE HEAT: PUSHING YOUR PROJECT'S POTENTIAL

Some compositions are so bold that they seem to explode off the page. Other compositions have all the right ingredients but never really take off. By asking the following questions you can more fully realize the potential of any assignment.

## Basic Arithmetic

1. Should anything be *added* to the design? If your composition lacks energy, consider adding another layer of information or increasing the illusion of space. Notice how texture changes the composition in figures 7.6A and 7.6B.

2. Should anything be *subtracted*? If the composition is cluttered, try discarding 25 percent of the visual information. Then, use the remaining shapes more deliberately (7.7A–B). Get as much as possible from every visual element. Economy is a virtue.

3. What happens when any component is *multiplied*? As shown in figures 7.8A and 7.8B, repetition can unify a design, add rhythm, and increase the illusion of space.

4. Can the design be *divided* into two or more separate compositions? When a design is too complicated, it may become impossible to resolve. Packing 20 ideas into a single design can diminish rather than improve communication. In figures 7.9A and 7.9B, a complicated source image has been separated into several different designs, creating a series of stronger images.

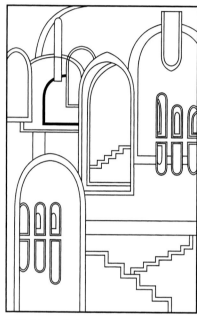

**7.6A** Linear design.

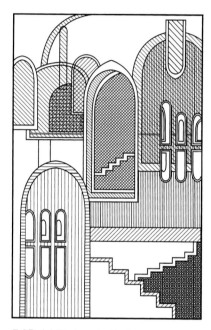

**7.6B** Adding invented texture.

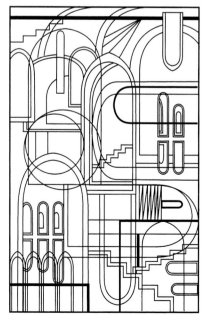

**7.7A** Visual clutter.

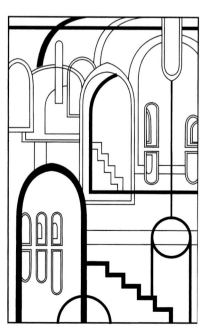

**7.7B** Visual clarity.

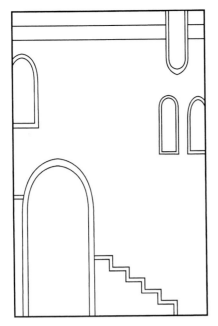

**7.8A** Basic composition.

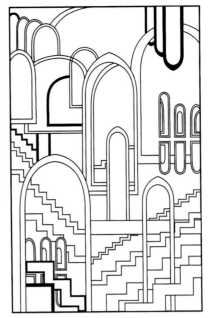

**7.8B** Elaborated composition.

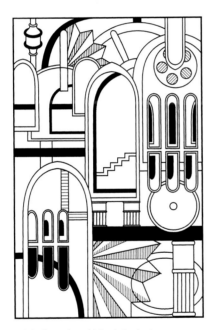

**7.9A** Completed labyrinth design.

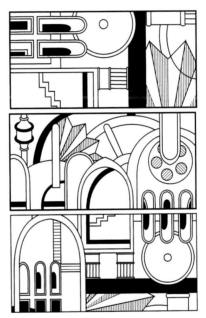

**7.9B** Divided labyrinth design.

## Transformation

Works of art and design present ideas in physical form. Each composition is strongly influenced by the materials used, the relationships created, and the viewing context chosen. Consider the following alternatives:

1. What happens when the material is changed? Even when the shapes stay the same, a silver teapot is very different from a glass, steel, or ceramic teapot. Sculptor Claes Oldenburg has used transformations in material extensively, often changing hard, reflective materials into soft vinyl. This form of transformation is especially effective when the new material brings structural qualities and conceptual connotations that challenge our expectations.

2. What is the relationship of the piece to the viewer? What is the relationship between the artwork and its surroundings? What

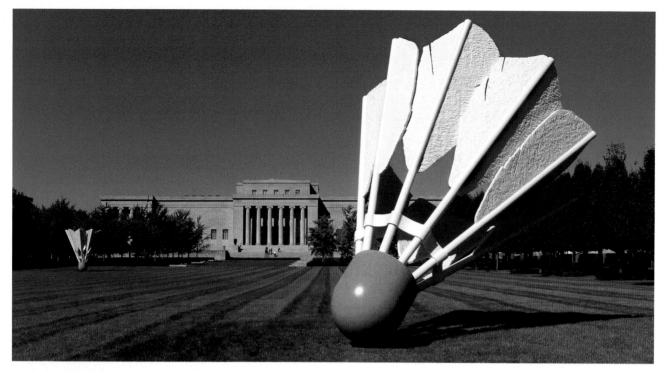

**7.10 Claes Oldenburg and Coosje van Bruggen, *Shuttlecocks*, 1994.** South facade of the Nelson-Atkins Museum of Art and the Kansas City Sculpture Park. Aluminum, fiberglass-reinforced plastic, urethane paint, approx. 19 ft 2⅜ in. h. × 16 ft diameter (5.9 × 4.9 m).

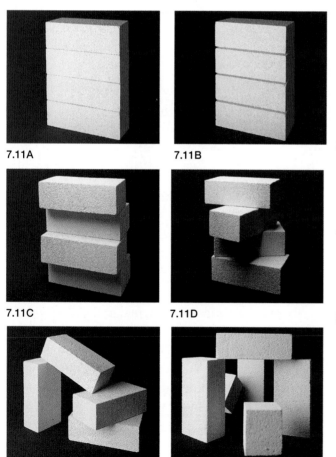

7.11A    7.11B

7.11C    7.11D

7.11E    7.11F

happens when a chair is reduced to the size of a salt shaker? Or when a 20-foot-tall badminton shuttlecock (7.10) is placed in front of a museum? How does any image change, both visually and conceptually, when size is dramatically reduced or increased?

3. Can a change in position increase impact? Working with the same four blocks, a seemingly endless number of solutions can be created (7.11A–F).

4. Is a physical object compelling from all points of view? Does the composition of the artwork encourage the viewer to view it from other angles?

5. Will a change in viewing context increase meaning? For example, a side of beef has a very different meaning when it is hung in a gallery rather than staying in a slaughterhouse. Likewise, pop artists, such as Andy Warhol and Roy Lichtenstein, brought new meaning to soup cans and comic books by using them as subject matter in their paintings.

## Reorganization

Time-based work, such as visual books, comic books, film, and video, is generally constructed from multiple images. Changing the organization of the parts of the puzzle can completely alter the meaning of the piece. For example, Angela contemplates entering the building in the sequence shown in figure 7.12. Using a different organization of the same three images, Angela now wonders what will happen when she opens the door at the top of the stairs (7.13). By repeating the image of Angela, we can present a dilemma: she is now in a labyrinth—which route should she take (7.14)?

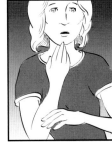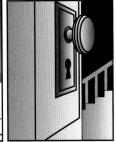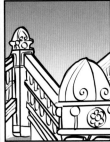

**7.12**

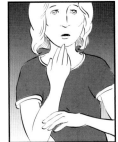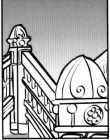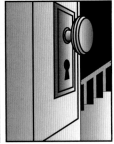

**7.13**

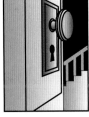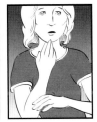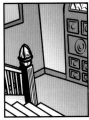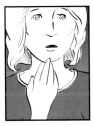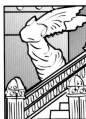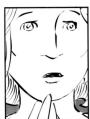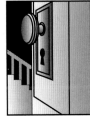

**7.14**

# CONCEPT AND COMPOSITION

Any compositional change affects the conceptual impact of an artwork. Henry M. Sayre provides a striking example in *A World of Art*.[1] A distilled version of his ideas follows.

Robert Rauschenberg's *Monogram* (7.15) is constructed from a stuffed goat, an automobile tire, and a painted plywood base. Seeking to combine painting and sculpture, Rauschenberg created three different versions of this piece. In the first version (7.16), he placed the goat on a shelf that

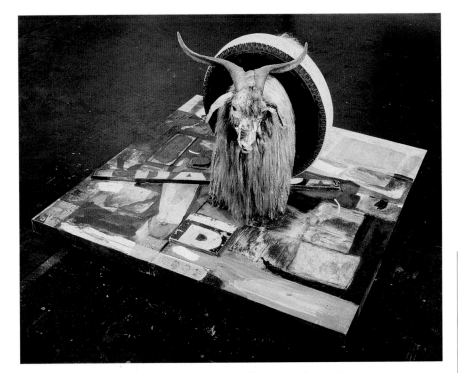

**7.15 Robert Rauschenberg,** *Monogram*, **1955–59.** Freestanding combine, 42 × 63¼ × 64½ in. (106.7 × 160.7 × 163.8 cm).

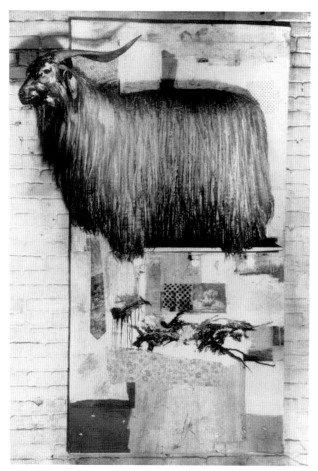

**7.16 Robert Rauschenberg, *Monogram*, 1st State, c. 1955.**
Combine painting: oil, paper, fabric, wood on canvas, plus stuffed
Angora goat and three electric light fixtures, approx. 75 × 46 × 12 in.
(190.5 × 114.3 × 30.5 cm). No longer in existence.

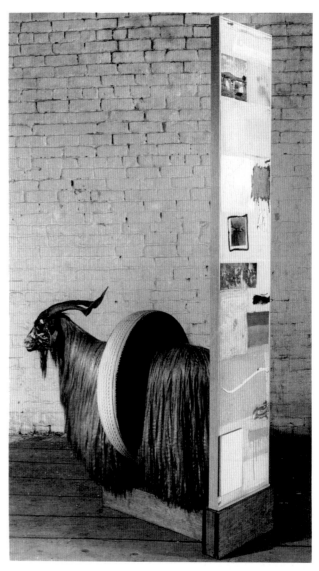

**7.17 Robert Rauschenberg, *Monogram*, 2nd State, c. 1956.**
Combine: oil, paper, fabric, wood, plus rubber tire and stuffed Angora
goat on wood, 115 × 32 × 44 in. (292 × 81.3 × 111.8 cm).

extended from the center of a 6-foot-tall painting.
This created a connection between the painting and
the goat but diminished its sculptural impact. In the
second version, Rauschenberg placed a tire around
the goat's midsection and moved the animal in front
of the painting (7.17). This enhanced its three-
dimensionality but created too much of a separation
between the animal and the painting. He finally hit
on the right combination when he placed the painting on the floor and positioned the goat in the
center. The painting retained its integrity as a two-
dimensional surface, the goat retained its physical
presence, and a highly unified combination of the
two elements was achieved. The addition of the tire
enhanced the goat's sculptural form and gave the
artwork a humorous twist.

# ACCEPTING RESPONSIBILITY

We have explored only a few of the many approaches
to critical thinking in this chapter. Every assignment
presents new possibilities for critiques, and each
teacher invents his or her own way to address the
needs of a specific class.

Regardless of the specifics, however, two facts
are inescapable. First, you will learn only what you
want to learn. If you reject out-of-hand the alternatives suggested, or if you avoid responsibility for
your conceptual and compositional choices, you
will gain nothing from the critique, no matter what
strategy is used. Second, there are no free rides.

Everyone in the class is responsible for the success of the session. It is often difficult to sustain your attention or honestly assess your work or the work of others. When you get a superficial response to a project, insisting on further clarification is not easy.

Every critique demands sincere and sustained attention from each participant. And, when the responses are supportive and substantial, remarkable improvements in works of art and design can be made.

## SUMMARY

- Using critical thinking, an artist or a designer can identify strengths and weaknesses in a project and determine the improvements that need to be made.

- Understanding the criteria on which a project will be judged helps focus critical thinking.

- Many artworks can be analyzed in terms of three basic aspects: form, subject, and content.

- Objective critiques focus on observable facts. Subjective critiques focus on feelings, intentions, and implications.

- Four common critique methods are description, cause and effect, compare and contrast, and greatest strength/unrealized potential.

- Many critique methods may be used when you are working on a long-term project. In every case, there are three primary objectives: explore alternatives, delete nonessentials, and strengthen essentials.

- Basic arithmetic, transformation, and reorganization can be used to increase compositional impact.

## KEYWORDS

cause-and-effect critique
compare/contrast critique
content

critique
descriptive critique
form

objective criticism
subject
subjective criticism

## IN DETAIL

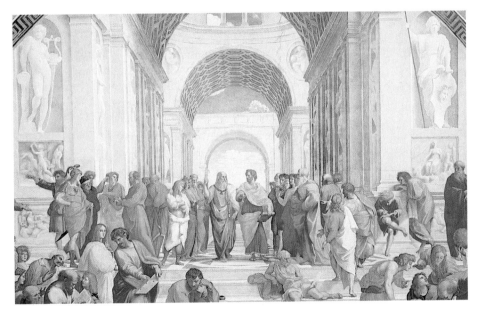

Commissioned as part of a group of four paintings decorating the apartments of Pope Julius II, *School of Athens* brings together two major approaches to philosophy. On the left, Plato points to the heavens as inspiration and clutches a book containing one of his famous dialogues. To his right, the practical Aristotle holds his book titled *Nichomachean Ethics* and gestures downward: his philosophy is more down to earth. An assortment of intellectual luminaries from Pythagoras and Ptolemy to Euclid fill the stage, while statues of Apollo (god of the arts) and Athena (goddess of wisdom) oversee the proceedings.

# Profile:
## Heidi Lasher-Oakes, Sculptor

The Infinite Journey: Exploring
Ideas in Art and Science

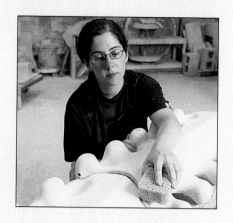

Heidi Lasher-Oakes is best known for her *Biological Abstractions Series.* Her exhibitions include "Seductive Matter, Sensual Form," which was installed in the Corcoran Art Gallery, and "In Three Dimensions: Women Sculptors of the 90's," which was held at the Snug Harbor Cultural Center. Educated at Reed College, the Pacific Northwest College of Art, and Syracuse University, Lasher-Oakes was awarded a residency at the Bemis Art Center in Omaha, Nebraska, and received a Pollock-Krasner Individual Artist Grant in 1997.

**MS:** What do art and science have in common?

**HL:** I have always believed that artistic and scientific methods are closely linked. A scientific experiment is aesthetically pleasing when it is simply and elegantly designed and takes into consideration all possible variables. On the other hand, the full exploration of an artistic idea requires the same rigor of inquiry and careful documentation as the exploration of a scientific hypothesis. In either discipline, if a process is aesthetically successful, it will lead to a coherent result. An aesthetic process requires that all components be ruthlessly considered and evaluated individually and as a unit. The aesthetic integrity of a process does not guarantee that the resulting artwork or experiment will be successful, but it does seem to guarantee that the subsequent work will not constitute a waste of time, either for the investigator or for the audience.

The Shakers have a philosophy of work that expresses this viewpoint simply: if you are going to do something, do it as well as you can.

**MS:** What is the connection between art and science in your work?

**HL:** The sculptures in my current *Biological Abstraction Series* are inspired by human anatomy and physiology, by the forms of cell and tissue structures as seen through an electron microscope, and by the relationships of these forms to manmade structures and objects. They also incorporate plant, animal, and rock forms. Science really provides the starting point for my artwork.

**MS:** Why are you a sculptor rather than a scientist?

**HL:** Art gives me a way to express my ideas and observations through the creation of physical objects. I am a haptic person, which means that I am as influenced by touch as I am by sight. I think this ties into a phrase common in our culture, "Let me see that!" which really means, "Give that to me: I want to hold it." To know a thing, I have to hold it, turn it over in my hands, take it apart, then put it back together.

**MS:** I'm intrigued by your strong emphasis on research, both in your own work and in the classes you teach. What is the value of research?

**HL:** Research is valuable for two reasons. It provides information for existing ideas and is a way of generating new ideas. Personally, I never know where research will take me. To my mind, the act of researching a subject is very much like exploring a hypertext site on the Internet—once you start clicking, you soon find that you have wandered far from your original reference point. While I understand the value of staying focused, it is the digressions and distractions that give me the best ideas, months or even years later.

Research is insurance. It provides context and fertilizes ideas. The more pieces of information you have, the more connections or associations you will be able to make. And associations are essential. Associative thinking is the ability to make original or unexpected connections. It is an essential part of creativity. Some people start out thinking this way, while for others it is a learned trait.

A wide range of interests seems to encourage associative thinking, so I keep my mind open. For example, I am currently reading a book on grasshoppers, two histories of military battle dress, a mystery novel by Antonia Fraser, three collections of American English proverbs, an introduction to chemistry, and a book by Jorge Luis Borges—and several others waiting in the wings!

MS: How do you get your ideas?

HL: Just about anything in my environment and experience can generate an idea—a book I read, a conversation, a walk in the woods.

MS: Your ideas are pretty complex. How do you communicate this information?

HL: Using association, I try to put as many ideas as possible into the forms I construct. For example, *Biological Abstraction III*, which depicts an ovary and associated seed structures, also embodies references to dandelion seeds, diving bells, and bomb casings. Each reference contains another piece of information which expands on a physical quality of the object and adds another layer of meaning. I'm not interested in making copies of the structures I study. Instead, I try to understand and express their essential forces and overriding themes.

MS: Please describe your working process.

HL: First, I identify a system for study. Since I am especially interested in human anatomy and physiology, I think of a system as an organ or group of organs in the human body. In this series, I have studied the female reproductive tract, the skin, the respiratory tract, and the inner ear.

Once I have chosen a system, I study it at microscopic and macroscopic levels to try to learn something about the relationship between its structure and function. Scale is really important:

the microscopic view reveals an astonishing level of complexity in the simplest of structures! During this phase, I also look for materials that share the structural and functional properties of my system's cellular building blocks. I experiment by combining these materials to see how they might work together. At the same time, I begin to make plans and drawings for different aspects of the piece. When I have gathered enough information to give me a solid foundation, I begin construction.

MS: It sounds so orderly! My creative process is much more chaotic.

HL: Actually, my process is definitely *not* as linear as it sounds! The research, while extensive, is never complete: all art-making requires a balance between analysis and intuition. The materials always have something new to teach me if I am willing to learn. This element of unpredictability can be frustrating and uncomfortable, but it is absolutely essential. If I play it safe, if I'm inflexible, too insistent on sticking to a set plan, the resulting piece will be dull and lifeless. For me, learning comes from experimenting and making mistakes. It is the desire to learn about my materials, myself, and the world around me that keeps me actively engaged during many hours of physical work.

MS: I think we can appreciate the function of science in our culture. What is the function of art?

HL: For me, art helps to stimulate thought, encourage contemplation, increase understanding, and express emotion. Like science, it gives us a way to see beyond everyday experience and embrace the complexity and beauty of our world.

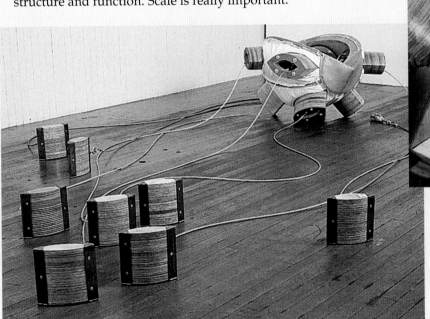

**Detail**

**Heidi Lasher-Oakes, Biological Abstraction III, 1996.** Wood, fiberglass, foam rubber, canvas, steel, dinghy anchors, rubber gasket material, fabricated and purchased hardware. Primary structure: 4 × 4 × 3½ ft; (1.21 × 1.21 × 1.07 m); length of entire assembly approx. 15 ft (4.5 m).

# Constructing Meaning

Cultivating creativity, seeking and solving visual problems, and developing critical judgment all require hours of hard work. Why are these skills so highly valued by artists and designers and so strongly emphasized by college teachers?

The answer is simple. At a professional level, art and graphic design projects are done in order to communicate ideas and express emotions. Turning elusive concepts into effective communication is not easy. Clay, ink, metal, fabric, and other physical materials must somehow stimulate an audience to see, understand, and respond. In this chapter, we will explore the essentials of visual communication and identify some of the strategies artists and designers use to construct meaning. Interviews with designer Ken Botnick and artist Roger Shimomura provide an insider's view of this process.

## BUILDING BRIDGES

### Shared Language

A shared language is the basis on which all communication is built. For example, if you are fluent in English and I am effective as a writer, the ideas I want to communicate in this chapter should make sense to you. On the other hand, if English is your second language, some of the vocabulary may be unfamiliar. In that case, you may have to strengthen the bridge between us by looking up words in a dictionary.

Figure 8.1 demonstrates the importance of shared language. For a reader of Chinese, the flowing brushstrokes form characters that communicate specific

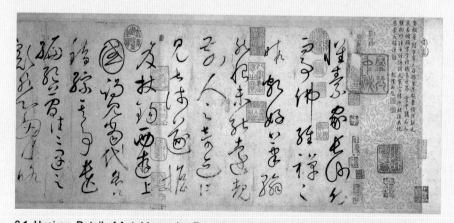

8.1 Huai-su, Detail of Autobiography, Tang dynasty, 7th–10th centuries. Ink on paper.

ideas. For those of us who know only English, the calligraphy is visually enticing but conveys no specific message. We cannot understand the characters.

## Iconography

Many visual images rely on cultural references to build meaning. **Iconography** (literally, "describing images") is the study of symbolic visual systems. Iconography plays a major role in all forms of visual communication.

Deborah Haylor-McDowell's *The Serpent Didn't Lie* (8.2) is loaded with cultural references. An anatomical diagram copied from Leonardo da Vinci's notebooks appears in the upper left corner, while the nude couple near the center is based on *The Kiss*, a sculpture by August Rodin. Einstein's computations for the theory of relativity appear in the upper right corner, and in the foreground, a baby takes his first steps. A snakeskin border surrounds the image. What does it all mean? Haylor-McDowell says:

> Ignorance may spare us the pain of difficult decisions. However, the price we pay is high. Can humankind's greatest gifts, emotion and intellect, mature in a world that is free of suffering? In the absence of adversity, will our humanness be lost?
>
> *The Serpent Didn't Lie* is based on a biblical text dealing with good and evil in the Garden of Eden. What is the price we pay for knowledge? The images I used in the composition deal with the complexities and responsibilities of our pursuit of knowledge.

Through a sophisticated use of iconography, the artist created a puzzle that is filled with ideas for us to unravel and explore. For those who understand the cultural references, this print presents a survey of types of knowledge in a compelling visual form. For those who do not understand the references, the print is simply a beautifully crafted collection of architectural and figurative fragments.

Graphic designers are especially aware of the importance of iconography. On a purely visual level, Milton Glaser's 1996 poster for the School of Visual Arts (8.3) is intriguing and evocative in itself. The hovering hat, shadowy figure, and curious text raise all sorts of questions. When we compare the

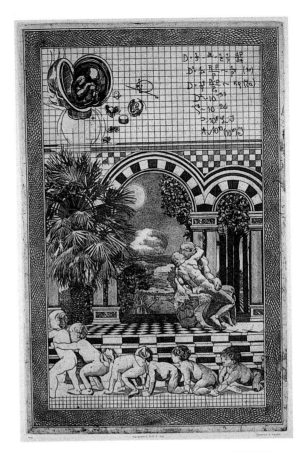

8.2 Deborah Haylor-McDowell, *The Serpent Didn't Lie*, 1997. Etching, 15 × 23 in. (38.1 × 58.42 cm).

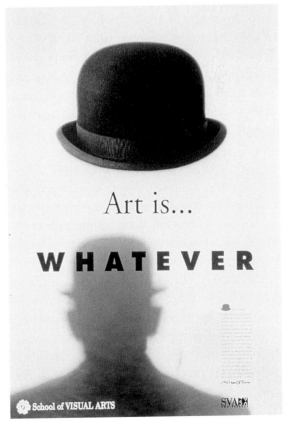

8.3 Milton Glaser, *Art is . . .*, 1996. Poster.

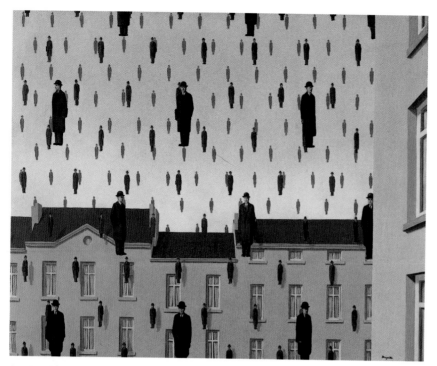

8.4 René Magritte, *Golconde*, 1953. Oil on canvas, 31¾ × 38⅝ in. (80.65 × 98.11 cm).

poster with surrealist René Magritte's *Golconde* (8.4), the ideas expand much further. In this and other paintings by Magritte, the man in the bowler hat represents anyone who is courageously navigating through the chaos of contemporary life. When we make the connection between Glaser and Magritte, the School of Visual Arts poster becomes poignant as well as provocative. Like the man in the bowler hat, each art student must find a path through the complexities of contemporary life in order to develop a meaningful approach to art and design.

## Audience

Just as films are targeted and rated for specific audiences, so many forms of visual communication are designed for a particular type of viewer. Illustrator Kenny Kiernan specializes in cartoons for preteens (8.5). The subject matter is light-hearted; the iconography is simple; the drawing style is exuberant. A very different approach was used for figure 8.6. Realizing that disfigurement is of greater concern than death for many teenagers, the designers have focused on the scarred face of a traffic accident survivor. Seeking to discourage drunk driving, they have targeted the teenager's greatest fear in order to drive home their message. Caillebotte's *Place de L'Europe*

*on a Rainy Day* (see figure 7.1A, page 142) presents yet another approach. It captures a quiet moment in time and space. There is minimal action, just the movement of groups of people within an architectural setting. This painting is compelling to a mature viewer yet lacks the action and excitement sought by a younger audience. To engage children, many museums use storytelling or other bridge-building activities when presenting paintings of this kind to school groups.

## Immediacy

When the bridge between the image and the audience is explicit, communication can occur almost instantaneously. When the iconography is elusive or complex, communication takes longer and is more varied. Each approach can be effective in the right time and place. When driving a car, our lives depend on the immediate message we receive when a traffic light turns red. When visiting a museum, we often seek greater complexity and emotional resonance.

Graphic designers generally seek a combination of immediacy, clarity, and resonance. For them, an effective poster or billboard can be understood at a glance. Figure 8.7 is an excellent example. The bold, white hangman immediately attracts attention, and the book title itself is simple and direct. The position of the figure's head adds an additional layer of meaning to this critique of capital punishment.

By comparison, *Solstice Greetings* (8.8) by Georgiana Nehl and David Browne requires extended viewer involvement. The collage includes a map, international postage stamps showing birds in flight, various pieces of patterned paper, a color chart, and butterflies, both dimensional and drawn. A tiny watch, two insects, three globes, two cubes, a child's jack, a circle, and a spiral orbit around the egg at the center of the composition. The message here is neither explicit nor immediate. As with Haylor-McDowell's work,

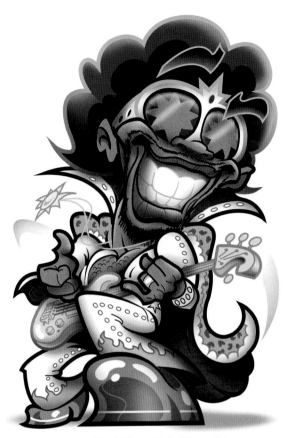

8.5 **Kenny Kiernan,** *Rock Stars.* Digital Vector Art.

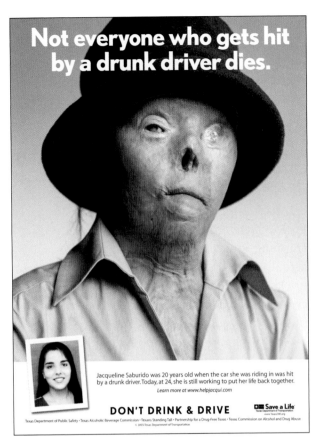

8.6 **Sherry Matthews & Associates.** Photography, poster.

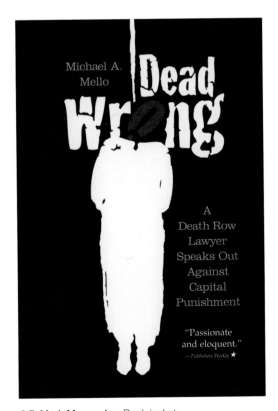

8.7 **Mark Maccaulay.** Book jacket.

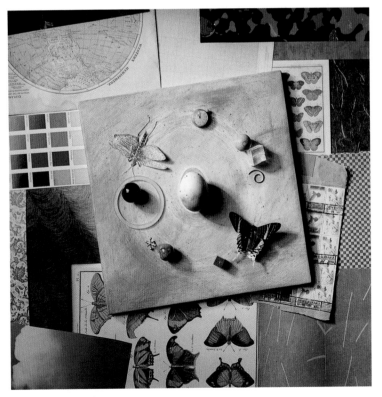

8.8 **Georgiana Nehl and David Browne,** *Solstice Greetings,* **1998.** Color photograph of constructed assemblage, 5 × 5 in. (12.7 × 12.7 cm).

the viewer must piece together a complex set of clues, then reach his or her own conclusions about journeys, the passage of time, and the transience of life.

## Stereotypes

A **stereotype** is a fixed generalization based on a preconception. On a benign level, when we use a stereotype, we ignore individual characteristics and emphasize group characteristics. For example, the broken wine glass in figure 8.9 is widely used on shipping crates to communicate fragility. Glass is actually a very versatile material that can be cast as bricks, spun into fiberoptic cables, and polished to create lenses. However, we are most familiar with fragile wine glasses and bottles. Relying on this *general* perception, the shipping label designer used a stereotype to communicate fragility.

Racial stereotyping, which is never benign, tends to exaggerate negative generalizations. Even when a positive assumption is made (such as "Asian-Americans are brainy overachievers"), the overall effect is demeaning. Rather than learning about an individual person, we make judgments based on our preconceptions.

Stereotypes are often used to create the bridge on which communication depends. Because they are based on preconceptions, stereotypes require little thought. The viewer responds automatically. In some situations, an automatic response is ideal. Four airport pictograms are shown in figure 8.10. Can you determine the meaning of each? If the designer is successful, even an exhausted traveler from New Zealand will be able to determine at a glance where to find a baggage locker, an elevator, or a toilet. Especially notice the use of the male and female stereotypes for the toilet pictograms. Despite the wide range of clothing worn by female travelers, the designers used a dress to create a stereotypical female.

## Clichés

A **cliché** is an overused expression or a predictable treatment of an idea. Phrases such as "Let's level the playing field" and "Think outside the box" are powerful the first time we hear them. However, when we hear them repeatedly, they lose their impact and become clichés. Visual clichés are equally predictable. Skulls representing death and seagulls representing tranquility may be effective at first but tend to become worn out when used repeatedly.

## Surprise

A shift in a stereotype or cliché upsets our expectations and challenges our assumptions. The resulting shock can surprise or delight an audience, making the message more memorable. Originally based on the cowboy stereotype, the Marlboro Man has been reinterpreted in figure 8.11. This ad, which begins like an ordinary cigarette commercial, quickly shifts from the heroic cowboy to a man with a hacking cough. At this point, the narrator suggests that "cowboys are a dying breed" because of the cancer caused by smoking. By breaking the stereotype, the designers attract the viewers' attention, challenge the conventional cigarette ad, and strengthen their nonsmoking message.

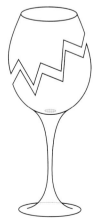

8.9 "Fragile" pictogram.

Baggage lockers 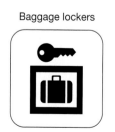  Elevator 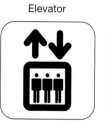  Toilets, men 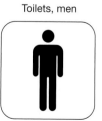  Toilets, women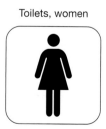

8.10 Roger Cook and Don Shanosky, images from a poster introducing the signage symbol system develped for the U.S. Department of Transportation, 1974.

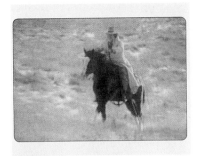
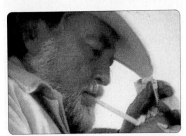
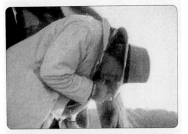

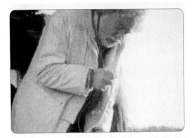
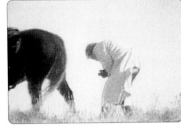
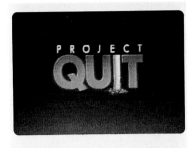

NARRATOR: No wonder cowboys are a dying breed. If

you need help quitting, tune into project QUIT, and take    control of your life.

PROJECT
QUIT

**8.11** Agency: Ruhr/Paragon, Minneapolis. Production: Lotter, Minneapolis. Details: TV, 30 seconds, color. First appearance: February 1988. Account Supervisor: Anne Bologna. Creative Director/Art Director: Doug Lew. Associate Creative Director/Copywriter: Bill Johnson. Agency Producer: Arleen Kulis. Production Company Director: Jim Lotter.

## Key Questions

- Are there any symbolic or cultural meanings embedded in your composition? Are these meanings consistent with the message you want to convey?
- Have you used a stereotype or a cliché? Does this strengthen or weaken your message?
- What audience do you want to reach? Is the form and content of your design appropriate for that audience?

## PURPOSE AND INTENT

Any number of approaches to visual communication can be effective. We simply choose the style, iconography, and composition that is best suited to our purpose.

Let's consider three very different approaches to human anatomy. *Arterial Fibrillation* (8.12) was developed for the cover of a medical journal. With equal training in art and science, medical illustrator Kim Martens combined anatomical accuracy with artistic

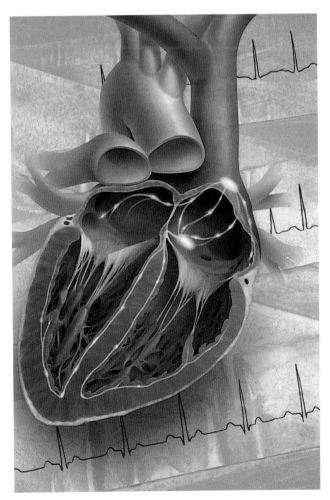

**8.12** Kim Martens, *Arterial Fibrillation*, 2000. Photoshop.

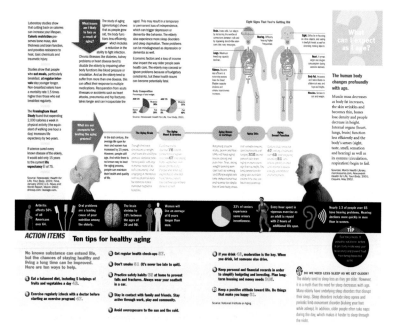

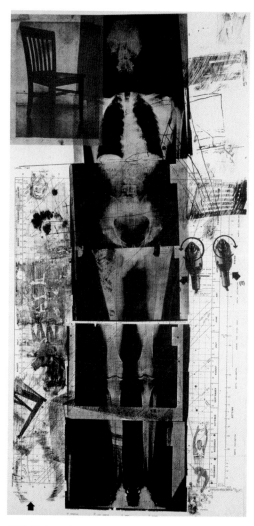

**8.13** Richard Soul Wurman, a page from *Understanding Healthcare.* Design Firm: Pentagram Design.

**8.14** Robert Rauschenberg, *Booster,* 1967. Lithograph and serigraph, printed in color, composition 71⅜₆ × 35⅛ in. (181.7 × 89.1 cm).

imagination to create this design. Intent on sales, the art director for the magazine requested an image that was both physically correct and visually enticing. Designed as an anatomical roadmap, *Understanding Healthcare* (8.13) had to present complex information in a clear and concise way. To make the text accessible to a general audience, the designers used a loose grid, dominated by vertical columns at the top and a strong horizontal band at the bottom. Arrows and other visual cues increase visual impact and help the reader navigate from page to page. *Booster* (8.14) is dominated by series of X-rays of the artist's body. In this unconventional self-portrait, Robert Rauchenberg combined a collection of personal X-rays with various examples of technological notation, including an astronomer's chart, diagrams analyzing the movement of drills and arrows, graphs, and an empty chair. The title adds further meaning, suggesting a connection to booster shots, booster rockets, and booster seats, which increase the height of an ordinary chair so that young children can sit at a table comfortably. Reduced to an X-ray image and surrounded by fragments of technological information, the artist becomes a cog in the machinery of mass culture.

## CONTEXT

The compositional context in which any image appears profoundly influences meaning. In figure 8.15, the juxtaposition of a quiet line of flood survivors with a propagandistic billboard makes us rethink the phrase "There's no way like the American way."

The social context in which an image appears is equally important. In figure 8.16, Winston Churchill, the prime minister most responsible for British victory during World War II, extends two fingers to create the "V for victory" gesture he used throughout the war. If we are familiar with Churchill and know about the desperate struggle of the British people during the war, we immediately make the correct connection. In figure 8.17, the same gesture communicates a very different idea. As part of the signage

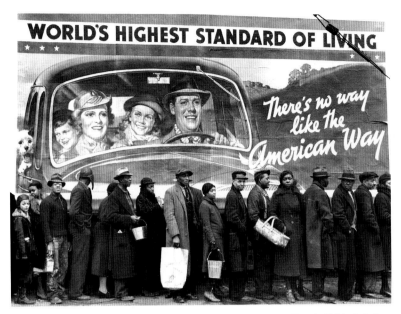

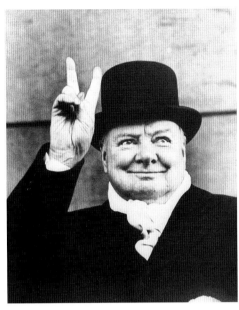

8.15 Margaret Bourke-White, *At the Time of the Louisville Flood*, 1937. Getalin silver print.

8.16 Alfred Eisenstadt, *Winston Churchill, Liverpool*, 1957. Getalin silver print.

for the Minnesota Children's Museum, the extended fingers now communicate the number two. Realizing that many young visitors to the museum may not be able to read, the designers used both a number and a gesture to communicate location. Finally, in Sean O'Meallie's *Out-Boxed Finger Puppets Perform the Numbers 1 Through 5 in No Particular Order* (8.18), the same gesture becomes a playful piece of sculpture as well as an indication of the number two. We now see the extended fingers in the context of a series of whimsical forms. In each of these three cases, the meaning of the two fingers depends on context.

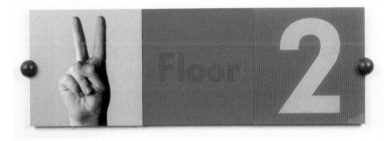

8.17 Minnesota Children's Museum, Pentagram design, NY, NY. Tracy Cameron and Michael Bierut, Designers.

# CONNECTIONS

Analogies, similes, and metaphors are figures of speech that link one thing to another. An **analogy** creates a general connection between unrelated objects or ideas, while a **simile** creates the connection using the words *as* or *like*, as in "She has a heart as big as Texas." A **metaphor**

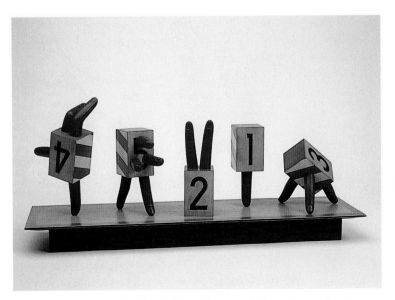

8.18 Sean O'Meallie, *Out-Boxed Finger Puppets Perform the Numbers 1 Through 5 in No Particular Order*, 1999. Polychromed wood.

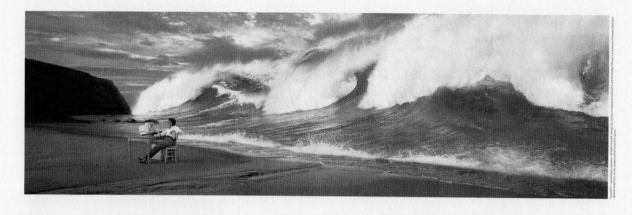

8.19 Iomega Corporation, "Y2K's coming. Don't just sit there."

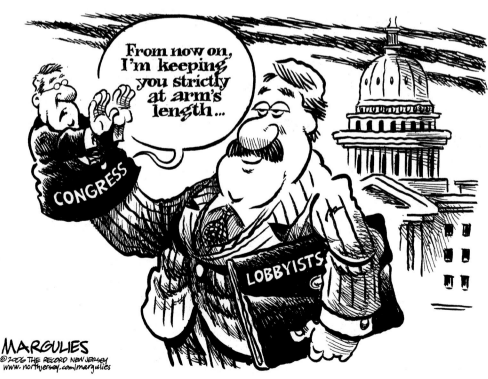

8.20 Jimmy Margulies, Editorial Cartoon, 2006.

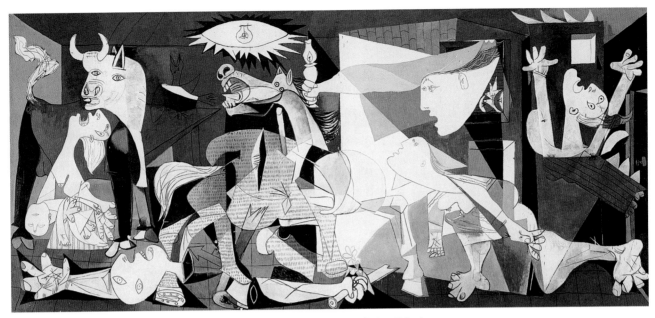

**8.21** Pablo Picasso, *Guernica*, **1937.** Oil on canvas, 11 ft 5½ in. × 25 ft 5¼ in. (3.5 × 7.8 m).

is more explicit: Speaking metaphorically, we would say "Her heart *is* Texas." As you can see, a substantial shift in meaning occurs when metaphor is used.

In all cases, the original word is given the qualities of the linked word. For example, when Robert Burns wrote the simile "My love is like a red red rose," he gave the abstract concept of "love" the attributes of a glorious, colorful, fragrant, thorny, and transient rose.

**Metaphorical thinking** can be used to connect an image and an idea. Take the phrase "I have butterflies in my stomach." This phrase is widely used to describe nervousness. Substitute other insects for butterflies, such as bees or wasps. How does this change the meaning? To push it even further, start with the phrase "My mind was full of clouds." What happens when "clouds" is replaced by mice on treadmills, rats in mazes, shadowy staircases, beating drums, screaming children—or even butterflies? When my mind is full of butterflies, I am happy, but butterflies in my stomach indicate fear. In addition to expanding your ideas, metaphors can help provide specific images for elusive emotions.

Metaphorical thinking and symbolism have always been used by artists and designers to strengthen communication. Exaggerated metaphors are especially common in advertising design. The massive wave that threatens the computer user in figure 8.19 is a metaphor for the destructive power of the Y2K computer bug that once seemed likely to create massive computer failures on January 1, 2000. Editorial cartoons also rely on metaphors. In figure 8.20, a congressional hand puppet vows independence from the very lobbyist who is controlling his vote. Picasso's *Guernica* (8.21) is also loaded with metaphors. In *A World of Art*, Henry Sayre offers the following description:

> The horse, at the center left, speared and dying in anguish, represents the fate of the dreamer's creativity. The entire scene is surveyed by a bull, which represents at once Spain itself, the simultaneous heroism and tragedy of the bullfight, and the Minotaur, the bull-man who for the Surrealists stood for the irrational forces of the human psyche. The significance of the electric light bulb at the top center of the painting, and the oil lamp, held by the woman reaching out the window, has been much debated, but they represent, at least, old and new ways of seeing.[1]

Rather than showing exploding bombs or collapsing buildings, Picasso filled his painting with abstracted animals, screaming humans, and various light sources. In so doing, he focused on the meaning and emotion of the event, rather than the appearance.

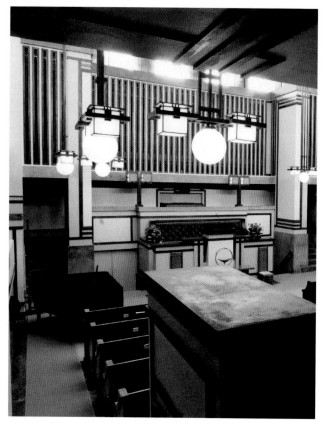

8.22 Notre-Dame Cathedral nave vaults, Chartres, 1194–1230.

8.23 Frank Lloyd Wright, Unity Temple interior, 1906. Oak Park, Illinois.

# AESTHETICS

## Definitions

In *Design in the Visual Arts,* Roy Behrens notes the difference between the words anesthetic and aesthetic. An **anesthetic** is used to induce insensitivity or unconsciousness. In an anesthetic state, we are numbed and disoriented. We may not be able to determine the size or location of objects or the sequence of events. On the other hand, **aesthetics** is the study of human responses to beauty. In an aesthetic experience, our feelings are enhanced and our understanding expands. As a result, an aesthetic experience tends to heighten meaning while an anesthetic experience tends to dull meaning. Dentists use anesthetics; artists and designers use aesthetics.

Aesthetic theories reflect community values, and thus vary greatly from culture to culture. For example, an exalted conception of Christianity dominated civic life during the Middle Ages in Europe. To express their faith, architects developed ingenious building strategies to create the soaring Gothic cathedrals we associate with that period (8.22). By contrast, intimacy and a sense of community were highly valued by the Unitarian congregation that commissioned Frank Lloyd Wrights' *Unity Temple* (8.23). The sanctuary is essentially a cube, with rows of seats facing inward from three sides. Congregants face each other while at the same time maintaining close contact with the minister. The *Pompidou Center* (8.24), by Renzo Piano and Richard Rodgers, offers a third approach to public architecture. From the outside, it looks more like a roller coaster than a major art museum. To emphasize the importance of technology in contemporary life, the blue ventilation ducts, red elevators, and green water pipes are highlighted rather than being hidden. Because cultural values are so variable, to conclude our discussion of meaningful design, we must delve into contemporary aesthetics.

## Postmodernism

Contemporary art and design is widely described as "postmodern." This description emphasizes the extent to which today's artists and designers seek solutions that challenge or exceed modernism. Thus, to understand contemporary aesthetics, we must first examine the basic characteristics of the previous aesthetic period.

In the arts, modernism is a general term that encompasses a wide range of individual movements. Beginning in Europe in the latter part of the nineteenth century, modernism became the dominant force in art and design from around 1915 to 1975.

In a sense, modernism rose from the ashes of World War I. After this devastating conflict, traditional attitudes and images seemed inadequate and out of date. Architects began to strip away traditional ornamentation to reveal the underlying structures and spaces in their buildings. Designers such as Marcel Breuer, Raymond Lowry, and Charles and Ray Eames used plastic, metals, and glass to mass-produce objects and images for an expanding consumer market. Artists such as Wassily Kandinsky, Naum Gabo, and Piet Mondrian valued abstraction over traditional representation. The international art world became a hotbed of experimentation.

Many modernists shared four fundamental beliefs. First, they were fascinated by **form,** which may be defined as the physical manifestation of an idea. "Less is more" became a mantra for designers, while "the form is the content" became a catchphrase for many painters. Second, modernists readily embraced new materials and methods of production. Especially in architecture, traditional materials such as wood, brick, and stone began to be replaced by concrete, plastic, and glass. Third, the early modernists strongly believed in the social significance of the arts. They wanted to bring art and design to the general population, rather than working for an elite. Finally, many modernists sought to understand and express universal truths. No longer satisfied with a conventional representation of reality, they began to develop a new visual language based on distillation and abstraction.

These four fundamental beliefs stimulated innovation in all areas of art, architecture, and design, and an enormous amount of brilliant work was produced. Over time, however, many modernists became trapped by their own success. Constructed from hard, reflective materials and dominated by right angles, modernist buildings often seemed cold and monolithic. Based on an underlying grid and typographical conventions, modernist posters often seemed predictable. Reduced to the most essential

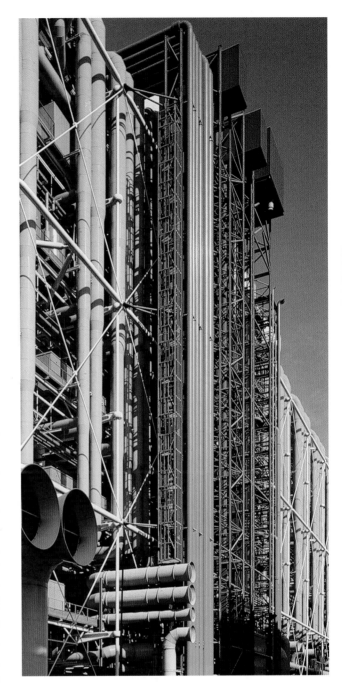

8.24 Renzo Piano and Richard Rogers, Pompidou Center, Paris, 1976.

forms, modernist painting and sculpture became detached from the chaos and complexity of contemporary life. It seemed that all the questions of modernism had been answered. Something had to change.

The 1966 publication of *Complexity and Contradiction in Architecture* set the stage for postmodern architecture. In it, architect Robert Venturi extolled the energy and ambiguities of renaissance architecture, saying

I like elements which are hybrid rather than "pure," compromising rather than "clean," distorted rather than "articulated," perverse as well as impersonal, boring as well as "interesting," conventional rather than "designed," accommodating rather than excluding, redundant rather than simple, vestigial as well as innovating, inconsistent and equivocal rather than direct and clear. I am for messy vitality over obvious unity.

At the same time, philosophers Jean-Louis Lyotard, Jacques Derrida, Michael Foucault, and Roland Barthes began to expand our understanding of the process of communication. They argued that both knowledge and communication are impermanent and conditional: there *are* no universal truths. The audience rather than the artist ultimately creates the meaning of an artwork; thus, meaning changes constantly. Furthermore, they tended to see knowledge as cyclical rather than progressive. They argued that we are pursuing a complex path with multiple branches rather than a grand journey that will culminate in human perfection.

Influenced by these theorists and seeking fresh ideas and approaches, many contemporary artists and designers reject the central tenets of modernism. For the postmodernist, context and content are as important as pure form. Postmodern use of materials tends to be omnivorous and irreverent. An exhibition may be constructed from trash, and fiberglass may be manipulated to mimic metal. Distinctions between "high art" (such as painting and sculpture) and "low art" (such as advertising and crafts) are considered artificial. And, since all aspects of visual culture are intertwined, the postmodernist may recycle images and ideas with impunity, "appropriating" them for use in a new context. Finally, for the postmodernist there are multiple rather than universal truths, and all truths are continually changing. As a result, where late modernism tended to be stable and reductive, postmodernism tends to be expansive and dynamic. As Venturi suggested, complexity and contradiction can be seen as strengths.

For the past 30 years, the collision between modernism and postmodernism has released an enormous amount of energy. Taboos have been broken repeatedly and the criteria for excellence continues to evolve.

## Visual Strategies

Five common characteristics of postmodern art and design follow.

**Appropriation** (the re-use of an existing artwork) is often used to create a connection between past and present cultural values. In *We Don't Need Another Hero* (8.25), Barbara Kruger borrowed a Norman Rockwell illustration in which a young girl admires her male counterpart's muscles. The emphatic text shifts the meaning from the original gender stereotype to a contemporary feminist statement.

**Re-contextualization** is another postmodern mainstay. Constructed from steel pins and placed in a gallery, Mona Hatoum's *Doormat* (8.26) forces us to rethink a commonplace object. As part of a series on racism, this artwork suggests that the opportunities offered by civil rights legislation may be as illusory as a welcome mat made of pins.

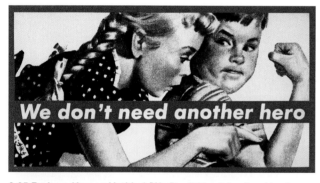

**8.25 Barbara Kruger, Untitled (We Don't Need Another Hero), 1987.** Photographic silkscreen, vinyl lettering on Plexiglas, 109 × 210 in. (276.9 × 533.4 cm).

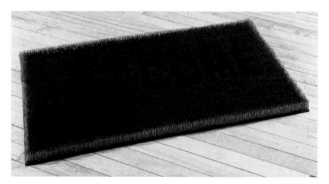

**8.26 Mona Hatoum, Doormat, 1996.** Stainless steel and nickel-plated pins, glue, and canvas, 1 × 28 × 16 in. (2.5 × 71 × 40.6 cm).

**Layering** is often used to create complex or even contradictory meanings. In *The Red Mean: Self Portrait* (8.27), Jaune Quick-to-See Smith reinterprets Leonardo da Vinci's famous drawing of ideal human proportions (8.28). As a renaissance man, Leonardo was fascinated by both perfection and the grotesque. In this drawing, he mapped out an idealized figure, radiating out from the navel in the center.

Despite its superficial similarity, the aesthetic basis for Smith's self-portrait is entirely different. Her circular outline simultaneously suggests a target, negation, and the four directions emphasized in Native American spiritual practices. A sign proclaiming "Made in America" combined with the artist's tribal identification number covers the chest of the figure and tribal newspapers fill the background. While the da Vinci drawing is simple and elegant, Smith's self-portrait provides a rich commentary on the complexities of her life as a Native American.

All of these examples demonstrate a fourth postmodern characteristic. Words and images are often integrated in order to expand emotional impact or to create conflict. For the postmodernist, contradiction and complexity are celebrated as facts of life and sources of inspiration.

Finally, **hybridity** may be defined as the creation of artworks using disparate media to create a unified conceptual statement. Mark Messersmith's *Edge of Town* (8.29) is an excellent example. As noted in Chapter Four, the illusion of space is complex and contradictory. At the center of the painting, a logging truck and a car full of hunters roar past each other, simultaneously pulling us into the image and pushing the composition outward. A group of frantic animals appears at the top, carved out of wood, and another narrative is presented in seven small boxes at the bottom. In these boxes, an animal sculptured from plastic trash bags, fragments of magazine photographs, decorative plastic plants, and shaped sheets of copper present an increasingly apocalyptic tale of the destruction of nature. Thus, in addition to the traditional oil paint used in the main image, Messersmith has added an improbable mix of nontraditional objects and materials. Visual and emotional punch are more important than technical purity.

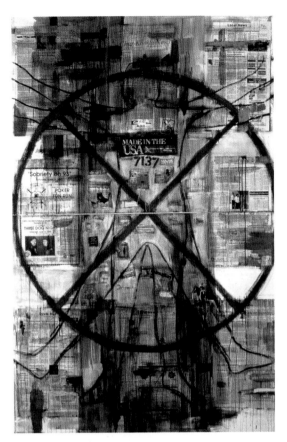

8.27 Jaune Quick-to-See Smith, *The Red Mean: Self-Portrait*, 1992. Mixed media.

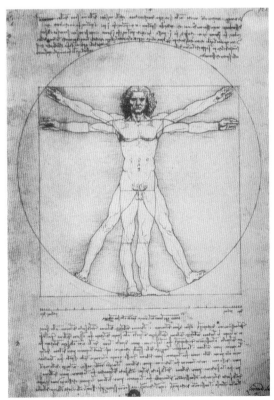

8.28 Leonardo da Vinci, *Proportions of the Human Figure* (after Vitruvius), c. 1485–90. Pen and ink, 13½ × 9¾ in. (34.3 × 24.8 cm).

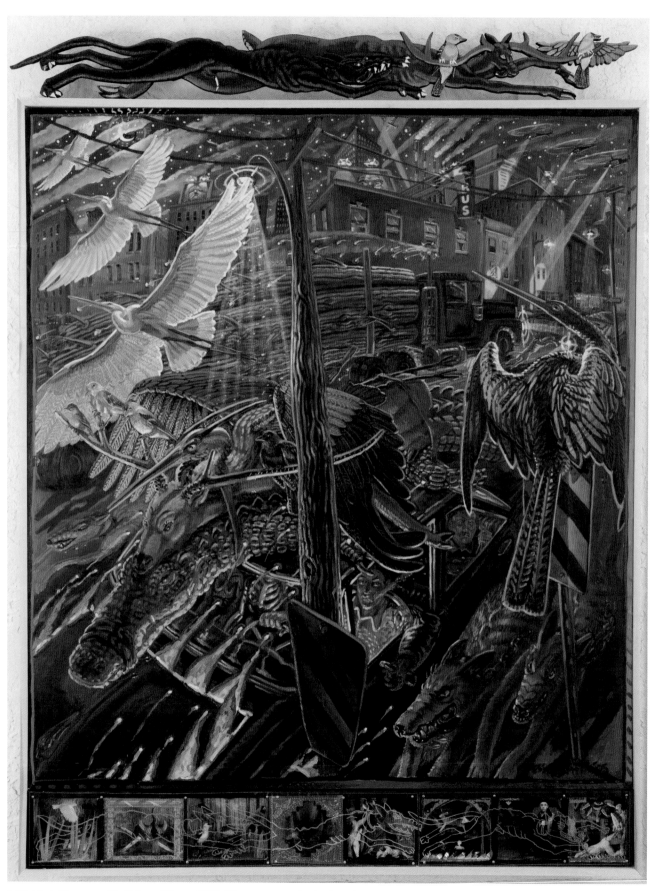

8.29 Mark Messersmith, *Edge of Town,* 2005. Oil on canvas and mixed media.

# DRAMA

Regardless of the medium used or the message conveyed, all communication can be strengthened through dramatic delivery. Even Martin Luther King's "I Have a Dream" speech loses much of its power when delivered in a flat, monotonous tone of voice. Just as a playwright sets the stage for the story he or she seeks to tell, so an artist can set the stage for visual communication.

All of the elements and principles of design described in this book can be used to increase compositional drama. To increase conceptual drama, we can:

- *Personify the idea.* When we identify with a character in a play, we become more empathetic and involved in the story. Likewise, when we identify with a character in a painting or a poster, we are much more likely to remember the idea or emotion being conveyed. For example, the shattered face of the woman in figure 8.6 makes an immediate connection. We look her in the eye and feel her sorrow.

- *Focus on essentials.* It has often been said that theater is "life with the boring parts left out." To be meaningful to an audience, the characters and events in a play must have a strong relationship to direct experience. However, a playwright rarely shows a character flossing his or her teeth. Too much detail clutters the composition, confuses the audience, and muddles the message. Including the right amount of information in just the right way can add drama to even the simplest idea.

- *Seek significance.* Any event, character, or time period can be used to create an effective play. Likewise, any object, event, or idea can be used in our quest for visual communication. A unique approach to a familiar subject or an insightful interpretation of personal and political events can add significance and increase impact.

# SUMMARY

- A shared language is the basis on which all communication is built.
- Iconography (the study of symbolic visual systems) provides us with a way to analyze the meaning of images and objects.
- Immediacy is often highly valued in graphic design. By comparison, many paintings require extended viewer involvement and longer viewing time.
- A stereotype is a fixed generalization based on a preconception. Stereotypes can easily create a bridge between the image and the audience.
- A cliché is an overused expression or predictable treatment of an idea. Even the most interesting image will lose its power if overused.

- A shift in a stereotype or cliché challenges our assumptions and can increase impact.
- Artists and designers choose the style, iconography, and composition best suited to their purpose. A mismatch between the type of image and its purpose creates confusion.
- The visual and social context in which an image appears will profoundly affect its meaning.
- Analogies, similes, and metaphors are figures of speech that link one thing to another. Metaphors are especially widely used in visual communication.
- Appropriation, re-contextualization, layering, word/image integration, and hybridity are five common strategies to create postmodern meaning.
- Dramatic delivery of a message enhances meaning.

# KEYWORDS

| | | | |
|---|---|---|---|
| aesthetics | cliché | layering | simile |
| analogy | form | metaphor | stereotype |
| anesthetic | hybridity | metaphorical thinking | |
| appropriation | iconography | re-contexturalization | |

# Profile:
## Ken Botnick, Graphic Designer

### Landscape of the Page: Conceiving and Composing Books

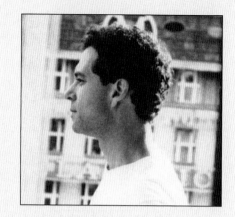

Ken Botnick has been making books for over 25 years. From 1979 to 1988, he and Steve Miller ran Red Ozier Press in New York City, producing over 50 limited-edition titles of contemporary poetry and fiction. From 1988 to 1993, Botnick was production and design manager of the art books at Yale University Press, with three of his book designs winning medals from the American Association of University Presses. He has also designed books for Princeton Architectural Press, Harry N. Abrams, Princeton School of Architecture, and the University of Alabama Press.

**MS:** Some artists pursue a very linear career path. Other artists, who are equally or even more interesting, come to art and design through a more circuitous route. Please describe your path.

**KB:** My origin is in landscape design. I trained in this field and worked on a whole range of projects, from community gardens to artist-designed parks. I was fascinated by the relationship of the parts to the whole and love physical materials, such as plants, soil, and stone.

**MS:** How, and why, did you shift to book design?

**KB:** For me, landscape design became more and more about proposals and paperwork and less and less about the actual designs and the doing.

Since I had been involved with books since my undergraduate years at the University of Wisconsin, joining my friend Steve Miller at Red Ozier Press seemed like the right move. I began to think of the words as the soil and the paper, the type and ink as the plants that grow from it. In quick order, Steve and I were partners and publishers running a very active press in New York City, working with the most amazing writers and artists. We took our jobs very seriously and made careful choices as to whom we would publish. When you are setting type or printing 150 copies of a book, you see the text differently. You get to read in a way that you would never do ordinarily.

**MS:** "Landscape" is an unusual word to associate with book design. What is the meaning of this title?

**KB:** Like a landscape, a well-designed book is full of nuances and complex relationships. The page size, the weight and texture of the paper, the size and style of the type, and the layout of information on the page all contribute to the reading experience. For me, the page is a construct that you move through, literally and figuratively. Like the window on a train, the frame remains constant, while the landscape continually changes.

**MS:** Please talk us through your design process for *The Bicycle Rider*, a novel in 100 sections by Guy Davenport. which was produced as a limited edition at Red Ozier Press.

**KB:** In designing typography for a text, I first ask "What are my emotional responses to the content of the story?" Throughout *The Bicycle Rider*, Davenport refers to Dutch painter Piet Mondrian and the primary colors he used in his mature work. Like the bicycle rider, Mondrian was a master of proportion, balance, and daring. Reds and blues pop up throughout the text. So, instead of using illustration, I used various typographic embellishments and created a title page inspired by Mondrian's paintings. The book was bound in a subtle brown handmade paper, with simple typography and color in order to play off the idea of the plain wrappers of not-so-plain books. This brown text paper is filled with red and blue fibers that echo the color of the ink.

Next, I assess my current visual surroundings, including other design books, painting, sculpture, and so on. When working on The Bicycle Rider, I was looking at a pamphlet of poems by Kenneth Patchen that had been printed during World War II, with big red numbers in the margins of each poem. This book seems to do everything "wrong" typographically, yet because of its great energy, it is one of my favorite books. To emulate Patchen, I selected a clear and classic-looking typeface, then adapted his bold red numbers for the section numbers. Combined with the classic typeface, these numbers added a syncopated beat to the pages.

**MS:** It seems that a lot of planning is required and that everything in your design is intentional.

**KB:** The planning has to be there to support the spontaneity. I especially enjoy working with students who are planning their projects. Making the dummies of a book, exploring alternatives, and giving shape to the ideas are the most enjoyable part of the process. Most people are surprised at how much planning happens before production, yet that is where the magic really happens.

The beauty of craft is that there are all these repetitive functions one must go through in the studio: cutting paper, setting type, cleaning the presses, printing. These hours are vital to the creative process because they place you into direct contact with the materials, physically and sensually. That is the fertile time when many of the best ideas are formed. Creativity is not segmented out into "big-idea time" versus "boring production time"—it is all part of a fluid process. Ideas are elusive. The more you try to trap them, the more they escape.

**MS:** From whom did you learn the most?

**KB:** Even though I never took a book course, I worked closely with book artist Walter Hamady during my last year at the University of Wisconsin. I went to his house to plant trees, then stayed on to cook a meal and talk. It was really about building a life. I learned that a personal investment in life and a willingness to pour all of your energy into an activity is crucial.

My collaboration with Steve Miller was also pivotal. When it is working well, a partnership can be a wonderful mirror, reflecting what you do especially well and what your partner does especially well. It also taught me a great deal about transforming a vision into reality.

**MS:** What advice do you have for my students?

**KB:** First, keep your eyes open: don't limit yourself through rigid self-definitions. If I had limited myself to architecture, I would never have become a graphic designer. Mindless careerism can be the path to ruin. Be willing to take side trips: they may change your life. Second, read, read, and read some more! The opportunities for learning are endless and through books, you can access the wisdom of the masters in all fields.

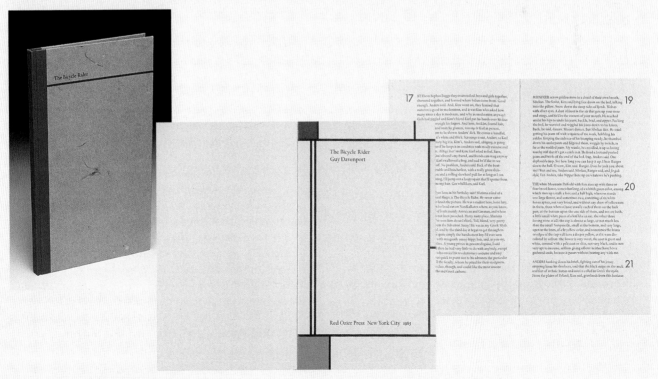

**Ken Botnick, *The Bicycle Rider*, 1985.** Guy Davenport, author. Letterpress printing, 5½ × 9½ in. (14 × 24 cm).

# Profile:
## Roger Shimomura, Artist
### Exploring Identity

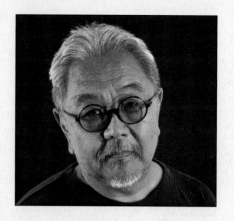

Roger Shimomura's paintings, prints, and theater pieces address sociopolitical issues of Asian America and have often been inspired by 56 years of diaries kept by his late immigrant grandmother. He has had over 100 solo exhibitions of his paintings and prints and has presented his experimental theater pieces nationally. Shimomura taught as a Distinguished Professor at The University of Kansas for 35 years and has been a visiting artist at over 200 universities, art schools, and museums across the country. His work is found in nearly a thousand museums and private collections, including the Whitney Museum of American Art, Chicago Art Institute, Smithsonian, and Philadelphia Museum of Art.

**MS:** How do you define stereotyping, and why is it the focus of your artwork?

**RS:** Racial stereotyping is an oversimplified opinion or mental snapshot of members of that race. It's the focus of my artwork because it has caused harm to not only Asian-Americans, but also every marginalized group in this country. This harm ranges from personal pain to larger legal actions that affect the entire community.

**MS:** What are the sources of your images?

**RS:** My sources range from old *Marvel* comic books to films by Kurosawa, from an image of Minnie Mouse to a geisha in an Utamaro print. Anything I see can generate an idea or become part of a composition.

Collecting objects and images that stereotype Japanese people is my current obsession. This includes Jap hunting licenses, slap-a-Jap club cards, postcards, ads, and movie posters featuring the buck-toothed, slant-eyed, yellow-skinned depictions of Asian people.

My collection of experiences is even more important. Following the Japanese attack on Pearl Harbor, my family was forcibly moved to Minidoka, a concentration camp in the southern Idaho desert. We were released two years later, when I was five years old. All through grade school and junior high, our favorite neighborhood game was not "Cowboy and Indians" but "Kill the Japs,"

bringing to life the values from the comics that I collected at that time. We reluctantly took turns being the "Jap," though we all preferred to be John Wayne, the most prolific Jap killer of the time. As a soldier during the Korean War, I was nicknamed "Pop-Up" because my fellow white officers thought I resembled the pop-up targets we used for target practice. All of these experiences feed into my exploration of stereotypes and racism.

**MS:** *Florence, South Carolina* is part of your "Stereotypes and Admonitions" series. Each painting in this series describes a single racist incident in a very straightforward, almost deadpan way. What is the advantage of this approach?

**RS:** It is the most direct and simplest way to tell a story of injustice. A verbal story accompanies the painting, making the content completely accessible. Hopefully, the work will resonate beyond the viewing, leading viewers to continue the conversation long after they leave.

**MS:** *Yellow Rat Bastard, Or How to Tell the Difference Between the Japanese and the Chinese* is much more complex. Can you talk us through this piece? What is the source and what do the various elements mean?

**RS:** *Yellow Rat Bastard* is a mixed media comparison between Roger (right panel) who is Japanese-American, surrounded by his current family, with his friend, Norman Gee, who is a Chinese-American painter.

It seems pretty simple. Each artist holds his respective country's chopsticks with an either short- or long-grained rice kernel, and is surrounded by appropriate cultural references. It gets complex when we look more carefully. Roger is married to a blonde-haired, blue-eyed Caucasian, has a daughter-in-law who is Filipina, and grandchild that is half Filipino and half Japanese. Norman is married to a Japanese-American (who studies Chinese Tai Chi). His children are half Chinese and half Japanese, as referenced by his daughter who holds a bao (Chinese bun) in one hand, and Makizushi (sushi roll) in the other.

Racist reminders are referenced by the WWII clichéd depiction of a *Yellow Peril Jap* looming behind Roger's portrait, while Fu Manchu peers out behind Norman's head. Both portraits are surrounded by contemporary pop icons from China and Japan.

Separating the two canvases is a shopping bag with the emblazoned words "Yellow Rat Bastard."

While this term was popularly used to describe the Japanese during WWII, it has been revived today, as the name of a trendy men's clothing store in New York City. Acting as a gesture to defuse the deadly yellow rat, the ears of a benign Mickey Mouse protrude out of the top of the bag. While non-Asian-Americans continue to have difficulty distinguishing between the Japanese and Chinese, the unfortunate fact is that many still view Asians as a generically alien race in this country.

**MS:** You are renowned as a teacher as well as an artist. What advice can you offer to beginning students?

**RS:** When my students came up to me and said that they didn't know what to paint, I would tell them to take a hard look at themselves first. It is important to consider whether there is significant value in sharing what you are experiencing in life. Sometimes the simplest approach to making art ends up being the most poignant.

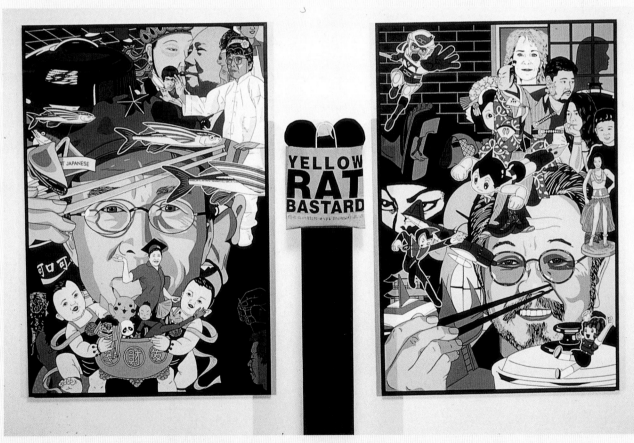

Roger Shimomura, Yellow Rat Bastard, 2006. Oil on canvas, 72 × 126 in. (182.9 × 320 cm).

## Visual Organization

Arnheim, Rudolph. *Art and Visual Perception: A Psychology of the Creative Eye.* Berkeley: University of California Press, 1974.

Arnheim, Rudolph. *Power of the Center.* Berkeley: University of California Press, 1999.

Berger, Arthur Asa. *Seeing Is Believing: An Introduction to Visual Communication,* 2nd ed. New York: McGraw-Hill.

Berger, John. *Ways of Seeing.* London: British Broadcasting Corporation, 1987.

Dondis, Donis. *A Primer of Visual Literacy.* Cambridge, MA: MIT Press, 1973.

## Two-Dimensional Design

Behrens, Roy R. *Design in the Visual Arts.* Englewood Cliffs, NJ: Prentice Hall, 1984.

Cheathan, Frank, Jane Hart Cheathan, and Sheryl A. Haler. *Design Concepts and Applications.* Englewood Cliffs, NJ: Prentice Hall, 1983.

Graham, Donald W. *Composing Pictures.* New York: Van Nostrand Reinhold, 1970.

Kepes, Gyorgy. *Language of Vision.* Chicago: Paul Theobald, 1944.

Lauer, David A., and Stephan Pentak. *Design Basics,* 5th ed. Orlando, FL: Harcourt, Brace and Company, 2000.

Myers, Jack Fredrick. *The Language of Visual Art: Perception as a Basis for Design.* Orlando, FL: Holt, Rinehart and Winston, 1989.

Ocvirk, Otto G., Robert E. Stinson, Philip R. Wigg, Robert O. Bone, and David L. Cayton. *Art Fundamentals: Theory and Practice,* 10th ed. New York: McGraw-Hill, 2006.

## Color Theory

Albers, Josef. *Interaction of Color.* New Haven, CT: Yale University Press, 1963.

Birren, Farber. *Light, Color and Environment.* New York: Van Nostrand Reinhold, 1982.

Gerritsen, Frans. *Theory and Practice of Color.* New York: Van Nostrand Reinhold, 1975.

Hornung, David. *Color: A Workshop Approach.* New York: McGraw-Hill, 2005.

Itten, Johannes. *The Art of Color.* New York: Van Nostrand Reinhold, 1974.

Kuppers, Harald. *Color: Origin, Systems, Uses.* New York: Van Nostrand Reinhold, 1972.

Linton, Harold. *Color Model Environments.* New York: Van Nostrand Reinhold, 1985.

Munsell, Albert H. *A Grammar of Color: A Basic Treatise on the Color System of Albert H. Munsell.* New York: Van Nostrand Reinhold, 1969.

Norman, Richard B. *Electronic Color.* New York: Van Nostrand Reinhold, 1990.

Pile, John F. *Interior Design.* New York: Harry N. Abrams, 1988.

Zelanski, Paul, and Mary Pat Fisher. *Color.* Englewood Cliffs, NJ: Prentice Hall, 1989.

## Creativity

Bohm, David. *On Creativity.* New York: Routledge, 2000.

Briggs, John. *Fire in the Crucible: Understanding the Process of Creative Genius.* Grand Rapids: Phanes Press, 2000.

Csikszentmihalyi, Mihaly. *Creativity: Flow and the Psychology of Discovery and Invention.* New York: HarperCollins, 1996.

Dewey, John. *Art as Experience.* New York: Capricorn Books, 1958.

Gardner, Howard. *Art, Mind and Brain: A Cognitive Approach to Creativity.* New York: Basic Books, 1982.

Gardner, Howard. *Creating Minds: An Anatomy of Creativity Seen Through the Lives of Freud, Einstein, Picasso, Stravinsky, Eliot, Graham, and Gandhi.* New York: Basic Books, 1993.

Gardner, Howard. *Frames of Mind: The Theory of Multiple Intelligences.* New York: Basic Books, 1985.

Lamott, Anne. *Bird by Bird: Some Instructions on Writing and Life.* New York: Anchor Books, 1998.

Le Boeuf, Michael. *Imagineering.* New York: McGraw-Hill, 1980.

Prince, George. "Creativity and Learning as Skills, Not Talents," *The Philips Exeter Bulletin,* 1980.

Shekerjian, Denise. *Uncommon Genius: How Great Ideas Are Born.* New York: Penguin Books, 1991.

Wallace, Doris B., and Howard E. Gruber, eds. *Creative People at Work.* New York: Oxford University Press, 1989.

## Concept Development

Adams, James L. *Conceptual Blockbusting.* Reading, MA: Addison-Wesley, 1986.

de Bono, Edward. *Lateral Thinking.* London: Ward Educational Limited, 1970.

Grear, Malcolm. *Inside/Outside: From the Basics to the Practice of Design.* New York: Van Nostrand Reinhold, 1993.

Johnson, Mary Frisbee. *Visual Workouts: A Collection of Art-Making Problems.* Englewood Cliffs, NJ: Prentice Hall, 1983.

Kelley, Tom. *The Art of Innovation: Lessons in Creativity from America's Leading Design Firm.* New York: Doubleday, 2001.

Lakoff, George, and Mark Johnson. *Metaphors We Live By.* Chicago: University of Chicago Press, 1981.

Shahn, Ben. *The Shape of Content.* Cambridge, MA: Harvard University Press, 1957.

Von Oech, Roger. *A Kick in the Seat of the Pants.* New York: Harper and Row, 1963.

Von Oech, Roger. *A Whack on the Side of the Head.* New York: Harper and Row, 1986.

Wilde, Judith and Richard. *Visual Literacy: A Conceptual Approach to Graphic Problem Solving.* New York: Watson-Guptil, 2000.

## Critical Thinking

Barnet, Sylvan. *A Short Guide to Writing About Art,* 6th ed. New York: Addison, Wesley, Longman, 2000.

Barrett, Terry. *Criticizing Photographs: An Introduction to Understanding Images,* 3rd ed. New York: McGraw-Hill, 2000.

Barrett, Terry. *Interpreting Art.* New York: McGraw-Hill, 2003.

Sayre, Henry M. *Writing About Art,* 3rd ed. Upper Saddle River, NJ: Prentice Hall, 1999.

Smagula, Howard, ed. *Re-visions: New Perspectives of Art Criticism.* Englewood Cliffs, NJ: Prentice Hall, 1991.

Tucker, Amy. *Visual Literacy: Writing About Art.* New York: McGraw-Hill, 2002.

bibliography

## Works Cited, Chapter Two

1. Johannes Itten, *The Art of Color* (New York: Van Nostrand Reinhold, 1974), p. 16.

2. Alexander Theroux, *The Primary Colors: Three Essays* (New York: Henry Holt and Company, 1994), p. 6.

## Works Cited, Chapter Three

1. Jean L. McKechnie, *Webster's New Universal Unabridged Dictionary* (New York: Simon and Schuster, 1983), p. 373.

## Works Cited, Chapter Five

1. Mihaly Csikszentmihalyi, *Creativity: Flow and the Psychology of Discovery and Invention* (New York: HarperCollins), pp. 55–76, 1996.

2. George Prince, "Creativity and Learning as Skills, Not Talents," *The Philips Exeter Bulletin*, June-October, 1980.

3. Anne Lamott, *Bird by Bird: Some Instructions on Writing and Life* (New York: Anchor Books, 1998), pp. 18–19.

## Works Cited, Chapter Six

1. Keith A. Smith, *Structure of the Visual Book* (Fairport, NY: The Sigma Foundation, 1991), pp. 17–18.

## Works Cited, Chapter Eight

1. Henry M. Sayre, *A World of Art*, 3rd ed. (Upper Saddle River, NJ: Prentice Hall, 2000), p. 496.

notes

# Glossary by
# Mary Stewart and Peter Forbes

## A

**abstract form** 1. a form derived from visual reality that has been distilled or transformed, reducing its resemblance to the original source. 2. a multiple image structure, such as a film, in which the parts are related to each other through repetition and visual characteristics, such as shape, color, scale or direction of movement.

**abstract shape** a shape that is derived from a visual source, but is so transformed that it bears little visual resemblance to that source.

**abstraction** the reduction of an image or object to an essential aspect of its form or concept.

**accent** a specific shape, volume, color, musical note, etc. that has been emphasized. Using an accent, a designer can bring attention to part of a composition and increase rhythmic variation within a pattern.

**accent color** a color that stands out from its surroundings. Often used to attract attention to a specific part a design.

**achromatic color** a color (such as black and white) that has no hue.

**act** a major division in a film or theatrical event. Acts are generally constructed from a group of sequences that increase in intensity.

**action-to-action transition** in comic books, the juxtaposition of two or more panels showing a sequence of actions.

**actual lines** lines that are physically present in a design.

**actual motion** motion that physically occurs in a design.

**actual time** the duration of an actual temporal event. For example, it takes less than a minute for the bowling ball to roll down the ramps in Jean Tinguley's *Chaos 1*.

**additive color** color created by combining projected beams of chromatic light. The additive color primaries are red, green, and blue and the secondaries are cyan, magenta, and yellow.

**additive sculpture** a physical object constructed from separate parts that have been connected using glues, joints, stitching, welds, and so on.

**aesthetics** the study of human responses to art and beauty.

**afterimage** in color theory, a ghostly image that continues to linger after the actual image has been removed.

**ambient light** the quality of light within an entire space or setting. For example, when we enter an open courtyard on a sunny summer afternoon, we are surrounded by warm ambient sunlight. Everything we see is colorful and bright.

**amplified perspective** the exaggerated use of linear perspective to achieve a dramatic and engaging presentation of the subject. Amplified perspective is often created using an unusual viewing position, such as a bird's eye view, accelerated convergence, or some form of distortion.

**analogous color** a color scheme based on hues that are adjacent on a color wheel, such as red, red-orange, and orange.

**analogy** a similarity or connection between things that are apparently separate and dissimilar. For example, when a teacher describes wet plaster as having the "consistency of cream," he or she is using an analogy.

**anesthetic** a chemical or action used to induce insensitivity or unconsciousness.

**anomaly** an obvious break from norm in a design.

**appropriation** a postmodern practice in which one artist reproduces an image created by another and claims it as his or her own.

**approximate symmetry** a form of balance that occurs when roughly similar imagery appears on either side of a central axis.

**armature** an internal structure created to strengthen and support a three-dimensional object.

**aspect-to-aspect transition** in comic books, the juxtaposition of two or more panels showing different views of a single setting or event. This transition is often used in Japanese comic books.

**assemblage** an additive method in which the artist or designer constructs the artwork using objects and images that were originally created for another purpose. Essentially, assemblage can be defined as three-dimensional collage.

**asymmetrical balance** equilibrium among visual elements that do not mirror each other on either side of an axis.

**atmospheric perspective** a visual phenomenon in which the atmospheric density progressively increases, hazing over the perceived world as one looks into its depth. Overall definition lessens, details fade, contrasts become muted and, in a landscape, a blue mist descends.

**attached shadow** a shadow that directly defines a form.

## B

**backlight** a light source positioned behind a person or object that can either create a silhouette or separate the person or object from the background.

**balance** the equal distribution of weight or force among visual units.

**base** a horizontal support for a physical object, such as a stone block supporting a bronze sculpture.

**beat** 1. a unit of musical rhythm that creates the pulse of a sound. 2. in acting, the most basic element in a story. A beat is an exchange of behavior, based on action and reaction.

**bend** one of the five major forces affecting structural strength.

**Bezold effect** a change in a single color that substantially alters our perception of the entire composition.

**boundary** the dividing line or edge between objects, images, or experiences.

**brainstorming** any of a number of problem-solving techniques that are designed to expand ideas and encourage creativity. List making, mapping, associative thinking, and metaphorical thinking are common strategies used.

**calligraphic line** derived from the Greek words for beautiful and writing, a flowing, and expressive line that is as personal as handwriting. Calligraphic lines generally vary in thickness and velocity.

**camera angle** the angle at which an object or event is viewed. An aerial view can provide the sweeping panorama needed to convey the enormity of a battle, while a low camera angle can provide an expansive view of the sky.

**carving** the removal of materials from a larger mass, gradually revealing an image or object. Carving is a subtractive process.

**cast shadow** a dark shape that results from placement of an opaque object in the path of a light source.

**categorical form** in film, a multiple image structure that is based on categories, or subsets of a topic. For example, a film on predators might begin with a discussion of wolves, then move on to lions, and conclude with a discussion of hawks.

**causality** the interrelation of cause and effect, based on the premise that nothing occurs without cause. Narrative film is based on causality: because the starting pistol was shot, the footrace began.

**cause-and-effect critique** a critique in which the viewer seeks to determine the cause for each visual or emotional effect in a design. For example, the dynamism in a design may be caused by the diagonal lines and asymmetrical balance used. Also known as formal analysis.

**centricity** as identified by Rudolph Arnheim, a compressive compositional force.

**characteristic texture** the inherent or familiar texture of a material. The gleaming reflective surface of a steel teapot, the transparent and reflective qualities of glass, and the gritty texture of clay are all characteristic textures.

**chiaroscuro** (from Italian meaning **"light-dark"**). The gradual transition of values to create the illusion of light and shadow on a three-dimensional form.

**chroma** the purity, intensity, or saturation of a color.

**chromatic gray** a gray made from a mixture of various hues, rather than a simple blend of black and white.

**chronology** the order in which events occur.

**cliché** an overused expression or a predictable visual treatment of an idea.

**close-up** in film, a type of framing in which the scale of the object shown is relatively large, as in a close-up of an actor's face.

**closure** the mind's inclination to connect fragmentary information to produce a completed form. Closure is an essential aspect of Gestalt psychology.

**codex** traditional bound-edged format used for modern books, with separate pages normally bound together and given a cover.

**collage** an image constructed from visual or verbal fragments initially designed for another purpose.

**color harmony** use of compatible colors to help unify a composition.

**color interaction** the way colors within a composition influence one another.

**color key** a color that dominates an image and heightens its psychological and compositional impact.

**color overtone** a secondary hue "bias" in a primary color. For example, alizarin crimson is a red with violet overtones, while scarlet is a red with orange overtones.

**color theory** the art and science of color interaction and effects.

**compare/contrast critique** a critique in which similarities and differences between two designs are analyzed. Often used in art history classes to demonstrate differences in approach between artists.

**comparison** recognition of similarity in two or more compositions. Often used in art history to demonstrate connections between images done by different artists or in different periods.

**complementary color** hues that oppose one another on a color wheel. When paired in a composition, complementary colors create contrast; when mixed, complementary colors produce a wide range of browns.

**composite** a new material created when two or more materials of differing strengths are fused together. Examples include Fiberglas and formcore.

**composition** the combination of multiple parts into a unified or harmonious whole.

**compression** the forcing or crushing of material into a smaller, denser condition and its visual dynamics and implied psychological effects.

**condensation** to be reduced to a denser form, as with the transition from a vapor to a liquid.

**cone of vision** in perspective drawing, a hypothetical cone of perception originating at the eye of the artist and expanding outward to include whatever he or she wishes to record in an illusionistic image, such as a perspective drawing. The cone's maximum scoping angle is 45–60 degrees; anything outside the cone of vision is subject to distortion.

**contact** the meeting point between visual or structural elements in a design.

**containment** a unifying force created by the outer edge of a composition or by a boundary within a composition.

**content** the emotional and/or intellectual meaning or message of an artwork.

**continuity** degree of connection or flow among compositional parts.

**contour line** a line that describes the edges of a form and suggests three-dimensional volume.

**contradictory texture** the unfamiliar use of a texture or the addition of an unusual texture to the surface of an object.

**contrast** the degree of difference between compositional parts or between one image and another. Contrast is created when two or more forces operate in opposition.

**contrasting colors** colors that are substantially different in hue, value, intensity, or temperature.

**convergent thinking** a problem-solving strategy in which a predetermined goal is pursued in a linear progression using a highly focused problem-solving process. Six steps are commonly used: 1. define the problem, 2. do research, 3. determine your objective, 4. devise a strategy, 5. execute the strategy, 6. evaluate the results.

**critique** any means by which the strengths and weaknesses of designs are analyzed.

**cropping** the manner in which a section of an image or a fragment of observed reality has been framed. For example, photographers select a fragment of reality every time they look through the view finder of the camera. Part of the scene is included, while the remainder is cut away. Photographs are often cropped further in the darkroom, leaving only the most significant information.

**cross-contour** multiple lines running over the surface of an object horizontally and/or vertically that describe its surface configuration topographically, as in mapping. This process is much like wireframing in three-dimensional computer modeling. Cross-contours can also be used in drawing to suggest three-dimensional form through tonal variation.

**crosscut** in film, an abrupt alternation between two or more lines of action.

**cross-hatching** a technique used in drawing and printmaking to shade an object using two or more networks of parallel lines. Darker values are created as the number of networks increases.

**curvilinear shape** a shape whose contour is dominated by curves and flowing lines.

**cut** in film, the immediate change from one shot or frame to another.

**definition** 1. the degree to which a shape is distinguished from both the ground area and from other shapes within the design. 2. the degree of resolution or focus of an entire image. Sharply defined shapes tend to advance while blurred shapes tend to recede.

**denouement** the outcome, solution, or point of clarification in a story.

**density** the extent to which compositional parts are spread out or crowded together. Visual connections generally occur easily in high-density compositions, while visual connections may be less obvious in low-density compositions.

**depth of field** the range of focus in a photographic image, from foreground to background. In a photograph with great depth of field, an object that is fifteen feet from the camera is in focus, as well as an object that is ten feet from the camera.

**descriptive critique** a critique in which the viewer carefully describes what he or she sees when observing a design.

**descriptive shape** a shape that is derived from specific subject matter and strongly based on perceptual reality.

**diegesis** the world created in a film or video.

**directed light** localized and focused light, such as a spotlight on a singer.

**direction** actual or implied movement of an element within a design.

**disharmony** combination of colors that clash with each other and appear to be jumping out of the picture.

**displacement** a forming method in which a solid material is physically forced into a new configuration. The stamping process used to mint coins is an example of displacement.

**dissolve** a transition between two shots during which the first image gradually disappears while the second image gradually appears.

**dissonance** the absence of harmony in a composition. Often created using disharmonious colors, shapes, textures, or sounds.

**distribution** the manner in which colors, shapes, or other visual elements are arranged within the format.

**divergent thinking** an open-ended problem-solving strategy. Starting with a broad theme, the artist or designer expands ideas in all directions.

**dominance** the principle of composition in which certain elements assume greater importance than others. Also see **emphasis.**

**duration** 1. the length of time required for the completion of an event; as in the running time of a film, video, or performance. 2. the running time of events depicted in the story (plot duration). 3. the overall span of time the story encompasses (story duration).

**dynamic** energetic, vigorous, forceful; creating or suggesting change or motion.

**dynamic form** a form that implies change.

**earth colors** colors made primarily from pigments in soil, and include raw sienna, burnt sienna, raw and burnt umber, and yellow ochre.

**earthwork** commonly, an artwork that has been created through the transformation of a natural site into an aesthetic statement.

**eccentricity** as identified by Rudolph Arnheim, an expansive compositional force.

**economy** distillation of a design down to the essentials in order to increase impact.

**editing** in film, selecting and sequencing the details of an event to create a cohesive whole.

**elements of design** basic building blocks from which designs are made. For example, the essential elements of two-dimensional design are line, shape, texture, color, and value.

**elevation** in orthographic projection, the front, back, and side views of an object or architectural structure.

**emotional advertising** use of emotion to sell a service, product, or idea. This strategy is often used when a product is neither unique nor demonstrably better than a competing product.

**emphasis** special attention given to some aspect of a composition to increase its prominence.

**environmental work (or environment)** an artwork that must be entered physically. Installations (which are usually presented indoors) and earthworks (which are usually presented outdoors) are two major types of environmental works.

**exaggerated advertising** pushing an idea to an extreme to make a point.

**exoskeleton** an external support structure.

**expansion** the extending outward of materials to fill more space.

**eye level or eye line** in linear perspective, the eye level is determined by the physical position of the artist. Sitting on the floor creates a low eye level while standing at an easel creates a higher eye level. Also known as the horizon line. All vanishing points in one- and two-point perspective are positioned on the eye level.

**fade** a gradual transition use in film and video. 1. In a fade-in, a dark screen gradually brightens as a shot appears. 2. In a fade-out, the shot gradually darkens as the screen goes black.

**fidelity** the degree of connection between a sound and its source. For example, when we hear the sound of a helicopter and see a helicopter on the screen, the sound matches with image, creating tight fidelity.

**figure** the primary or positive shape in a design; a shape that is noticeably separated from the background. The figure is the dominant shape in a figure-ground relationship.

**figure/ground reversal** an arrangement in which positive and negative shapes alternatively command attention.

**fill light** a diffused light used to lower the contrast between light and dark areas in cinematic and theatrical lighting.

**filtration** the process of separating a solid from a liquid by passing it through a porous substance such as cloth, charcoal, or sand.

**flashback** in film, an alternation in chronology in which events that occur later in a story are shown first.

**floodlight** a softly defined light with a broad beam.

**flying buttress** a type of exoskeleton commonly used by medieval architects in creating cathedrals.

**focal point** primary point of interest in a composition. A focal point is often used to emphasize an area of particular importance or to provide a strong sense of compositional direction.

**form** 1. the physical manifestation of an idea, as opposed to the content, which refers to the idea itself. 2. the organization or arrangement of visual elements to create a unified design 3. a three-dimensional composition or unit within a three-dimensional composition. For example, a sphere, cube, and pyramid are all three-dimensional forms.

**formalism** an approach to art and design that emphasizes the beauty of line, shape, texture, etc. as ends in themselves rather than as means to express content. Strictly formalist works have no explicit subject matter.

**format** the outer edge or boundary of a design.

**fractured space** discontinuous space that is created when multiple viewpoints are combined within a single image.

**frame** a single static image in film or video.

**freestanding work** an artwork that is self-supporting and is designed to be viewed from all sides.

**function** the purpose of a design or the objective that motivates the designer. For an industrial designer, the primary purpose of a design is often utilitarian. For example, he or she may be required to design a more fuel-efficient automobile. For a sculptor, the primary purpose of a design is aesthetic: he or she seeks to create an artwork that engages the viewer emotionally and intellectually.

**fusion** the combination of shapes or volumes along a common edge.

**geometric form** a three-dimensional form derived from or suggestive of geometry. Examples include cubes, spheres, tetrahedrons, etc.

**geometric shape** a shape derived from or suggestive of geometry. Geometric shapes are characterized by crisp, precise edges and mathematically consistent curves.

**Gestalt psychology** a theory of visual perception that emphasizes the importance of holistic composition. According to this theory, grouping, containment, repetition, proximity, continuity, and closure are essential aspects of visual unity.

**gesture drawing** a vigorous drawing that captures the action, structure, and overall orientation of an object, rather than describing specific details. Often used as a basis for figure drawing.

**gloss** 1. in writing, words of explanation or translation inserted into a text. 2. a secondary text within a manuscript that provides comments on the main text.

**gradation (or shading)** any gradual transition from one color to another or from one shape or volume to another. In drawing, shading created through the gradation of grays can be used to suggest three-dimensional form.

**graphic relationship** the juxtaposition of two or more separate images that are compositionally similar. For example, if a basketball is shown in the first panel, an aerial view of the round free-throw zone is shown in the second, and the hoop of the basket itself is shown in the third, a graphic relationship based on circles has been created.

**gravity** the force that tends to pull all bodies toward the center of the Earth.

**grid** a visual or physical structure created from intersecting parallel lines.

**grisaille** a gray underpainting, often used by Renaissance artists, to increase the illusion of space.

**group** in sequential structure, a collection of images that are related by subject matter, composition, or source. For example the trombone, trumpet, and tuba are all members of the group known as the brass section in an orchestra.

**grouping** visual organization based on similarity in location, orientation, shape, color, and so on.

**gutter** in bookbinding, the center line of a book, where the two pages are joined.

**hand-held** a small-scale object that can be held in your hands.

**Happening** an assemblage of improvised, spontaneous events performed by the artist and audience alike, based on a general theme. There is no rehearsal, and any location, from a parking lot to a factory interior, can be used. The Happening is most commonly associated with Alan Kaprow and is a precursor to performance art.

**hard-sell advertising** an advertising approach in which a major point is presented in a clear, direct manner. The narrative is usually linear, and the message is usually explicit.

**harmony** a pleasing or soothing relationship among colors, shapes, or other design elements.

**hatching** a technique used in drawing and printmaking to create a range of gray tones using multiple parallel lines.

**high definition** sharply focused visual information that is easily readable. High definition creates strong contrast between shapes and tends to increase clarity and immediacy of communication.

**horizon line** in linear perspective, the line on which all vanishing points are positioned. More accurately described as the eye line or eye level.

**hue** the name of a color (such as red or yellow) that distinguishes it from others and assigns it a position in the visual spectrum.

**human scale** a design that is roughly our size.

**humorous advertising** use of humor to sell a service, product, or idea. By entertaining the viewer, the designer can make the message more memorable.

**hybridity** the creation of artworks using disparate media to create a unified conceptual statement.

**iconography** the study of symbolic visual systems.

**illusionary space** the representation of an object or scene on a two-dimensional surface to give it the appearance of three-dimensionality.

**imbalance** the absence of balance.

**implied line** 1. a line that is suggested by the positions of shapes or objects within a design. 2. a line that is suggested by movement or by a gesture rather than being physically drawn or constructed.

**implied motion** the suggested change in location of a figure or object.

**implied time** the suggested location or duration of an event.

**installation** an artwork or a design that presents an ensemble of images and objects within a three-dimensional environment.

**intensity** 1. the purity, saturation, or chroma of a color. For example, fire engine red is a high-intensity color, while brick red is a low-intensity color. 2. in time design, the power, concentration, and energy with which an action is performed or the quality of observation of an event.

**interdisciplinary art** the combination of two or more different disciplines to create a hybrid artform.

**interdisciplinary thinking** use of skills and knowledge from more than one discipline.

**in the round** a three-dimensional object that is self-supporting and is designed to be viewed from all sides, as in free-standing sculpture.

**invented texture** a form of visual texture that has been created without reference to perceptual reality.

**joint** a physical connection between elements or parts in a three-dimensional object. Some joints are fixed, such as ones that are bolted together, while others can be moved, as with a hinge or a ball-and-socket joint.

**junction** 1. the place at which objects or events meet. 2. a physical intersection between elements or parts in a three-dimensional object.

**key light** a primary source of illumination.

**kinesthetics** the science of movement.

**kinetic form** a form that actually moves.

**lap dissolve** in film, a dissolve in which two shots are temporarily superimposed.

**layered space** compositional space that has been deliberately separated into foreground, middle ground, and background.

**layering** a postmodern practice in which an accumulation of multiple (and often contradictory) visual layers is used to create a single artwork.

**line** 1. a point in motion, 2. a series of adjacent points, 3. a connection between points, 4. an implied connection between points. Line is one of the basic elements of design.

**linear perspective** a mathematical system for projecting the apparent dimensions of a three-dimensional object onto a flat surface. Developed by artists during the Renaissance, linear perspective is one strategy for creating the illusion of space.

**line weight** variation in line thickness.

**long shot** in film, a type of framing in which the scale of the subject shown is relatively small, as with an image of a human figure within a landscape.

**loudness** the amplitude of a sound wave; the volume of a sound.

**low definition** blurred or ambiguous visual information. Low-definition shapes can increase the complexity of the design and encourage multiple interpretations.

## M

**maquette** a well-developed three-dimensional sketch, comparable to a two-dimensional thumbnail sketch.

**mass** a solid three-dimensional form.

**matrix** a three-dimensional grid.

**medium shot** a type of framing in which the scale of the subject shown is of moderate size, as in view of an actor from the waist up.

**metaphor** a figure of speech in which one thing is directly linked to another dissimilar thing. Through this connection, the original word is given the qualities of the linked word. For example, when we say "she's a diamond in the rough" we attribute to a woman the qualities of an unpolished gem.

**metaphorical thinking** the use of metaphors or analogies to create visual or verbal bridges.

**meter** the basic pattern of sound and silence in music or positive and negative in design.

**model** in three-dimensional design, a model is a technical experiment or a small-scale version of a larger design.

**modeling** the process of manipulating a pliable material (such as clay) to create a three-dimensional object.

**moment-to-moment transition** in comic books, a transition in which a character or situation is simply being observed over time. This transition is often used in Japanese comic books but rarely in American comic books.

**monochromatic color scheme** a color scheme based on variations in a single hue. For example, a light, pastel blue, a medium navy blue and a dark blue-black may be used in a room interior.

**monumental objects** objects that are much larger than humans.

**movement** in design, the use of deliberate visual pathways to help direct the viewer's attention to areas of particular interest.

**myth** a traditional story collectively composed by many members of a society. The creation of the world, sources of evil, the power of knowledge, and even the nature of reality may be explained through these grand expressions of the imagination.

## N

**negative shape (or ground)** 1. a clearly defined area around a positive shape or form. 2. a shape created through the absence of an object rather than through the presence of an object.

**nonobjective shape** shapes created without reference to specific visual subject matter.

**non-sequitur transition** the juxtaposition of multiple frames or shots that have no obvious conceptual relationship.

## O

**objective criticism** the assessment of strengths and weakness in a design solely based on the visual information presented.

**one-point perspective** a form of linear perspective in which the lines receding into space converge at a single vanishing point of the eye level or horizon line.

**opponent theory** an explanation for the electric glow that occurs when two complementary colors are placed side by side.

**organic shape** a shape that visually suggests nature or natural forces. Also known as biomorphic shape.

**organizational lines** lines used to create the loose linear "skeleton" on which a compositional can be built. Also known as structural lines.

**orientation** the horizontal, vertical, or diagonal position of a composition or design element.

**orthographic projection** a drawing system widely used by artists and designers to delineate the top, bottom and four side views of a three-dimensional object. Unlike perspective drawing, which is designed to create the illusion of space, an orthographic projection is constructed using parallel lines that accurately delineate six surfaces of an object.

**overlap** placement of one shape in front of another to create the illusion of space.

**oxidation** a common form of chemical change used in creating a patina (or colored surface) on a metal sculpture.

## P

**pace** the rate of change in a temporal event.

**panel** a single frame in a comic book.

**pattern** a design created through systematic repetition. Many patterns are based on a module, or repeated visual unit.

**pedestal** a vertical support for a sculptural object.

**performance art** a live presentation, often including the artist, usually combining elements from a variety of art forms, such a film, video, theater, and dance.

**permanence** the degree of durability, or resistance to decay, in a given material or design.

**physical texture** actual variation in a surface.

**picture plane** in linear perspective, the flat surface on which a three-dimensional image is mentally projected.

**pitch** in music, the relative highness or lowness of a sound. Pitch is determined by wave frequency, as compression and expansion occurs within the sound wave.

**plane** a three-dimensional form that has length and width but minimal thickness.

**plan view** the top view of a three-dimensional object or architectural structure, drawn orthographically or freehand.

**plinth** horizontal support for a sculptural object.

**plot duration** the running time of the events depicted in a story.

**polyhedra (or polyhedrons)** multi-faceted volumes.

**positive form** an area of physical substance in a three-dimensional design.

**positive shape (or figure)** the principle or foreground shape in a design and the dominant shape or figure in a figure-ground relationship.

**primary colors** colors from which virtually all other colors can be mixed. The additive (or light) color primaries are red, green, and blue. The subtractive (or pigment) color primaries are yellow, magenta red, and cyan blue.

**primary contour** the defining edges of a physical object, such as the extremities of a carved sculpture.

**principles of design** the means by which visual elements are organized into a unified and expressive arrangement. Unity and variety, balance, scale and proportion, rhythm, illusion of space, and illusion of movement are commonly cited as the principles of two-dimensional design.

**process colors** in four-color process printing, refers to the subtractive primary colors: yellow, magenta, and cyan, plus black.

**proportion** the relative size of visual elements within an image.

**prototype** a well-developed model, as with the fully functional prototype cars developed by automobile companies.

**proximity** the distance between visual or structural elements or between an object and the audience.

**pure forms** circles, spheres, triangles, cubes, and other forms created without reference to specific subject matter.

**radial symmetry** a form of balance that is created when shapes or volumes are mirrored both vertically and horizontally, with the center of the composition acting as a focal point.

**rational advertising** a type of advertising in which logic and comparisons of quality are used to sell a service, product, or idea. A rational approach is most effective when the message is compelling in itself or the product is truly unique.

**realistic advertising** use of a familiar setting or situation to involve the viewer and relate a product, service, or idea to use in everyday life.

**re-contextualization** a postmodern practice in which the meaning of an image or object is changed by the context in which it is placed.

**rectilinear shape** a shape composed from straight lines and angular corners.

**reflected light** light that is bounced off of a reflective surface back into space.

**refracted light** light that has been bent as it passes through a prism.

**relief** sculpture in which forms project out from a flat surface. The degree of projection ranges from low to high relief.

**repetition** the use of the same visual element or effect a number of times in the same composition.

**representation** commonly, the lifelike depiction of persons or objects.

**representational shape** a shape derived from specific subject matter and strongly based on visual observation.

**rhetorical form** a type of sequential organization in which the parts are used to create and support an argument. Often used in documentary films.

**rhythm** 1. presentation of multiple units in a deliberate pattern. 2. in filmmaking, the perceived rate and regularity of sounds, shots, and movement within the shots. Rhythm is determined by the beat (pulse), accent (stress), and tempo (pace).

**rhythmic relationship** the juxtaposition of multiple visual elements or images to create a deliberate pulse or beat.

**saturation** the purity, chroma, or intensity of a color.

**scale** a size relationship between two separate objects, such as the relationship between the size of the Statue of Liberty and a human visitor to the monument.

**scene** in film, continuous action in continuous time and continuous space.

**scene-to-scene transition** in comic books, the juxtaposition of two or more frames showing different scenes or settings.

**scope** conceptually, the extent of our perception or the range of ideas our minds can grasp. Temporally, scope refers to the range of action within a given moment.

**screenplay** the written blueprint for the film; commonly constructed from multiple acts.

**secondary colors** hues mixed from adjacent primaries. In paint, the secondary colors are violet, green, and orange.

**secondary contour** the inner edges of a physical object, such as the internal design and detailing of a carved sculpture.

**section** in orthographic projection, a slice of an object or architectural structure that reveals its internal structure and detail.

**sequence** 1. in filmmaking, a collection of related shots and scenes that comprise a major section of action or narration. 2. in narrative structure, any collection of images that have been organized by *cause and effect*. In a simple sequence, action number two is caused by action number one. In a complex sequence, there may be a considerable delay between the cause and the effect.

**series** in sequential structure, a collection of images that are linked simply, as with cars in a train.

**serious advertising** advertising that treats a topic in a somber or solemn manner. Often used for public service announcements, such as drunk driving commercials.

**setting** the physical and temporal location of a story, the props and costumes used in a story, and the use of sound.

**shade** a hue that has been mixed with black.

**shading** in drawing, a continuous series of grays that are used to suggest three-dimensionality and create the illusion of light.

**shape** a flat, enclosed area created when a line connects to enclose an area, an area is surrounded by other shapes, or an area is filled with color or texture.

**shear** a force that creates a lateral break in a material.

**shot** in film, a continuous group of frames.

**side light** a light positioned to the side of a person or object. Can be used to dramatically increase the sense of dimensionality.

**sight line** 1. a viewing line that is established by the arrangement of objects within one's field of vision. 2. a straight line of unimpeded vision.

**simile** a figure of speech in which one thing is linked to another dissimilar thing using the word "like" or "as." Through this connection, the original word is given the qualities of the linked word. For example, when we say "he's as strong as an ox," we attribute to a man the strength of an animal.

**simultaneous contrast** the optical alteration of a color by a surrounding color.

**site-specific artwork** an artwork is specifically designed for and installed in a particular place.

**skeleton (or endoskeleton)** a structure that provides internal support.

**soft-sell advertising** an advertising approach that uses emotion, rather than reason, to sell a service, product, or idea. The narrative is often nonlinear and ideas or actions may be implied.

**solidification** a forming method in which a liquid material is poured into a mold or extruded through a pipe, then allowed to harden.

**space** the area within or around an area of substance. The artist/designer defines and activates space when constructing a three-dimensional object.

**spatial context** the space in which a sound is generated. A sound that is played outdoors behaves differently than a sound that is played in a small room.

**spatial relationship** the juxtaposition of two or more images that are spatially different, such as a close-up, medium shot, and a long shot.

**split complementary** a complementary color plus the two colors on either side of its complement on the color wheel.

**spotlight** a light that creates a small, clearly defined beam.

**static** a composition that is at rest or an object that appears stationary.

**static form** a form that appears to be stable and unmoving.

**stereotype** a fixed generalization based on a preconception.

**story duration** the overall length of a story.

**subject** the person, object, event, or idea on which an artwork is based.

**subjective criticism** the assessment of strengths and weaknesses in a design based on nonobjective criteria, such as the narrative implications of an idea, the cultural ramifications of an action, or the personal meaning of an image.

**subject-to-subject transition** in comic books, the juxtaposition of two or more frames showing different subject matter.

**subordinate** of secondary importance. See **emphasis.**

**subtractive color** hue created when light is selectively reflected off a colored surface.

**subtractive sculpture** a forming method in which materials are removed from a larger mass. Carving, drilling, cutting, and turning on a lathe are all subtractive processes.

**symbolic color** a color that has been assigned a particular meaning by the members of a society. For example, in the United States, the white color of a wedding gown symbolizes purity, while in Borneo, white symbolizes death.

**symmetrical balance** a form of balance that is created when shapes are mirrored on either side of a central axis, as in a composition that is vertically divided down the center.

**take** in film or video, one version of an event.

**tangibility** the substantiality of an object or the degree to which an object or a force can be felt.

**temperature** the physical and psychological heat suggested by a color's hue.

**tempo** the pace at which time-based art and music occurs. A fast tempo is generally used in action films while a slow tempo is usually used in a dramatic film.

**temporal relationship** how the shots in a film relate in time.

**tension** the extension of an object through stretching or bending.

**tertiary color** a hue that is mixed from a primary color and an adjacent secondary color.

**testimonial advertising** use of a trustworthy character or celebrity to provide endorsement for a product, service, or idea.

**texture** the visual or tactile quality of a form. Texture can be created visually using multiple marks, physically, through surface variation, or through the inherent property of a specific material, such as sand as opposed to smooth porcelain.

**three-point perspective** a form of linear perspective in which the lines receding into space converge at two vanishing points of the eye level (one to the left of the object being drawn and one to the right of the object being drawn) plus a third vanishing point above or below the eye level. Used when the picture plane must be tilted to encompass an object placed above or below the eye level.

**three-quarter work** a physical object that is designed to be viewed from the front and sides only.

**timbre** the unique sound quality of each instrument. For example, a note of the same volume and pitch is quite different when it is generated by a flute rather than a violin.

**tint** a hue that has been mixed with white.

**tone** a hue that has been mixed with black and white.

**torque** the distortion of an object through a twisting movement. Also known as **torsion.**

**transition** the process of changing from one state or form to another. For example, the surface of a metal sculpture as it shifts from a smooth to a rough surface or the manner in which a computer drawing morphs from one form to another.

**translucent** a surface that permits passage of light.

**transparent** a surface that permits the passage of light, such as clear plastic or glass.

**triadic harmony** a color scheme based on three colors that are equidistant on a color wheel.

**tromp l'oeil** a flat illusion that is so convincing the viewer believes the image is real. From a French term meaning "to fool the eye."

**two-point perspective** a form of linear perspective in which the lines receding into space converge at two vanishing points of the eye level (or horizon line), one to the left of the object being drawn and one to the right of the object being drawn.

**typestyle** the distinctive quality of the letterforms within a given font. For example, Helvetica has a very different look than Palatino type.

**unity** compositional similarity, oneness, togetherness, or cohesion.

**value** the relative lightness or darkness of a surface.

**value distribution** the proportion and arrangement of lights and darks in a composition. Also known as **value pattern.**

**value scale** a range of grays that are presented in a consistent sequence, creating a gradual transition from white to black.

**vanishing point** in linear perspective, the point or points on the eye line at which parallel lines appear to converge.

**variety** the differences that give a design visual and conceptual interest; notably, use of contrast, emphasis, differences in size, and so forth.

**viewing time** the time an audience devotes to watching or exploring an artwork.

**visual book** an experimental structure that conveys ideas, actions, and emotions using multiple images in an integrated and interdependent format. Also known as an artist's book.

**visual movement** use of continuity to create deliberate visual pathways. Often used to direct the viewer's attention to areas of particular importance in the composition.

**visual texture** texture created using multiple marks or through a descriptive simulation of physical texture.

**visual weight** 1. the inclination of shapes to float or sink compositionally. 2. the relative importance of a visual element within a design.

**vitalistic sculpture** a sculpture that appears to embody life in an inanimate material, such as Fiberglas, stone, or wood.

**volume** 1. an empty three-dimensional form. 2. in two-dimensional design, a three-dimensional form that has been represented using the illusion of space. 3. in time design, the loudness of a sound.

**volume summary** a drawing that communicates visual information reductively, using basic volumes, such as sphere, cubes, and cylinders, to indicate the major components of a figure or object.

**volumetric** three-dimensional in nature.

**weight** the visual or physical heaviness of an object.

**wipe** in film, a transition in which the first shot seems to be pushed off the screen by the second. Wipes were used extensively in *Star Wars.*

# Introduction

*Page xv:* Photos courtesy of the author.

*xvi T:* Collection: Editon 1: Museo Nacional Centro de Arte Reina Sofia, Madrid. Edition 2, Los Angeles County Museum of Art, Modern and Contemporary Art Council Fund. Photo: Gary McKinnis.

*xvi B:* Collection Toni Greenbaum, NY. Photo: Keith E. LoBue.

*xvii T:* Designers: Bill Cannan, Tony Ortiz, H. Kurt Heinz. Design Firm: Bill Cannan & Co. Client/Mfr. NASA Public Affairs.

*xvi B:* Hans-Jürgen Syberberg, Parsifal, 1982.

*xviii:* Installation,Venice Bienniale, Chiesa de San Stae, Venice, Italy. Courtesy of Paula Cooper Gallery, NY.

*xix T:* The Museum of Modern Art, Film Stills Archive.

*xix B:* Designers: James E. Grove, John Cook, Jim Holtorf, Fernando Pardo, Mike Boltich. Design Firm: Designworks/USA. Client/Mfr: Corona Clipper Co.

*xx B:* Le Bassin des Nympheas (Water Lilly Pond), 1904, Claude Monet. Denver Art Museum Collection: Funds from Helen Dill bequest, 1935.14. © Denver Art Museum 2005.

*xxi:* © 2007 Samuel L. Francis Foundation/Artists Rights Society (ARS), NY.

*xxii:* Collection, University of Illinois at Urbana, Champaign. Photo courtesy of the artist © Alice Aycock, 1994.

*xxiii:* TM & © 2005 Marvel Characters, Inc. Used with permission.

*xxiv:* Wassily Kandinsky, Several Circles (Einige Kreise), January-February 1926. Oil on canvas, $55\frac{1}{4} \times 55\frac{3}{8}$ inches. The Solomon R. Guggenheim Museum, New York. Gift, Solomon R. Guggenheim, Founding Collection. 41.283. © 2007 Artists Rights Society (ARS), New York/ADAGP, Paris.

# Chapter One

*Page 1 T:* Collection of David Geffen, Los Angeles. © Jasper Johns/Licensed by VAGA, NY.

*1 B:* Courtesy Scott Hull Associates.

*3 L:* The Sidney and Jarriet Janis Collection, Digital Image © The Museum of Modern Art, NY/Licensed by SCALA/Art Resource, NY.

*3 R:* AP/Wide World Photos.

*4 TL:* © 2007 Barnett Newman Foundation/Artists Rights Society (ARS), New York.

*4 TR:* Iris & B. Gerald Cantor Center for Visual Arts at Stanford University. Gift of Dr. And Mrs. Louis J. Rattner, (CCVA 1968.13).

*4 RC:* Collection of David Lebrun, Courtesy of Koplin Gallery, Los Angeles.

*4 B:* © British Museum.

*5 TL:* Attributed to Tawaraya Sotatsu, Japanese (active c. 1600–1640) and Hon'ami Koetsu, calligrapher, Japanese (1558–1637). Flying Cranes and Poetry, Edo Period (1615–1868). Handscroll section mounted as a hanging scroll; ink and gold paint on tinted paper, $7\frac{5}{8} \times 6\frac{9}{16}$ inches. The Nelson-Atkins Museum of Art, Kansas City, Missouri. Gift of Mrs. George H. Bunting, Jr., 73-27. Photograph by Mel McLean.

*5 TR:* The Spencer Museum of Art, University of Kansas.

*5 BR:* © Alfred Leslie.

*6 LC:* Reproduction courtesy The Minor White Archive, Princeton University. © 1989 by The Trustees of Princeton University. All Rights Reserved.

*6 BL & R:* Vatican Museums, Vatican State. Scala/Art Resource, NY.

*7 TL:* Digital Image © The Museum of Modern Art/Licensed by SCALA/Art Resource, NY. © 2007 Artists Rights Society (ARS), NY/ADAGP, Paris.

*7 TR:* Courtesy of David Mach.

*7 BR:* Musée du Louvre, Paris. © Réunion des Musées Nationaux/Art Resource, NY.

*8:* The Museum of Modern Art, The Sidney and Harriet Janis Collection. Digital Image © 2001 The Museum of Modern Art/Licensed by Scala/Art Resource, NY. © 2007 The Pollock-Krasner Foundation/Artists Rights Society (ARS), NY.

*9 TL:* PATH Station Maps, Louis Nelson Associates Inc, NY. Artist: Jennifer Stoller, Louis Nelson. © Louis Nelson Associates for the Port Authority of New York & New Jersey.

*9 TR:* Courtesy of Joel Peter Johnson.

*9 B:* Courtesy of Pentagram Design.

*10 B:* Art & Artifacts Division, Schomburg Center for Research in Black Culture, The New York Public Library, Astor, Lenox and Tilden Foundations.

*11 TL:* Photograph © 2001 The Detroit Institute of Arts, Gift of Edsel B. Ford, 33.10.N.

*11 C:* Courtesy Bantam Books.

*11 R:* Galleria Moderna Venice, Italy. Cameraphoto Arte, Venice/Art Resource, NY.

*11 BL:* Carin Goldberg, Cover of Ulysses, by James Joyce, 1986. Random House Vintage Books. Art Director: Edith Loseser.

*12 B:* Philadelphia Museum of Art: Purchased with the Edward and Althea Budd Fund, the Adele Haas Turner and Beatrice Pastorius Turner Memorial Fund, and with funds, 1981-94-a, b.

44 T: School of Art, Ohio University.

44 B: © Kenneth Noland/Licensed by VAGA, NY.

45 T: MANUAL/Suzanne Bloom/Ed Hill.

46 BL: © Nicora Gangi.

46 BR: © David Hockney/Gemini G.E.L.

47 L: Smithsonian American Art Museum, Washington, DC/Art Resource, NY.

47 R: © 2007 Succession H. Matisse, Paris/Artists Rights Society (ARS), NY.

49 T: Courtesy of National Trust for Historic Preservation.

49 B: Collection, Albright-Knox Art Gallery, Buffalo, NY. Gift of Seymour H. Knox, 1956. © 2007 Estate of Arshile Gorky/Artists Rights Society (ARS), NY.

50 BL: © Guy Goodwin.

50 BR: "Chromatics", 1970. Gerald Gulotta, Jack Prince, Arzberg, Porzellanfabrik. Block China Company, American, founded 1963. Porcelain, printed. Dallas Museum of Art, gift of Gerald Gulotta.

51 BR: © 2007 The Estate of Francis Bacon/Artists Rights Society (ARS), NY/DACS, London.

52 T: National Gallery of Art, Washington, DC, Alfred Stieglitz Collection, Bequest of Georgia O'Keeffe. © 2007 The Georgia O'Keeffe Foundation/Artists Rights Society (ARS), NY.

52 B: © Joel Katz Design Associates.

53 T: Musée d'Orsay, Paris. Réunion des Musées Nationaux/Art Resource, NY. Photo: Herve Lewandowski.

53 B: South Australian Museum. © 2007 Artists Rights Society (ARS), NY.

54 L: © 2007 The Estate of Francis Bacon/Artists Rights Society (ARS), NY/DACS, London. Tate Gallery, London/Art Resource, NY.

54 R: Courtesy of Steve Quinn.

55 T: © Wolf Kahn/Licensed by VAGA, NY.

55 B: University Art Museum, University of California, Berkeley, Gift of the artist.

56 T: Astor, Lenox and Tilden Foundation, Spencer Collection, The New York Public Library/Art Resource, NY. © 2007 Succession H. Matisse, Paris/Artists Rights Society (ARS), NY.

56 B: © Nancy Crow. Photo: J. Kevin Fitzsimons.

57 TR: Whitney Museum of American Art, New York; Purchase, with funds from the Friends of the Whitney Museum of American Art, 60.63. © Estate of Willem de Kooning/Artists Rights Society (ARS), NY.

57 BL: PATH Station Maps, Louis Nelson Associates Inc, NY. Artist: Jennifer Stoller, Louis Nelson. © Louis Nelson Associates for the Port Authority of New York & New Jersey.

57 BR: Collection of Michael Krichman. Courtesy of Vernon Fisher.

58: © Andrew Wyeth. Lent by Professor and Mrs. Charles H. Morgan, Amherst, MA. Mead Art Museum, Amherst College, on extended loan to the Museum from the Estate of Charles H. Morgan (AC EL.1984.51).

59 T: Richard Diebenkorn, American (1922-1993). Interior with a Book, 1959. Oil on canvas, 70 × 64 inches. The Nelson-Atkins Museum of Art, Kansas City, Missouri. Gift of the Friends of Art, F63-15. Photograph by E. G. Schempf.

59 B: © Sandy Skoglund.

60 T: © Joe Spadaford.

60 B: The Minneaplis Institute of Arts, Gift of the P.D. McMillan Land Company.

61 TL: OUR FEAR IS THEIR BEST WEAPON. A few weeks before the Zimbabwe parliamentary elections in June 2000, the redeployment of the 5th Brigade into Matebeleland has added a psychological twist to the state's continued intimidation campaign. In the 1980's the infamous Red berets' were responsible for the notorious 'Gakuruhundi' campaign that left thousands of Ndebele dead and the area traumatised. Photomontage: Chaz Maviyane-Davies.

61 TR: Repainted by Jim Kewanwytewa, Oraibi, Museum of Northern Arizona.

61 BR: The Museum of Modern Art, New York. Gift of the Celeste and Armand Bartos Foundation. Digital image © The Museum of Modern Art/Licensed by Scala/Art Resource, NY. © Jasper Johns and U.L.A.E./Licensed by VAGA, NY.

62 T: Staatliche Kunstsammlungen der DDR. Kupferstichkabinett Dresden. © 2007 Artists Rights Society (ARS), NY/VG Bild-Kunst. Bonn.

62 BL: Staatsgalerie Stuttgart. © 2007 Artists Rights Society (ARS), NY/VG Bild-Kunst. Bonn.

62 BR: National Gallery of Art, Washington, DC. Gift of Robert and Chris Petteys. Photograph © 2001 Board of Trustees, National Gallery of Art, 1956.1 © 2007 Artists Rights Society (ARS), NY/VG Bild-Kunst. Bonn.

63: South Australian Museum. © 2007 Artists Rights Society (ARS), NY.

64–65: Courtesy of Ann Baddeley Keister.

# Chapter Three

Page 67 TL: Courtesy Scott Hull Associates.

67 TR: Philadelphia Museum of Art, #1991-19-1/CelminsViga.

67 BR: Staaliche Museen zu Berlin. Photo: Jorg Anders, Preussiher Kulturbesitz, Nationalgalerie/ NG57/61. © 2007 Artists Rights Society (ARS), NY/ VG Bild-Kunst. Bonn.

68 B: The British Library, London.

69 B: Courtesy of Larry Moore for Creative Club of Orlando.

70 T: © Aaron Macsai.

70 B: Vatican Museums. Photo: A. Bracchetti-P. Zigrossi. Scala/Art Resource, NY.

71 T: Toledo Museum of Art, Toledo, OH. Purchased with funds from the Libbey Endowment, gift of Edward Drummond Libbey (1972.4). © 2007 Frank Stella/Artists Rights Society (ARS), NY.

71 R: Musée du Louvre, Paris. © Réunion des Musées Nationaux/Art Resource, NY.

72 L: Designers, Illustrators: Traci Dalberko, Dennis Clouse. Photo: Marco Prozzo. Client: Intiman Theatre, Seattle, WA.

72 R: © Copyright The Andy Warhol Foundation/ ARS, NY. Photo Credit: The Andy Warhol Foundation, Inc./Art Resource, NY.

73 L: Syracuse University Library, Department of Special Collections, Syracuse, NY.

73 R: Faith Ringgold © 1988. Solomon Guggenheim Museum, New York. Gift, Mr. and Mrs. Gus and Judith Lieber, 1988. 88.3620.

74: Courtesy of Joan Dobkin.

75 L: © Berenice Abbott/Commerce Graphics Ltd, Inc.

75 R: © British Museum.

76: © Ansel Adams Publishing Rights Trust/CORBIS.

77 T: © Anthony Kersting.

77 B: Courtesy of the Allan Stone Gallery, NY.

78 TR: San Francisco Museum of Modern Art, Gift of Tracy O'Kates. © 2007 Judy Chicago/Artists Rights Society (ARS), NY.

78 BL: Wadsworth Atheneum, Museum of Art, Hartford, CT. The Ella Gallup Sumner and Mary Catlin Sumner Collection Fund (1952.52).

80 T: Hirshhorn Museum and Sculpture Garden, Smithsonian Institution, Washington, DC. Gift of Joseph H. Hirshhorn Foundation, 1972 (HMSG 72.205).

80 B: Courtesy of Frank Miller, Edina, MN.

81 T: Museo de Arte Moderno, Mexico. D.F. Schalkwijk/Art Resource, NY.

81 B: Courtesy of the artist and Mary Boone Gallery, NY.

82 C: Michael Bierut, Design Firm: Pentagram, NY. Client: Designing New York Committee. © Pentagram.

83 TL: Albright-Knox Art Gallery, New York. Gift of Seymour H. Knox, 1967.

83 B: Photo: David Caras.

84 TL: Philadelphia Museum of Art/Bridgeman Art Library. © 2007 Artists Rights Society (ARS), NY/ADAGP, Paris/Estate of Marcel Duchamp.

84 TR: Publisher: Art Center: College of Design, Pasadena, CA. Emphasis by isolation.

84 CR: Photo: Doug Yaple.

85 T: © Jacey, Shannon Associates.

86 T: © Robert Crawford.

86 C: Wadsworth Atheneum, Museum of Art, Hartford, CT. Ella Gallup Sumner and Mary Catlin Sumner Collection (1951.40).

87: Syracuse University Library, Department of Special Collections, Syracuse, NY.

88: Courtesy of Bob Dacey.

89: From a cover of MIRIAM'S CUP by Fran Manushkin, illustrated by Bob Dacey. Published by Scholastic Press, a division of Scholastic Inc. Illustration © 1998 by Bob Dacey. Used by permission.

90: Courtesy of Bob Dacey.

# Chapter Four

Page 91 L: Trinity College Library, Dublin.

91 R: Alte Pinakothek, Munich. Scala/Art Resource, NY.

92: Stanza della Segnatura, Vatican Palace, Vatican State/ Scala/Art Resource, NY.

94 R: Harvard University Art Museums, Fogg Art Museum, Gift of Paul J. Sachs, M3188.

95 T: Museo del Prado, Madrid. Bridgeman-Giraudon/Art Resource, NY.

95 B: The Metropolitan Museum of Art, Rogers Fund, 1907 (07.123). Photograph © 1996 The Metropolitan Museum of Art.

96: National Palace Museum, Taipei, Taiwan.

97 L: Glasgow Museums: The St. Mungo Museum of Religious Life and Art. © 2007 Kingdom of Spain, Gala-Salvador Dali Foundation/Artists Rights Society (ARS), NY.

97 TR: © David Hockney.

98 TL: Robert Stackhouse, Inside Running Animals/Reindeer Way, 1977. Watercolor and charcoal on paper, 59¾ × 39¼ inches. From the Collection of the John and Maxine Belger Family Foundation.

98 BL: Courtesy of Ann Strassman and Kidder Smith Gallery.

155: Stanza della Segnatura, Vatican Palace, Vatican State. Scala/Art Resource, NY.

156–157: © Heidi Lasher-Oakes.

# Chapter Eight

*Page 158:* Collection of the National Palace Museum, Taipei, Taiwan.

*159 T:* Courtesy of the artist.

*159 B:* Courtesy of Milton Glaser Studio.

*160:* The Menil Collection, Houston.

*161 TL:* © Kenny Kiernan, Mendola Ltd.

*161 TR:* Courtesy of Jacqui & Sherry Matthews Advocacy Marketing.

*161 BL:* Michael A. Mello, Dead Wrong: A Death Row Lawyer Speaks Out Against Capital Punishment. © 1997.
Cover design and illustration by Mark Maccaulay. Reprinted by permission of The University of Wisconsin Press.

*161 BR:* Courtesy of Georgiana Nehl.

*163 T:* Ruhr/Paragon, Minneapolis.

*163 B:* Courtesy of Kim Martens.

*164 L:* Courtesy of Richard Saul Wurman, wurrmanrs@aol.com and Pentagram.

*164 R:* © Robert Rauschenberg/Licensed by VAGA, NY.

*165 TL:* Margaret Bourke-White/TimePix/Getty Images.

*165 TR:* Alfred Eisenstadt/TimePix/Getty Images.

*165 CR:* Michael Bierut & Tracey Cameron/Pentagram. Photo: Don F. Wong.

*165 B:* Courtesy of Sean O'Meallie. Photo: Ric Helstrom.

*166 T:* © 1999 Iomega Corporation.

*166 B:* Courtesy of Jimmy Margulies.

*167:* Museo Nacional Centro de Arte Reina Sofia, Madrid/Bridgeman Art Library, NY. © 2007 Estate of Pablo Picasso/Artists Rights Society (ARS), NY.

*168 T:* © Paul M.R. Maeyaert.

*168 B:* AP Images.

*169:* A.F. Kersting.

*170 T:* Barbara Kruger, "Untitled" (We don't need another hero). 109" by 210", photographic silkscreen/vinyl, 1987. © Barbara Kruger. Collection: Fisher Landau Center for Art, Long Island City, New York. Courtesy: Mary Boone Gallery, NY.

*170 B:* Courtesy of Alexander and Bonin, NY.

*171 T:* Courtesy of Jaune Quick-to See Smith and Lewallen Gallery.

*171 B:* © Bridgeman Art Library, London/SuperStock.

*172:* Courtesy of Mark Messersmith.

*174–175:* Courtesy of Ken Botnick.

*176–177:* Courtesy of Roger Shimomura.

photo credits

Index

index

Index

index

index

Index

207